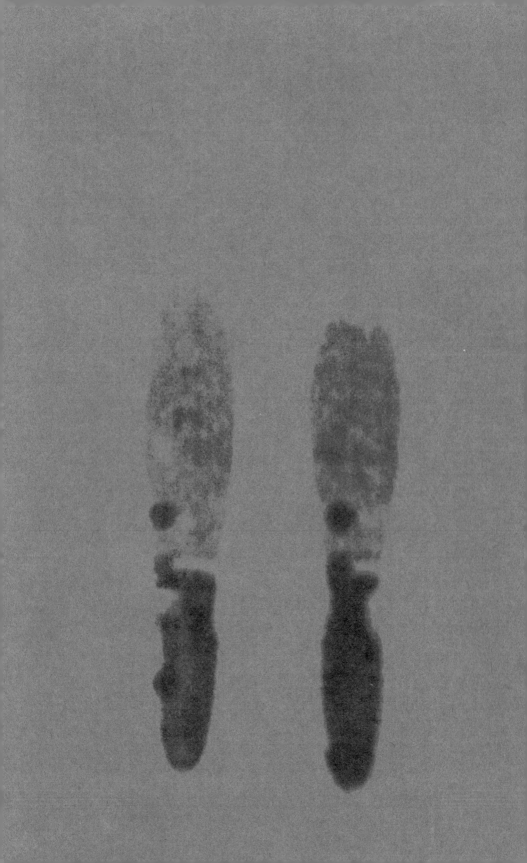

DUEL for the DUNES

DUEL
FOR THE
DUNES

Land Use Conflict
on the Shores
of Lake Michigan

KAY FRANKLIN and
NORMA SCHAEFFER

University of Illinois Press
URBANA AND CHICAGO

This book is printed on acid-free paper.

Library of Congress Cataloging in Publication Data

Franklin, Kay.
  Duel for the dunes.

  Bibliography: p.
  Includes index.
  1. Nature conservation—Indiana—Indiana
Dunes National Lakeshore. 2. Land use—Indiana
—Indiana Dunes National Lakeshore.
3. Environmental policy—Indiana—Indiana Dunes
National Lakeshore. 4. National parks and reserves—
United States—History. 5. Indiana Dunes National
Lakeshore (Ind.). I. Schaeffer, Norma. II. Title.
QH76.5.I6F72 1983   333.78'4   82–25601
ISBN 0–252–01034–5

You may frequently win a battle, but you can never win the war. Whenever one threat is put down, another immediately arises: the struggle is endless, and conservationists must always be ready to rally their forces for another fight. Even triumphs carry their own dangers.
—Alfred A. Knopf

Contents

Preface

In the summer of 1821 General John Tipton led a surveying team from Corydon, Indiana, through the village of Chicago in Illinois to an area near the southeastern shore of Lake Michigan for the purpose of determining the boundary between Indiana and Illinois. Tipton dismissed the wind-swept and stark shoreline he came upon as inhospitable to settlers and of little value to either state.

On October 18, 1966, U.S. Senator Paul A. Douglas of Illinois addressed the Senate to pay tribute to the thousands of dedicated people who had, over the previous eight years, worked hard with him to preserve that same tract of land termed worthless by General Tipton 145 years earlier. Senator Douglas clearly had a different view, calling the Dunes of northwest Indiana "a significant part of America's natural heritage."

The nearly century and a half that separated these two events is the subject of the first and largest of this two-part treatment of the history of the conflict over the value and use of the Indiana Dunes. In these first seven chapters, authors Kay Franklin and Norma Schaeffer lead the reader carefully through the changing scenery and sentiments of the controversy: through the early days of territorial expansion and industrial push in the Midwest, the budding American conservation movement, and first efforts to shield the fragile ecology of the Dunes from the effects of economic growth; through the intense rivalry between Indiana and Illinois to attract heavy industry and the renewed interest of major steel corporations to capture a growing share of the midwestern market by building plants and gaining access to deep water ports in the lakeshore area.

The authors' narrative, woven from the threads of geology and social history, describes individual effort and massive economic change, well-made plans and inadvertent mishaps. The story is fascinating and, at the hands of these two gifted writers, comes alive as a classic struggle between two dominant strains in the American national character: the desire to force the land to yield its riches to ensure progress and prosperity as against the desire to protect another type of resource . . . the one that serves the human spirit. The reader slowly learns that the natural forces that first gave rise to the Dunes are a metaphor for the ebb and flow of power between the interests that shape the debate—those of development and those of conservation. The authors deftly draw portraits of the main actors in the dispute: nineteenth-century landscapers and frontier businessmen, committed environmentalists, and a range of political actors from feisty Republican clubwomen to U.S. Senators and Representatives.

The denouement of *Duel for the Dunes* came in 1966 with congressional approval of a 6,500-plus acre Indiana Dunes National Lakeshore, a solution which reflected a compromise between conservationists and champions of economic expansion.

In the second part of the book, Kay Franklin and Norma Schaeffer shift their focus from Capitol Hill to the offices of the National Park Service, which has the responsibility of translating legislative intent into rules and regulations. The bureaucracy now becomes the battleground for the conflict over national values.

Duel for the Dunes is ultimately much more than a well-researched chronicle of the Lake Michigan shore area or a moving account of Senator Douglas's lonely crusade to save the Dunes as a national treasure. This book instructs us in political decision-making in America. For example, we can trace how constituencies take shape around divergent interests and project their controversy into the public arena. We can see how outcomes vary depending on which arena of struggle is chosen: the federal, state, or local level. We learn how congressional styles of policy-making differ from those of the Executive branch.

As a former member of Congress who for twenty-two years represented a district in northern Indiana and who knew and worked with many of the people presented in these pages, I found this aspect of the book—its reflections on American politics—particularly insightful and intriguing.

Duel for the Dunes is a compelling reminder, if one were needed, that politics in a democracy is a never-ending cycle of conflict and compromise. There are no final solutions, only shifting forms. Like the sands of the dunes . . .

John Brademus
President, New York University

Acknowledgments

Without the help and support of scores of people we could not have completed *Duel for the Dunes*. Their belief in the project's worth buoyed us during eight long years of research and writing. We appreciate their many unique contributions.

The staffs of more than a dozen libraries, archives, and research facilities eased our way through an endless morass of data. Professionalism and competence always accompanied their valuable aid. We offer special thanks to Bill Brace of Rosary College who repeatedly demonstrated that libraries can unearth just about anything and to members of the Reference Department of the Michigan City Public Library for patience, availability, and always willing assistance.

Close to fifty interviews and conversations with participants in the Dunes struggle greatly enhanced our understanding of complex issues; the recollections of these people provided background, color, and depth. All individuals, even those who suspected that we disagreed with their positions, treated our effort with courtesy and respect. Thanks to: George Applegate, Birch Bayh, William Beecher, Toby Boccanegra, John Bowers, Hazel Bowers, John Canright, Mae Chester, Emily Taft Douglas, Tom Dustin, Ron Engel, Floyd Fithian, Edward Frank, Laura Gent, Ken Gray, Clinton Green, Charles A. Halleck, Lois Howes, Ralph Joseph, Earl Landgrebe, William Lieber, George Lively, John Lyons, Abner Mikva, Jerry Olson, Merrill Ormes, Edward Osann, Edward Osann, Jr., George Palmer, Betty Prang, Charlotte Read, Herb Read, Marian Reed, Martha Reynolds, Leonard Rutstein, Joseph Sax, Howard Shuman, Warren Stickle, Elizabeth Troy, Sylvia Troy, Stewart Udall, John Van Ness, Matthew Welsh, Lee White, and James R. Whitehouse.

Several academic advisers supported and encouraged our research. Their willingness to consider the merit of the work rather than our formal credentials opened many doors; their time, effort, and generosity on our behalf reflected the best traditions of intellectual inquiry and educational purpose. For help in fitting the Indiana Dunes conflict into a national environmental, historical, and political framework, and for reading, editing, and constructively criticizing the manuscript, we offer gratitude to Professors Lynton K. Caldwell, David A. Caputo, and Phillip VanderMeer. Consultants Malcolm Collier, Tom Cresswell, Lou Hasencamp, and Lance Trusty have also earned our thanks.

Margaret S. Schoon heads the "beyond the call of duty" department. She produced the book's index, relieving us of a prospect that had filled us with dread. Our appreciation also goes to typists Mary Daskais, Lisa Dlutkowski, and Frances Piest as well as to Ann Bishop, Florence Broadie, Betty and Milt Freudenheim, Jim Jonz, Paul Marshall, Bill Rickman, Bernie and Lois Weisberg, and Joan Wolfe for advice, ideas, and solace. Finally, we thank Robert L. Franklin, M. David Schaeffer, and our children for help in ways too numerous to mention.

Prologue

When contemporary events resurrect issues from the past, old conflicts seem newer than tomorrow's headlines. Matters that address fundamental values especially appear and reappear on the nation's political agenda. If separated by a decade or a generation from their last emergence, such questions may emit an aura of recent birth; almost always, they instead represent old problems in new and modern dress.

Early in the 1980s Ronald Reagan enacted policies that reactivated the long-standing debate about how best to use the nation's resources. The president eloquently defended an environmental ethic based on economic development, private interest, and states' rights. Together with Secretary of the Interior James Watt, Reagan revived the impassioned duel between his philosophical forebears and conservationists that had raged over the Indiana Dunes for more than half a century. His beliefs returned the arguments of Dunes's antagonists to a national forum and resubjected them to mass scrutiny. The pronouncements of Reagan and Watt demonstrated the continuing currency of the issues raised by the Dunes controversy and once again underscored its importance as a prototype of conflict between competing American values.

Midway through his first term, Watt had proposed a change in the Interior Department's seal. To the undiscerning, his conception looked identical to the original: a buffalo posed against a mountain peak. While the eyes of Interior's animal gazed to the left, however, the head of Watt's beast turned firmly, steadfastly to the right.[1] The secretary's perhaps facetious design for the seal accorded with his fervent design for the department. Under Watt's controversial stewardship, far more than the buffalo's head had turned to the right.

Watt undertook his shake-up with full awareness of his position's far-reaching power. Charged with overseeing over 400 million acres of land, one-fifth of the nation's acreage, the Interior Department has responsibility for both preservation and development of this vast holding. Wilderness and wildlife protection, mineral and mining activities, water resources, and Indian affairs all fall under the department's purview. In addition, through the National Park Service, Interior controls the 333 national parks, monuments, recreation areas, preserves, seashores, rivers, parkways, wilderness areas, forests, and wildlife refuges that make up the national park system.[2] The secretary heads "one of the most controversial and sensitive departments in government affecting as it does so many conflicting interests."[3] He wields enormous discretionary power and authority; his decisions and policies affect the expenditure of billions of dollars.[4] Moreover, unlike decisions of other governmental bodies, those made by Interior often produce irreversible results.

Through the three interlocking strategies of budget control, personnel appointments, and administrative fiat, Watt set out to reverse departmental policies that had enjoyed bipartisan support for over twenty years. From his first days in office, environmentalists watched in horror as he decimated their hard-won gains. He attacked established policies on public land and natural resources, leasing, regulatory reform, and wildlife management. In addition, he supported Reagan administration initiatives on the relaxation of pollution controls, which lowered standards for air and water purity, and on the reduced enforcement of laws to control hazardous wastes and toxic substances. He tampered with virtually every aspect of Interior's mission.[5] His actions drew outraged but impotent fire from "environmental extremists," Watt's contemptuous designation for all opponents of his values and policies.

Moreover, frontal attacks on the national parks released the ire of a large, heterogeneous constituency. While many Americans knew little of Interior's vast operation, hardly any lacked at least some acquaintance with the parks. Most considered them a national treasure and regarded them with affection and respect. Indeed, they used the parks extensively. In 1980, 300 million people—one American in four—visited a national park unit.[6] Therefore, Watt's proposed moratorium on expenditure of funds for park acquisition, including lands already authorized by Congress, encountered widespread opposition. The funding cuts—down from the $333 million recommended by the Jimmy Carter administration to $45 million "to be used in special cases"—not only threatened to halt new purchase of lands but also to prevent completion of such existing parks as Redwood National Park, Santa Monica Mountains National Recreation Area, and Indiana Dunes National Lakeshore.[7]

Watt's potshots at the parks embodied fundamental beliefs, long held in America, which maintained that the nation had already protected any land worth preserving—that of the vast unsullied West—

and now needed to learn to manage what it owned. This view particularly opposed urban national parks because, as "merely minor playgrounds," they failed to meet National Park Service (NPS) criteria for admission into the system. Parks supporters accused the secretary of creating a "hit list of national parks or other areas which the Department would request the Congress to de-authorize."[8] They took seriously his declared intention to have the department turn parts of the system over to state and local governments, fearing especially the prospective loss of recreational areas and urban holdings.

Watt's remarks to the Conference of National Park Concessioners in March 1981 fueled concern. At the meeting he acknowledged his "bias for private enterprise" and promised to call upon the concessioners to "be involved in areas that you haven't been allowed to be involved in before."[9] "I will err on the side of public use versus preservation," he declared. "We will use the budget system to be the excuse to make major policy decisions."[10]

Watt charged that the parks suffered primarily from deteriorating facilities remediable by increased restoration and development. He requested that Congress amend the Land and Water Conservation Act in order to provide money for park development and maintenance.[11] Watt's avowed willingness to subvert the fund, heretofore limited exclusively to land acquisiton, caused visions of roads, bridges, buildings, and sewers to dance through environmentalists' heads. They regarded such emphasis as a path to "first rate plumbing . . . in a second rate park system."[12]

Meanwhile, NPS officials spoke of more serious and irreversible hazards. The agency's 1980 State of the Parks Report to Congress pointed out over 4,000 identifiable dangers to the parks' natural and cultural resources. These threats, not Watt's concerns, elicited NPS's most urgent attention.[13]

Congress did not always take well to Watt's assaults on the national park system. The legislators rejected his budgetary recommendations and voted $150 million for land acquisition in fiscal year 1982. Nevertheless, that sum represented a sharp reduction from $550 million, the average appropriation of the previous five years.[14] Under fierce pressure from the public and Congress, Watt backed off from some of his more extreme plans for the parks. He neither disavowed his beliefs nor altered his intentions, but he did bow to political practicality and tone down his more incendiary rhetoric while waiting for the storm to pass.

Although environmentalists assailed Watt's ideology, conservatives and business-oriented individuals praised his programs and policies. They had long waited for the political pendulum to swing away from preservation and back to use and development of public land. In Watt, they had a staunch advocate for their interests. The *National Review, Business Week, Conservative Digest, Reader's Digest*, and *Saturday Evening Post* joined the lesser-known, nonliberal press in supporting the Watt-Reagan road to "restoring America's greatness." They eagerly touted Watt's philosophy of multiple use and balanced management of the nation's resources.

Seldom had a secretary of the interior aroused such universal enmity among the environmentally minded public. From his controversial confirmation hearings on, both his motives and his manner called forth unprecedented fury and outrage from those who differed with him. Watt's scriptural fervor mocked the philosophies upon which the environmental movement had rested from its conception. Primarily religious, America's early conservation doctrine preached the oneness of man with nature and all creation. Such wonders as national parks became the earth's cathedrals, necessary for repose and renewal both then and in the future. Watt's religion, a born-again version of Christianity, on the other hand, taught that "the Earth is merely a temporary way station on the road to eternal life. It is unimportant except as a place of testing to get into heaven. The Earth was put here by the Lord for his people to subdue and to use for profitable purposes on their way to the hereafter."[15] He operated within a framework of values radically different from those that motivated environmentalists. He drew conclusions about the use of public lands that opposed their solutions in all respects, and his high position allowed him to translate his private values into public policy.

Before Watt had held office for a year, over one million Americans signed petitions demanding his removal. Environmental groups, often at odds with each other, united behind the "Dump Watt" campaign. Even the National Wildlife Federation, the largest, most conservative and Republican organization, signaled to Reagan to get rid of Watt. Although many analysts and much of the media saw Watt as a political liability to the Reagan administration, they failed to realize that his combativeness and Reagan's silken sincerity comprised two faces of the same ideological coin. In Watt, Reagan had found exactly the kind of Interior secretary he most wanted. Further, while Watt's actions, which attacked preservation values, subverted environmental protection laws, and destroyed supporting governmental agencies, alarmed large parts of the nation, they did not really represent anything new. Watt had, in fact, resurrected values as old as the nation itself, themes born again for the 1980s to comply with the philosophies of the new purveyors of power.

The national awareness of and concern for environmental values had culminated in the 1960s with the passage of landmark federal environmental protection legislation, which gave the government extensive new authority. Almost simultaneously, however, two movements arose, expressing views vastly different from those of the environmentalists. Both groups, spearheaded by simmering disaffection for increased federal power, represented values identical with those that had conflicted with preservationists since the early twentieth century—and that later fueled Interior's program for the 1980s.

In the Rocky Mountain West a potent combination of oil and mining interests, livestock owners, ranchers, farmers, and cowboys unfurled the first effort, the Sagebrush Rebellion, which sought to loosen oppressive restriction on the uses of public lands (which comprise about 60 percent of the acreage in eleven western states).

The second antigovernment movement emerged from within the national parks. There, inholders—owners of property inside of the parks—took issue with proposed new legislation that recommended accelerated purchase by the NPS of private property in the older parks and that intended the gradual elimination of all inholdings. A self-styled activist named Charles Cushman founded the National Inholders' Association, a group initially dedicated to "protect[ing] the environment of our national parks and property rights from blind bureaucracy."[16] Inevitably, Cushman and the Sagebrush Rebels found each other, and with Sagebrush support Cushman expanded his operation still further.

Moreover, Watt and Cushman sang in perfect harmony. The National Inholders' Association provided a ready-made lobbying constituency for Watt's policies. In gratitude Watt appointed Cushman to the prestigious and influential National Parks Advisory Board, thus legitimizing the man, his methods, and his mission. Cushman's tactics emasculated new preservation legislation and persuaded Watt to crusade against the NPS and any additions to the national park system.

Observers of the long contest for dominance over land in the Indiana Dunes did not find Watt's ideas unfamiliar. The secretary and his plans, programs, and policies struck a reminiscent chord because his dealings with the national parks rekindled the long-standing dispute between preservation and development, public good and private interest, and federal participation and state control that had once divided the Indiana Dunes. His actions caused rearticulation of the underlying values affecting land use in the Dunes and reexamination of the governmental decision-making process that had both created a park and encouraged industrial expansion. Though time and location differed, much remained unchanged. New faces and new voices did not conceal old arguments, motivations, philosophies, and rhetoric. The old problems did require new solutions, however, for while the debate continued, the land disappeared.

NOTES

1. "Interior Department Seal to Change," Gary *Post Tribune*, Apr. 7, 1982.
2. Chuck Williams, "The Park Rebellion," *Not Man Apart*, June 1982, p. 12.
3. Elizabeth Drew, "Secretary Watt," *New Yorker*, May 4, 1981, p. 104.
4. Ron Wolf, "God, James Watt, and the Public's Land," *Audubon*, May 1981, p. 58.
5. Friends of the Earth, Natural Resources Defense Council, Wilderness Society, Sierra Club, National Audubon Society, Environmental Defense Fund, Environmental Policy Center, Environmental Action, Defenders of Wildlife, and Solar Lobby, *Indictment, the Case against the Reagan Environmental Record* (Washington, D.C., Mar. 1982), p. 15.
6. Ibid.
7. Drew, "Secretary Watt," p. 124.
8. Philip Shabecoff, "Watt Seeks New Trails for National Parks," New York *Times*, May 24, 1981.
9. Ibid.
10. Drew, "Secretary Watt," p. 129.
11. Friends of the Earth et al., *Indictment*, p. 15.
12. Ibid.
13. Robert Cahn, "Nation's Oldest Park Fends off New Incursions," *Christian Science Monitor*, June 14, 1982.
14. Friends of the Earth et al., *Indictment*, p. 16.
15. Wolf, "God, James Watt," p. 65.
16. Williams, "Park Rebellion," p. 14.

DUEL for the DUNES

PART I THE LONG WAR

Between the dawn of the twentieth century and 1966, major industries and conservationists competed for control of the Indiana Dunes. Early in the fierce and historic conflict, proponents of growth and development reenacted the nation's economic history as they attempted to industrialize Indiana's Lake Michigan shore. To their surprise, an opposing faction arose, dedicated to saving the Dunes as a national park. Over the decades preservationists stubbornly and persistently rejected economic uses of the land, thereby defying dominant, traditional American values. During the same years developers, together with political allies, single-mindedly pursued their time-tested vision of progress. Aided by mentors in Indianapolis and Washington, the two forces fought out these clashing philosophies on the Dunes battlefield.

Part I examines the protracted controversy between the two parties. It follows the manipulations of U.S. Steel and Bethlehem Steel, a half century apart, as these corporations attempted to gain prominence in the Midwest. It portrays the desperate yearning of northwest Indiana's boosters for a federally financed port to catch up and keep up with Chicago's economic lead. It documents the unwavering determination of scientists and conservationists to prevent the destruction of the Indiana Dunes, a beautiful, fragile, and unique natural area of worldwide scientific reputation.

The first six chapters present the actors on both sides of the conflict, their motives, strategies, triumphs, and disappointments. They follow the formation of advocacy groups for each position and trace the development of relevant legislation. The narrative analyzes the events in terms of values, politics, and the decision-making process. Chapter seven discusses the dynamics of presidential compromise and its ultimate effect on the struggle.

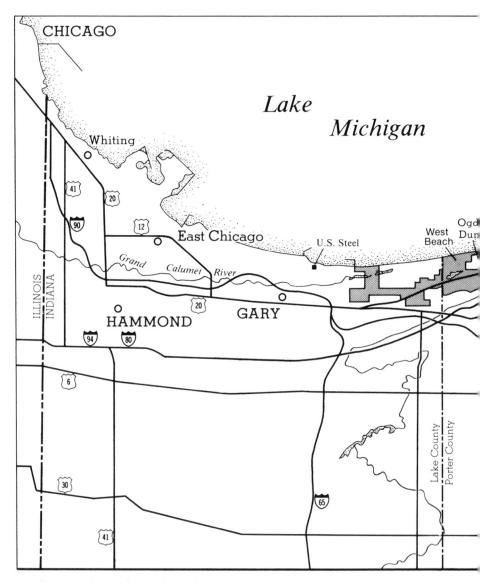

Northwest Indiana after Industrialization

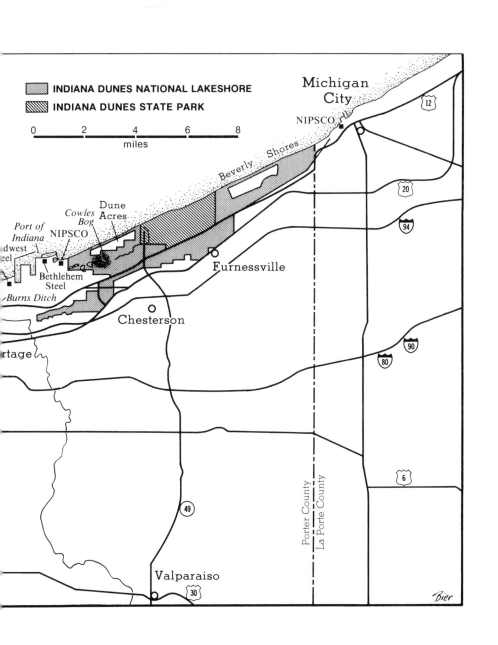

INDIANA DUNES NATIONAL LAKESHORE

INDIANA DUNES STATE PARK

0   2   4   6   8
            miles

Michigan
City

NIPSCO

12

Beverly Shores

20

94

Dune
Acres

Cowles
Bog

Port of
Indiana

NIPSCO

dwest
eel

Bethlehem
Steel

Burns Ditch

Furnessville

rtage

Chesterson

90

80

6

49

Porter County
La Porte County

Valparaiso

30

Bier

1 Battleground

Indiana's Lake Michigan coastline of the 1980s displays the full range of uses made possible by nature and devised by an industrial society. In the space of forty-five miles, tank farms, steel mills, and power plants intermingle with dunes and forests. Murky smoke clouds the routes of migratory birds; game fish and factory effluent combine beneath the lake's surface; luxurious private homes dot the high sand hills, while the cool woods conceal ramshackle summer cottages. Two parks, the Indiana Dunes State Park and the Indiana Dunes National Lakeshore, exist side by side, separated only by mutual distrust and a barbed wire fence. Many governmental bodies and agencies, many interest groups, and many individuals claim jurisdiction over this shoreline region. It has taken more than a century of discord and struggle to fragment the Indiana Dunes. Evolving social values and changing politics have produced the present land use pattern.

Had the values of the nineteenth century prevailed, such incompatible land use would likely not have occurred in the Dunes. Almost universally, Americans of the 1800s accepted growth and development as the nation's most worthy goals. Fresh from the carefully husbanded, crowded lands of Europe, pioneers and settlers responded to the limitless frontier with boundless energy and determination to subdue the wilderness. In contrast with what they left behind, America's vastness inspired optimistic confidence in the future. The will to develop the nation's God-given resources permeated nineteenth-century thinking and action. The citizenry cleared the forests, plowed the prairies, fenced the plains, harvested the lakes and rivers, and mined the earth beneath the mountains, believing in their right and obligation to make productive use of what they found.

The young nation could afford to make mistakes. It possessed more of everything—land for farming, wild animals for food and clothing, more forests, more rivers, more hills, and more potential for wealth and a new prosperous life than the combined imaginations of the Old World could fathom. The amount of work required for success seemed minuscule when measured against the universal expectation of dazzling rewards. No permanent failures existed in the minds of these Americans. One could always push further into a new frontier with the anticipation of finding an equally rich supply of resources. America existed for use, for building on and building up, and if, in the process, the people misused or wore out parts of its territory, more and still more lay ahead.

The industrial revolution of the century's second half provided the means for full realization of these national aspirations. It produced an increased standard of living, large urban centers of wealth and commerce, effective and efficient transportation systems, and machinery to build, manufacture, and expand, seemingly without end. No one could lose in this new world of opportunity. While the common man reveled in a newly acquired right of ownership, living out his often hard life beholden to no one, men like the Vanderbilts, the Guggenheims, and the Morgans busied themselves carving the nation into private dynasties. These men and their kind no longer contended for gold, jewels, spices, and silk, for centuries the plunder of the Old World. Instead they battled for control of railroads, mines, and steel mills, the riches of the New.

Even the immigrants toiling in the new industrial gloom did so as a *rite de passage* to a betterment they knew would come. As the industrial revolution absorbed the native labor supply, it allowed Europe's displaced millions to find homes, jobs, and rapid resettlement. By the beginning of the twentieth century the national pursuit of growth, development, and economic gain had succeeded overwhelmingly. America led the industrial nations of the world.

In Indiana far-sighted leaders had attempted to protect the state's economic future even before its admission to the Union. Controversy about the Lake Michigan shoreline first erupted in 1787, when the Northwest Ordinance fixed the original boundaries of Ohio, Indiana, and Illinois, leaving Indiana without lake frontage. Jonathan Jennings, delegate to Congress from the Indiana Territory, recognized correctly that access to the world's sixth largest lake would increase Indiana's economic potential. Despite the popular wisdom of the time, which considered much of the land in the territory poor in quality, especially near Lake Michigan, Jennings proposed extensive boundary changes. Because they proved too extreme to suit Michigan Territory, much of whose shoreline Jennings coveted, he reluctantly scaled down his plans. In 1816 Congress passed his amended bill, adding 1,100 square miles to Indiana, including forty-five miles of lakeshore.

Although congressional action had legally settled the northern boundary, the equally difficult task of surveying the line between Indiana and Illinois remained. Early in 1821 Indiana's first governor, the same Jonathan Jennings, appointed General John Tipton as commissioner to conduct the boundary survey in conjunction with a commissioner from Illinois. By May the project had started.

WORTHLESS LAND

Late in the evening of Tuesday, May 15, 1821, John Tipton and a black boy named Bill departed from Corydon, Indiana's first state capital. From there they headed west to Vincennes, where, on the 18th, they met Illinois's representative, Samuel McClintoc. The two commissioners spent the rest of May and most of June establishing their procedure; they hired John McDonald of Knox City as surveyor, at $4.50 a mile, and obtained all necessary personnel. When they had completed the arrangements, they traversed the 235 miles between Vincennes and the village of Chicago, detouring on the last day of June to attend an inspection of arms at Fort Dearborn. Following the noon ceremony, they proceeded to Chicago, where they planned to spend the night as guests of Dr. Alexander Wolcott, Indian agent for the region.

The village consisted of nine or ten houses situated on both sides of the Chicago River, all occupied by French traders and their families. Tipton described the settlement as lacking in "any kind of civil government."[1] *Wolcott had a comfortable home, however, and the delegation spent a pleasant evening drinking wine and receiving information about the next day's destination, the lake-rivers country.*

Having already put in a supply of pork and flour, they departed at daybreak and proceeded to the Indian villages at the junction of the "Calliminks," later known as the Grand and Little Calumet rivers. They then stopped and hired Indians to assist them in crossing horses and baggage to the north side of the Grand Calumet, where they planned "to run out the state line until it intercepts the lake."[2]

The next evening the weather made Tipton wish for the warmth of Wolcott's home. "The wind commensed Blowing a strong gale from the north and has continued all this day (which happily ride us of our common ennimy the muscheeters). [It] is so cold, I had to ware my grate coat all day. We encamped on the shore under some pine bushes, the wind increaseing and verry cool."[3] *When the wind finally died down, Tipton and his party viewed the Lake Michigan shore for the first time and found little to recommend it. "Covering the shore are small pine and cedar trees very few large enough for building or other use. Most of the way, the margin of the lake is lined with small hills of white sand rising five to ten feet above the country in back of them."*[4] *Tipton dismissed the lake country brusquely. "It is my opinion the hills are formed by the sand beating out of the Lake by the waves when it becomes dry. The hard wind which pervails here from the north drives it into those heaps. Immediately behind those hills the country falls off into ponds and marshes that never can admit of settlement nor never will be of much service to our state."*[5] *Having completed its work there, the surveying team vacated the Indiana Dunes without regret.*

In the thirty years following Tipton's journey, few settlers found their way to northern Indiana. Prior to 1850 southerners migrating northward from North Carolina, Maryland, Virginia, Tennessee, and Kentucky had populated the fertile banks of southern Indiana's waterways, the Ohio, the Whitewater, the Wabash, and the White rivers. They scrambled to purchase land parcels—some as small as forty acres—from federal land agents at $1.25 per acre and disciplined themselves to the rigors of pioneer existence in the expectation of a better, richer, and freer life. In contrast, settlers who headed west from New York, Pennsylvania, and New England in the 1830s and 1840s tended to bypass Indiana altogether. Deterred by the swampy, inhospitable land of northern Indiana, at the time reputed as unsuitable for agriculture, easterners tended to follow the Erie Canal to the Great Lakes and then proceed by boat to northern Ohio and southern Michigan and, in later years, to Illinois and Wisconsin.

Nonetheless, by 1850 a sparse population had settled Lake and Porter counties, two of the three counties that include the Indiana Dunes. Lake County claimed a population of 3,991 at that time, and Porter, 5,234. Few of these inhabitants, however, lived north of the Little Calumet River.[6] Instead they farmed the more arable land to its south. Despite the relative richness of that land, and despite ingrained qualities of independence, self-reliance, and self-sufficiency, these pioneers found that physical isolation, poor transportation facilities, and the high cost of tools and equipment produced an existence far less comfortable than the life they had imagined.

Even after 1850 few settlers saw any reason to contradict Tipton's disparaging conclusions about the Indiana Dunes. Accurately they regarded the lake country as both enemy and obstacle. In contrast to adjacent land to the south, the Dunes proved a pioneer's nightmare. It consisted of sand hills, thick woods, or unnavigable, mosquito-filled swamps. Located far from adequate transportation, the Dunes provided nothing of practical value for the settler.

A less agrarian-minded individual of that period might have agreed more with the observations of William Keating, U.S. War Department geologist, who had explored Indiana's Lake Michigan shoreline in 1823. "The view towards the north was boundless; the eye meeting nothing but the vast expanse of water, which spread like a sea, its surface at that time as calm and unruffled as though it were a sheet of ice. Towards the south the prospect was limited to a few yards, being suddenly cut off by a range of low sand hills which arose to heights varying from 20 to 40 feet, in some instances rising perhaps to upwards of 100 feet. . . . The sand hills are undulating and crowned at their summit with a scrubby growth of white pine and firs, while the brow which faces the lake is quite bare."[7]

Situated only thirty-five miles across Lake Michigan's waters from embryonic Chicago, the Dunes presented a splendid, primitive wilderness unlike any other in the nineteen states. Its formation had begun about 10,000 years before, when the waters of ancient Lake Chicago, precursor of Lake Michigan and product of the retreating glaciers of the Wisconson period, began to recede. During the next 9,000 years, the water level of Lake Chicago dropped a number of times. These changes in lake level, large, sudden, and unexplained, resulted in a series of dune ridges extending northward to the present shore of Lake Michigan. The Dunes country, nestled between these ancient and new shorelines, offered a unique, various, and ever-changing spectacle to the receptive eye. No single aspect lacked the characteristic, startling beauty of the whole: fine white beaches deposited for eons by angry lake storms, low dunes held stable by marram grass and sand cherry, woods composed of both northern and southern pine, ancient climax forests of beech and maple, and, no less breathtaking, the bogs, ponds, and swamps between the shoreline ridges. The Dunes exhibited a collage of contrasts, delicate and lush, stationary and moving, living, changing, dying, and living again.

Inhabited only little and lately by man, the Dunes long abounded with plant and animal life. Here many species reached their geographical limits, living side by side in uncommon proximity. Here, compressed in harmonious balance, flora and fauna belonging to the Arctic, the tropics, and the desert found a new home and thrived alongside the less flamboyant natives. Through the years the Potawatomi and other Indian tribes traversed the Dunes, marking trails that later became the railroad beds and highways of "civilized" man. Although they engaged in seasonal hunting and berry-picking, they did no damage to the Dunes environment. Despite the presence of both Indians and the occasional white settlers, the Dunes remained largely unobserved and undisturbed by man over the centuries of its evolution. Far into the nineteenth century it continued unappreciated and unwanted, indeed unnoticed, until long after the surrounding area achieved significant agricultural and industrial development.

By the 1850s those westbound settlers who previously shunned northern Indiana had thrust Chicago forward. Merely an unimportant trading post at the mouth of a marshy river prior to 1830, Chicago in two decades catapulted its geographical assets into a booming metropolitan success. The Erie Canal's completion in 1825 linked the Atlantic states to the Great Lakes, thus shifting the pathway of western movement north from the former Ohio River route and making Chicago the gateway to the frontier. Service industries sprang up to accommodate those poised to test the western wilderness; the city grew.

A further impetus toward greatness came with the unprecedented proposal to build a canal through the Chicago portage, known since the first European explorations in 1673 as the link between two river basins, the St. Lawrence and the Mississippi.[8] Congress allowed 284,000 acres to be sold, for the most part to raise construction funds for the canal. Completion seemed almost superfluous, for the concept alone put Chicago on the map. In 1848, however, the Illinois and Michigan Canal did open, joining the Mississippi River to the Great Lakes. That substantial connection solidified Chicago's position as a water gateway and established the city as a commercial hub. By 1857 Chicago's population had swelled from 12,000 to 74,000. The emerging midwestern capital had surpassed St. Louis as a livestock, grain, and shipping center.

Though crucial to Chicago's rise, the Illinois and Michigan Canal experienced early disfavor. A mere nine years after its glorious initiation, the railroads advanced sufficiently to rival water transport as a carrier of goods and people, making the canal virtually obsolete.[9] Rail developers quickly capitalized on Chicago's advantages; the city became the core of America's transcontinental route by 1869. Industry of all sorts tumbled in on the heels of expanding railroads. From the mines and forests of upper Michigan and Minnesota, lake vessels hauled iron ore to the waiting blast furnaces and lumber to supply the unending building boom. Railroads brought produce from the South and West, as well as hogs, cattle, and sheep to supply Chicago's sprawling meat-packing industry. Chicagoans recognized and maximized the natural advantages of their city. If its Indian name meant skunk or wild onion as many alleged, who cared? Others claimed the name meant powerful, and Chicago certainly qualified for that designation in the fifty years following its incorporation.[10] Transportation, industry, money, and people—by the 1880 census, half a million of them—combined to make Chicago the major city of the Midwest and the second largest in the nation.

Earlier in the century, however, other sites had competed for Chicago's position. Between 1830 and 1840 three other cities sprang up at the southern end of Lake Michigan, each hoping to become a major commercial center. In 1832 Michigan City, Indiana, developed on the site that two years earlier marked the northern terminus of the Michigan Road, a route from Madison, Shelbyville, and Indianapolis. In the expectation of its becoming a major shipping port, city boosters requested federal aid to build a harbor. Tipton, then Indiana's U.S. senator, convinced Congress to spend $2,000 to construct what he believed might become the Midwest's biggest port. Though federal appropriations began in 1836, the harbor took many years to become even reasonably operational. Too shallow and plagued by constant need for dredging, Michigan City's harbor lacked sufficiently noisy political mentors to insure that the necessary federal grants continued.[11]

The second of Chicago's potential rivals, Indiana City, would have developed in Lake County near the old mouth of the Grand Calumet River if its promoters had proved successful. Due to the panic of 1837, the project remained on paper, another in the ranks of similarly fated Indiana dream cities.[12]

The third rival, Porter County's City West, looked more promising. Speculators from Michigan City and Porter County attracted twenty families, as well as a hotel, a sawmill, a blacksmith shop, and a store. They based hopes for success on a proposed canal that was to link Lake Michigan with the Kankakee River. With the completion of this grandiose project, City West, together with the neighboring settlement of Waverly, confidently expected "to draw the trade of the whole county to City West and the Lake."[13] And why not? Plans for the canal included a huge water wheel for production of manufacturing power. Stage lines providing transportation east and west traversed the site. Furthermore, the state legislature seemed committed to massive expenditures for canals and roads, some of which might surely find its way to a northern Indiana project.

Since the 1820s Indiana had watched as neighboring states undertook programs of road and canal building at public expense. Although conservative Hoosiers predicted a financial debacle from such plans, the politicians who favored them triumphed, promising farmers that "an extra hen and a chicken would pay for the additional taxes."[14] In January 1836 the General Assembly authorized the Internal Improvements bill, a massive public works hodgepodge including three canals (construction had already begun on two), several railroads, and a turnpike or two. In all, the legislature authorized eight projects, increasing state indebtedness to $10 million, a mighty sum in those days, considering that the entire state's annual income only came to $75,000.

Everything that could have gone wrong did. Farmers, who knew an opportunity to get rich quick when they saw one, speculated wildly, forcing land prices up and up. Gross mismanagement prevailed, alongside inefficiency, political favoritism, and out-and-out graft. Construction costs inflated because of the unwillingness of contractors to cooperate in the interests of economy. Unanticipated maintenance problems (the voracious appetites of Indiana muskrats not the least of them) surfaced. Completion sagged further and further behind as prices doubled. Only one of the eight projects, the Wabash and Erie Canal, reached completion. The others, abandoned at various stages of work, either were transferred to private hands or remained in their unfinished states. This first legislative attempt to sponsor public works almost became the last. The state defaulted, coming agonizingly close to bankruptcy.

Aghast at this unexpected result, Indiana took determined steps to prevent a repetition of such fiscal irresponsibility. Its second constitution, written in 1851, prohibited the state from going into debt. Although this provision limited continued state support of public works and economic development, it did not dampen the legislative taste for it. Future state administrations would find ingenious methods of circumventing the constitutional restrictions.

By 1836 the future of City West seemed so bright that banks issued mortgages for all available property; the money flowed in. Though Congress had not yet approved federal aid for the canal and Michigan City harbor, it dispatched an investigating committee headed by the acclaimed statesman and national hero, Daniel Webster. He visited City West on July 1, 1837, as he concluded a leisurely tour of the West. Local boosters, convinced that their soil far surpassed that of Michigan City for harbor purposes, tried by all means, including lavish entertainment, to convince Webster of the vital importance of their project. Polite but noncommittal, he continued east, stopping in Michigan City, where harbor promoters provided even more royal festivities.

Without political backing, City West failed to qualify for the federal appropriation, while the Michigan City harbor received additional funds.[15] Those splendid dreams of a Porter County harbor, which would make City West the mercantile capital of the Midwest, disintegrated and with them City West itself. Future Porter County boosters would revive that dream often, reminding themselves that Michigan City and Chicago, the only two cities at the southern end of Lake Michigan to survive and succeed, received federal subsidies for harbor development while all those without such funds had failed.

Although northern Indiana's dream cities of the 1830s failed to materialize, developers and boosters in Lake and Porter counties never abandoned their envy of Chicago, nor their attempts to emulate its success. Eventually, as Chicago realized the economic potential of its strategic location, a similar, albeit slower, phenomenon occurred in the Dunes counties of Porter and Lake.

Compared with Chicago, Indiana got a late start. Dunes swamp had prevented development of the railroads during the earliest waves of construction. In 1850, however, Congress ceded swamp lands to their host states provided that they apply all proceeds from sales to reclamation. Two years later the Indiana General Assembly enacted legislation regulating the sale, drainage, and reclamation of such marshland. Before long, far-sighted speculators unloaded the drained and profitable product on the hungry railroads. Between 1852 and 1854 the price of worthless Dunes swamp skyrocketed from $1.25 to $42.95 per acre.[16]

The Dunes then began to feel the impact of Chicago's economic expansion. Whereas in 1850 fewer than 100 people lived in the Lake County Dunes north of the Little Calumet River, rail access and cheap land prices produced an instant population of speculators. The Dunes may not have been good for farming, but it did not take long to find a multitude of other uses. Dunes sand, in seemingly endless supply, provided the most obvious, most profitable product. Only the drunken expansion of Chicago's environs threatened the limits of this enormous resource. Cities and towns filled their swamps with it. Contractors used it by the carload, and the rampaging railroads could not get it fast enough. The overhead could not have gotten lower: sand-mining companies backed a railroad siding into the nearest dune, chuted or shoveled sand into a waiting car, and thereby provided round-the-clock supply and a profit to match. They often loaded at the extravagant rate of 300 cars every twenty-four hours. Some concerns, unwilling to pay property owners for their sand, found a free supply by using the sandsucker, a machine that took the sand directly from the shallow lake bottom. Chicago rose, expanded, flourished, and rebuilt itself after its great fire on sand from the Indiana Dunes. While not as extensive as the sand-mining industry, other Dunes products also made good money. Lumber, berries, ice, fish, and game caused everyone to look at this formerly worthless land in a new and golden light.

Meanwhile, civic leaders in Lake and Porter counties, observing Chicago's dizzying rise, panted in anticipation of their share in the bonanza. Although the geographical potential that gave rise to Chicago existed east of the state line as well, no similar miracle occurred in Indiana. By this late date Chicago had completely captured the Midwest market. The possibility, which had existed in the 1830s, for a northern Indiana town to become a major metropolitan center no longer existed. Despite a few sporadic successes prior to the 1880s the ambitious schemes of promoters to attract industry and wealth to northern Indiana resulted largely in frustration and failure. Infant towns, widely separated by impassable terrain, competed fiercely, attempting first one scheme and then another to create, induce, lure, or steal some industry. But the little that materialized did not go around. A mere pittance as compared with Chicago's, the scarce supply served to remind everyone of the lasting rivalries between neighboring towns, adjoining counties, and northwest Indiana and the now great city of Chicago.

A. J. BOWSER

Toward the end of the nineteenth century, when boosterism held sway as the nation's favorite sport, A. J. Bowser of Chesterton, Indiana, joined the scramble to put his town on the map and keep it there. Born next door in Valparaiso in 1862, Bowser moved to Chesterton in 1884 as owner and publisher of the Chesterton Tribune. Although only twenty-two, his six years of experience as a printer and newspaperman assured success for the Tribune as well as a position of leadership for himself. Promoting the progress of the community became Bowser's obsession. With his whole being he believed in his friend and neighbor, the whole-souled, prosperous, God-fearing, and contented local farmer. A promotional genius with the soul of a robber baron, he made it his mission, and that of the Tribune, to beat the drum for Chesterton, home of his manhood. In the fashion typical of his day, Bowser did not bother to confine his views to the editorial page. They appeared wherever and whenever he chose. Consider page 1, August 10, 1900: "Hoosiers are not fools, and the conditions which have brought prosperity to the country at large prevail here as fully as anywhere else in the country." Read page 5, July 6, 1900: "endorse the GOP for its record of business prosperity, stable currency, and patriotic Americanism. The threat to prosperity has always rested in the ranks of the Democratic party as well as in its incapacity to properly manage our public affairs." His fervor reflected an old-fashioned, flag-waving, horn-blowing patriot who promoted God, motherhood, the Republican party, country, county, Chesterton, and, last but not least, A. J. Bowser.

Like his counterparts everywhere, Bowser had more pies than he had fingers to put in them. Although he loved the Tribune first, he promoted his real estate interests with almost equal vigor. A handy vehicle to publicize any of Bowser's projects, the Tribune played its part in his most ambitious project. The rivalry between Chesterton and Porter, its neighbor about a mile to the east, concerned Bowser greatly. He knew the sparse business and industry would not go around and that neither town could exist merely as a settlement for retired farmers. So Bowser dreamed and schemed of merging the two into an industrial metropolis of 50,000 people. That in 1883 a brick yard employing forty people comprised Porter's most outstanding asset and that Chesterton's organ factory reached a total of 125 workers by the beginning of the next decade might have satisfied most, but not Bowser. He contacted some moneyed Chicagoans, whom he knew through his real estate business. With their backing he formed the Chicago-Porter Home Investment Company and then promoted it to the skies. For the better part of five years Bowser seemed a prophet as well as an optimist, but in the long run the scheme did not amount to much. Despite excursion trains from Chicago serving free beer and lunches, despite the promise of an opera house, a water works, and an electric light company intended for the masses of industries eager to relocate, the company (by 1895 renamed the Porter Land and Manufacturing Company) went bankrupt. To nobody's surprise, the court appointed none other than attorney A. J. Bowser to oversee the proceeding.

Because of his local prominence and business interests, politics came naturally to Bowser. By the time of his election to the Porter County Council in 1902, the readers of the Tribune had long acquaintance with his political predilections. Each preelection issue, under a Bowser byline, carried detailed front-page instructions showing how to cast a ballot for the Republican candidates. The Democratic hopefuls might as well not have existed—if indeed they did—for they rated nary a mention in any Bowser publication. The 40 percent of the populace who voted for the Democrats had to find a copy of the Porter County Herald, which listed its candidates and unblushingly omitted the Republicans.

Following a four-year stint in the council, Bowser graduated to the Indiana senate, where he represented both Lake and Porter *counties, and served until 1910. There, and perhaps unknowingly, he made a lasting mark on history. He sponsored a land reclamation bill, known as the Made-Land bill, which allowed heavy industry, then waiting in Indiana's wings, to acquire free land by filling in Lake Michigan's waters. This legislation set the stage for the Dunes country to compete as the biggest steel-producing region in the United States.*

With the Made-Land bill as his swan song, Bowser retired from public life and devoted himself to his still impressive business interests, including, of course, the Chesterton Tribune, *and to a long life editorially monitoring the community welfare.*[17]

Early failures and a late start notwithstanding, Lake County's superior location, combined with its cheap and formerly useless land, its access to surface as well as water transportation, and its proximity to a readily available labor supply, finally brought industrialization at the end of the nineteenth century on a scale undreamed of only a few decades earlier. Long-term, flirtatious wooing of Chicago industries by Indiana's Lake County cities achieved first success in 1889, when Standard Oil decided to build a major oil refinery in Whiting, Indiana. By the 1880s the revolting stench of crude oil, together with the visible dangers of its piping and storage, had dampened Chicago's enthusiasm for such industries. Expelled from Illinois, Standard Oil arrived, greatly welcomed, in Indiana. The event ushered in an industrial expansion that would make Commissioner Tipton's worthless land among the most economically productive and valuable in the nation. Moreoever, the 1892 discovery of rich iron ore in Minnesota's Mesabi range prompted the steel industry to seek further productive capacity in the Chicago area. Chicago, however, had run out of space for the kind of heavy industry that needs cheap land and abundant water. Furthermore, in its incarnation after the great fire, the city had developed a rudimentary refinement that eschewed the more noxious elements of the industries which had previously sustained it. This forced steelmakers to look elsewhere. If the coming of Standard Oil marked the initial stage in Indiana's romance of industry, the arrival of steel revealed a still greater passion and created profound and lasting changes.

Already venerable by the late 1880s, Chicago's iron industry had started sixty years earlier with small foundries along the Chicago River. Iron and steelmaking expanded rapidly there, spurred on by an insatiable market. The industry benefited from the vast ore deposits of the Lake Superior ranges, newly transportable via the Soo

Canal, the accessibility of Indiana, Illinois, and Appalachian coal and limestone easily shipped from Michigan, Indiana, Illinois, and western Lake Erie. For fifty years ironmaking remained in the same location, not moving southward until 1880, when Illinois Steel built its South Works. Then outside the city limits, South Works marked the beginning of a long search for sites combining inexpensive land and plentiful water to meet an ever-accelerating demand for steel.[18] As steelmaking concentrated in the unincorporated areas south of the city, older plants along the Chicago River fell into disuse and eventually disappeared. The steel companies now preferred sites along the Calumet River and Lake Michigan, in part owing to federal development of the South Chicago harbor begun in 1870. Furthermore, these locations offered accessibility to lake transportation for bringing in ore, coal, and limestone and for shipping out finished products, features highly prized by the industry. The Great Lakes provided low-cost transportation, unparalleled access to raw materials without further transshipment by rail, and easy proximity to markets.

Increased urbanization of midwestern and western states made Chicago ideally suited for distribution of finished steel products. In fact, regional consumption then accounted for one-fourth of the country's output of steel. By 1876, for example, Chicago's production of steel rails comprised one-third of the national total. Chicago steelmakers could supply a waiting market because their proximity to fabricating industries, as well as rail and water transportation, permitted efficient and economical distribution.[19] Economies resulting from these advantages allowed Chicago to rival the older eastern producers.

Consolidation and elimination of competition permitted cost cutting. By the turn of the century only five companies produced the Midwest's entire output. In addition, industrial integration, that is, internal control of raw materials and their transport, as well as control of the use of by-products and subsidiary fabricating plants, strengthened their position still further.[20] The early 1900s saw a race for expansion in the industry among existing midwestern companies. Only constant increases in facilities and capacity could keep pace with the continuing demand.

In 1901 some 200 steel companies combined to create U.S. Steel. The new giant used a variety of monopolistic practices to capture 60 percent of the nation's steel market. Concerned with shutting out competition and maintaining industry-wide supremacy, U.S. Steel searched for a new site, hopefully "midway between the Minnesota ore and the coal fields of the south," from which to rule the Midwest market.[21] Expansion of existing facilities had proved impractical, but several new locations looked feasible. Planners required a lakeshore site large enough to provide room for later placement of fabricating industries as well as one with sufficient space for housing the workers. In addition, they preferred a minimum of governmental regulations pertaining to harbor and breakwater construction. Whereas Illinois law dealing with submerged lands impeded development of harbor facilities, Indiana, due to the efforts of the forward-thinking Bowser, permitted and encouraged lakefront industrial development. At last, the needs of heavy industry coincided with desires longheld in the Dunes counties. U.S. Steel's selection of undeveloped lands in Indiana's Lake County solved the company problem while satisfying the most fervent hopes of Lake County's promoters.

In 1904 U.S. Steel selected A. F. Knotts, former mayor of Hammond, Indiana, and acting-attorney for the steel company, to choose a site and become the broker for the new plant. Because of his experience and knowledge, Knotts surpassed all other candidates for the job. Though a self-made, self-educated man, as mayor he had demonstrated the necessary intelligence and ability to improve Hammond's manufacturing capacity. He knew northern Indiana, especially the Dunes area, well and applied all his native shrewdness and capability to the company's assignment. When asked if he thought the proposed site could be obtained at a good price, Knotts replied, "It is said that every man has his price, which I doubt, but there is no question but what the holders of large tracts of unoccupied lands would sell them at a good price. When one purchases the land for business or industrial purposes he does not purchase the land but [instead] the location."[22]

Knotts first scouted the Porter-Furnessville-Chesterton area but found that, despite Porter County boosters' well-known interest in industrialization, prices there had jumped too high. Then Knotts, together with Eugene J. Buffington, president of U.S. Steel's newly named Indiana Steel Company, selected a lower-priced site in Lake County, perfect for their purpose. Close to Chicago's enormous and seemingly limitless market, it bordered Lake Michigan, provided the largest lake vessels with sufficient water depth, abutted established rail transport, and seemed cheap enough. Huge by any standard, the tract comprised 9,000 acres with over seven miles along Lake Michigan's shore.

Knotts's memoirs describe the politics of site approval at the turn of the century. "The company had to get federal authority to establish a city and to use the lake front and water supply. Federal Representative, Judge E. D. Crumpacker, drew up the bill to clarify that point and the matter was then taken up with the War Department [predecessor of the Army Corps of Engineers] instead of Congress to avoid petty politics and the War Department approved the project. Then the Indiana Legislature approved the Made Land bill and the Navigation Department granted permission to change the Calumet River."[23]

Even though industrial expansion eastward from Chicago had populated parts of Lake County, the chosen site remained wilderness. A. F. Knotts's brother, Tom, later recalled, "The site Gary was a primeval jungle, a barren waste of sand dunes and impassable morasses inhabited by small wild animals."[24] "The territory was traversed by several lines of railroads but otherwise it was [as] remote from the world as the fastness of Canadian forests."[25] Undesirable though it appeared—characteristic marshes covered with scrubby, tangled growth and dunes, the swampy Grand Calumet, neither river nor land—this land had been held by speculators awaiting the inevitable industrial purchasers. To avoid price escalation, the company conducted its land purchase negotiations with utmost secrecy. In 1906, as manager of the Gary Land Company, Knotts completed these transactions with assistance from his younger brother, Tom.

SETTLING GARY

"Although I was just a year old when we came to Gary, much later I asked my mother questions about it while she was still alive and I wrote it down. My folks lived in Hammond in 1905 where my father, Tom, was on the police force. He was a jovial man with a great sense of humor. He liked people—a natural-born politician, I guess you might say. He had gone through the eighth grade and then, like his brother A. F., he hired himself out as a teacher. For four years he taught school at a Sioux Indian Reservation in South Dakota. At any rate, my uncle, who was doing the buying for U.S. Steel, wanted him to come over to the site at Gary and be there in the summer of 1906. The Michigan Central train ran through there and Uncle A. F. thought people would get off and be interested in buying land. A. F. wanted someone there on the spot. Mother told me she knew my father was doing work for my uncle but she hadn't known exactly what he was doing. It was all kept very quiet because they didn't want the land prices to go up. Evidently they were pretty successful.

"I had four older brothers and I was a year old. My dad came home to lunch one day and said, 'How would you like to go on a *nice long camping trip?' The boys were immediately enthusiastic and wanted to know where, and he said, 'Over in the sand hills.' He told them there was a river there and they could have a canoe and they could go fishing.*

"My mother was taken by surprise but later he told her what my uncle had in mind. She wasn't too sure she wanted to do it. The boys were so enthusiastic—and my dad said, 'Would you try it for the summer?' Well, she agreed. My mother was very much of a pioneer-type woman—born in a log cabin and had grown up on a farm and had always known how to work hard and do everything, so she agreed.

"My father and my uncle made the arrangements—they came down on the train and brought a well digger with them. After they located three spots and put down wells, my father's partner came ahead and put down a wooden spar and wooden sides. Then they put a tent part over the top. It was a big tent—we were a good-sized family.

"When it came to moving, my mother decided, of course, they'd have to have beds, and they'd have to have an eating table, and she wanted her sewing machine and some dressers—so they loaded all this on a wagon pulled by a couple of horses. They started from Hammond early in the morning. My brother, Gene, came along and he carried his pet hen. They had to wind through the sandy ruts and trails around marshes and sloughs, and over hills so it was quite a long trip. It took almost all day. Later in the day, my father and mother and three brothers and I came on the Michigan Central to Tolleston, and there my father hired a buggy from one of the Bormans who had a grocery store there. They wound their way around from Tolleston in the buggy and, of course, my father was so heavy that I imagine he walked most of the way because it got to be too much for the horses. Mother said that as we came along, she saw her furniture all put off there, piece by piece, along the side of the road because it had gotten too heavy. Later, the men had to bring the moving wagon back and pick up the other pieces and bring them on.

"We arrived there quite late in the afternoon and that tent was the only thing there. Mother had prepared food for that night which she sent ahead in the wagon—a huge pan of baked beans, home-made bread, gingerbread—enough for us and the carpenter who was just finishing up.

"The carpenter then built another hut for cooking. They divided the main tent into three sections and put up curtains across on

ropes. We had a double bed and dresser in each corner. In the center section was a large oblong table and chairs. My mother tells how I often times rolled out of bed and got between the wooden sides of the tent and out in to the sand. The cook shack had an ice box and cooking stove and a place to store home canned goods. Mother had to keep a lot of staples because the closest grocery store was in Tolleston. My brothers had to walk the two miles to Tolleston for provisions and it was not a straight walk because they had to walk around the marshes. Mother would say that sometimes when she'd send my brothers for meat, it would spoil before they got back. We lived in that tent until fall and after we moved into it people did start getting off the train there so I guess it was worth it."[26]

U.S. Steel's plans for its Indiana facility followed a tradition begun by Scotch-born Robert Owen at the beginning of the nineteenth century. Owen and his disciples, like Francis Cabot Lowell and George Pullman, believed that industries had a social responsibility to their workers that included, among other benefits, housing, medical care, and facilities for worship, education, and cultural programs.[27]

In 1905 company engineers began secretly to design the plant. Its first superintendent, William P. Gleason, arrived in June 1906 to oversee the construction. About the same time A. F. Knotts, manager of the Gary Land Company, proceeded with the construction of the town, named for Judge Elbert H. Gary, chairman of the board of U.S. Steel. Knotts and Buffington, president of the Gary Land Company, hoped their new town would avoid both the exploitation and the paternalistic interference in workers' lives that had characterized Pullman and similar company towns. Instead, Buffington believed in Gary as an honest attempt to insure adequate living conditions near a steel-producing plant, not as a product of company domination.

Although officials expected the town to stay within the confines of what the steel company owned, it grew beyond those bounds almost immediately, causing friction between town and mill. Tom Knotts, Gary's first mayor and a fiery Democrat, often found himself in the position of defending town interests against those of the mill owners. In 1907 A. F. Knotts resigned, under pressure, from the Gary Land Company, having been accused of tending to his own interests—particularly Gary real estate—instead of those of Indiana Steel. Mill officials had experienced much conflict, caused, in their view, by the Knotts brothers.[28]

Despite the problems, contemporary observers viewed Gary as a modern miracle. To a nation intoxicated with the idea of modern industrial power, Gary symbolized the zenith. Stories about the founding of Gary and the coming of U.S. Steel became the substance of modern myth. People marveled at the heroic exploits involved in making it a reality. Gleason told of the monumental feats that U.S. Steel had accomplished:

> The mill site had to be raised 15 feet. The Lake depth had to be increased with suction pipes, great hills leveled, and sloughs filled. We moved as much dirt as the Panama Canal and moved a river 100 yards away. We had to lay a great water tunnel 80 feet below the surface, a mile out into the lake [having] a capacity of five million gallons a day. Tracks for three trunk lines had to be moved and the Grand Calumet had to be straightened for a distance of two miles.
> A great harbor had to be built, with a canal 5500 feet long, 250 feet wide, and a turnaround 750 feet in diameter . . . also to protect the harbor, a breakwater a mile long . . . mountains of concrete were poured, 160,000 tons of steel were used and a thousand men were employed.[29]

In erecting the Gary Works, hailed as the greatest steel plant in the world, U.S. Steel destroyed the Lake County Dunes forever. The creation of plant and town symbolized the predominant values of the previous fifty years—boosterism, economic growth, urbanization, and industrialization. That same half century saw America move from survival on the raw frontier to universal recognition as the greatest manufacturing power in the world. The nation optimistically believed that limitless growth, industrial advancement, and technological supremacy led to a strong society and a good life. Few Americans questioned these values. The political system at all governmental levels eased the way to their fulfillment by rapidly enacting legislation that encouraged industrial development. From its start in Chicago, industrialization sprawled inexorably eastward, passionately welcomed by Indiana, whose municipal and state governments hastened to provide quick and favorable laws. Northern Indiana had long awaited this time.

For centuries the Dunes had stood in self-contained isolation, remote, inaccessible, undisturbed by man. In less than 100 years this worthless land acquired incalculable economic value. By 1910, however, though industry had erased most of the Dunes in Lake County, the Porter County Dunes remained pristine and unspoiled. In increasing numbers people gathered there, in appreciation. They thus joined the small but growing nucleus seeking preservation.

NOTES

1. John Tipton, *The John Tipton Papers*, comp. Glen A. Blackburn (Indianapolis: Indiana Historical Bureau, 1942), p. 267.
2. Ibid.
3. Ibid., p. 271. Although Tipton was in many ways very able and informed, he lacked the benefits of a formal education; his somewhat original spelling is reproduced here.
4. Ibid.
5. Ibid.
6. Powell A. Moore, *The Calumet Region* (Indianapolis: Indiana Historical Bureau, 1959), p. 79.
7. Federal Writers' Project, *Indiana: The Calumet Region Historical Guide* (East Chicago: Gorman Printing Co., 1939), p. 20.
8. John Husar, "Early Waterways Spurred Development of Chicago Area," Chicago *Tribune*, Sept. 21, 1980.
9. Ibid.
10. "Chicago," *Encyclopedia Britannica* (1974), 4: 208.
11. W. A. Briggs, "Chicago's Rivals, Part 1," Valparaiso *Vidette Messenger*, Jan. 17, 1935.
12. Moore, *Calumet Region*, p. 78.
13. Briggs, "Chicago's Rivals, Part 2," Valparaiso *Vidette Messenger*, Jan. 24, 1935.
14. George S. Cottman, *Indiana: Its History, Constitution and Present Government*, rev. ed. (Indianapolis: Bobbs Merrill, 1935), p. 88.
15. Briggs, "Chicago's Rivals, Part 2."
16. Moore, *Calumet Region*, pp. 93–94.
17. Ibid., pp. 125–30, 405–6. Thomas H. Cannon, H. H. Loring, and Charles J. Robb, eds., *History of the Lake and Calumet Region of Indiana*, vol. 2 (Indianapolis: Historian's Association, 1927), p. 688.
18. Phyllis Bate, "The Development of the Iron and Steel Industry of the Chicago Area, 1900–1920" (Ph.D. diss., University of Chicago, 1948).
19. Ibid., p. 207.
20. Ibid., p. 210.
21. "Birth of Gary," Gary *Post Tribune*, May 20, 1956.
22. Ibid.
23. Local History Scrapbooks, Gary Public Library.
24. "Tom Knotts' Own Story," Gary *Post Tribune*, June 3, 1956.
25. Ibid.
26. Authors' interview with Hazel Bowers, daughter of Tom Knotts, Edgewood, Ind., 1976.
27. "Industrial and Organizational Relations," *Encyclopedia Britannica* (1974), 9: 497.
28. Moore, *Calumet Region*, pp. 237–343; Cannon, Loring, and Robb, eds., *Lake and Calumet History*, 1: 739–70.
29. Gary Local History Scrapbooks.

CHAPTER 2 Conservation's First Defeat

As the nineteenth century ended, new voices questioning the effects and results of the nation's unchallenged economic materialism began to gain attention. Previously, most citizens believed in a "divine imperative," which held the vast continent and its natural resources as the raw materials, first of agricultural and later of industrial production. The sacredness of private property and the individual owner's right to use his land as he wished formed the fundamental tenets of this credo. Now the resulting conditions and consequences caused concern. In a mere hundred years Americans had transformed a wilderness into a highly productive agrarian and manufacturing society and had also created sufficient wealth and leisure to produce a new middle class that fostered different values. Adhering to the dominant belief in inevitable progress through economic growth, this group also supported endeavors designed to enhance the quality of life.

In the cities the settlement house movement tried to ameliorate working and living conditions of the urban poor. Overcrowded slums, densely packed streets, and the absence of recreational space led to provisions for playgrounds and parks. In the country threats of development and destruction of the remaining bits of untouched nature fueled a call for preservation. Beginning with prophets like Henry David Thoreau and George Perkins Marsh, a small but growing group of adherents had promoted governmental preservation of the land for aesthetic, moral, and scientific purposes. Their message meant little to pioneer farmers or to the developers of the country's mines, mills, and factories. By the late 1880s the impetus for preservation had grown, demanding intervention by government to check profligate exploitation of the country's natural resources.

Both wings of the conservation movement favored governmental action, though their purposes differed sharply. The more radical aesthetic conservationists urged political action to preserve land solely for nonutilitarian ends: beauty, open space, solitude, wildlife protection. The more moderate utilitarian conservationists promoted governmental protection of the land and its resources for orderly, efficient use. Both groups claimed that future generations would benefit from their programs. To a nation that had heretofore viewed the proper role of government as limited to defense and mail delivery, either choice required a change of direction in public policy. Beginning in the 1890s, the adherents of utilitarian conservation, headed by Gifford Pinchot, gained widespread support. In the next decade Pinchot, who became President Theodore Roosevelt's director of the Forest Service, advanced this brand of conservation. Roosevelt stated its credo: "Conservation does not mean nonuse or nondevelopment. It does not mean tying up the natural resources of the states. It means the utilization of those resources under such regulation and controls as will prevent waste, extravagance and monopoly, but at the same time, not merely promoting but encouraging such use and development as will serve the interests of the people generally."[1]

At the turn of the century the aesthetic conservationists could look with pride on the expanding city and state park movement, but their influence on the national level remained minimal. The city park movement had begun in 1858 with Frederick Law Olmstead's and Calvert Vaux's transformation of Manhattan swamp into New York City's Central Park. Other large cities, including Chicago, San Francisco, and Boston, followed in the succeeding decades. Twin motives accounted for the spread of municipal parks: the social welfare goal of providing open space for urban populaces and the economic hopes of real estate speculators, who saw land values increase in areas adjacent to parks. Railroads, too, promoted parks in order to provide attractions along their rights-of-way.

The national park movement originated with the establishment of Yellowstone in 1872. By the turn of the century these preserves included Sequoia, Yosemite, and Mt. Rainier. They resulted from the urgings of a tiny band of citizens who believed that "the natural 'wonders' of the United States should not be handed out to a few profiteers, but rather held in trust for all people for all time."[2] Every square inch of these protected lands, however, came from western federal holdings or from donations by state governments. Congress never spent any money to buy park land. National parks evolved from a "concentration on protecting unique scenery" and "monumentalism," which enhanced American prestige and national identity.[3] Moreover, the legislators in approving these preserves demanded assurance that they had no economic value. The authorization of some national parks even included provisions for development of mineral rights and other activities not consonant with the aim of unspoiled preservation.[4] This congressional stance derived, in part, from the political weakness of the aesthetic conservationists. Unlike practical conservationists, who controlled the Forest Service, they lacked a government agency to espouse their cause. In addition, no nationwide preservation organization of any importance then existed. The first such grass-roots group, the Sierra Club, began in 1892 and focused on protecting scenic resources in California and other western states. No other organization, truly national in scope or membership, had formed, except the tiny American Civic Association. However, its president, J. Horace McFarland, almost made up in tenacity what his group lacked in numbers or influence.

Yet, in spite of the divergent ends sought by these two branches of the conservation movement, their existence and their unified emphasis on the role of government in land use provided the climate for the coming struggle to protect the Indiana Dunes. Without the emergence of this new national conservation ethic, saving the Dunes would have remained a slogan. The immediate impetus for preservation of the Dunes resulted from the development of a conservation base in Chicago.

Chicago came into the twentieth century confident of a booming future. A "can-do" spirit permeated business and industrial leaders, who had already rebuilt the central city on a vast scale after the 1871 fire had reduced the downtown to ashes. Certain of continued economic growth, Chicago's rich and powerful, spurred on by a growing new middle class of professionals and business managers, turned their enthusiasm and energy to cultural, civic, and humanitarian endeavors.[5] The World Columbian Exposition of 1893 reflected these interests and, in turn, stimulated further activity. The exposition's "White City," with its thousands of exhibits demonstrating worldwide advances in the arts and sciences, presented a vision of an ordered, beautiful environment. The city's elite and the thousands of exposition visitors contrasted its harmonious world with the wretched physical conditions prevalent in Chicago's smoky, noisy, filthy, chaotic neighborhoods. If the fairgrounds could emerge from marshy lakefront in a matter of months, why not transform the mucklands of Fort Dearborn into a great and beautiful city?[6]

A civic renaissance resulted. In almost startling succession came the development of the University of Chicago campus, the construction of new skyscrapers, and the Burnham plan, an ambitious and farsighted attempt at city design emphasizing open space. Chicago's leading citizens contributed millions of dollars and their prestige in support of all of these projects. Jane Addams's settlement houses thrived. To start *Poetry Magazine,* Harriet Monroe found it easy to raise one hundred dollars each from twelve contributors.

Moreover, unlike Indiana, Chicago already had a proud record of preserving open space and its lakefront. In the previous decade Chicago's leaders had convinced the Illinois legislature to provide for the establishment of three publicly financed park commissions. By 1891 the commissions had spent $24 million to establish eight big parks, including two along the lakefront, twenty-nine smaller ones, and thirty-five miles of broad boulevards. Chicago, its boosters proudly boasted, had become a city circled by parks.[7] In addition, after long litigation, the courts upheld Asa Montgomery Ward's contention that Chicago's lakefront belonged to its citizens and not to private interests.

In 1905 the Illinois state legislature again responded to Chicago's civic ferment by authorizing a million-dollar bond issue to acquire and improve small parks and playgrounds on Chicago's west side, where most of the city's immigrants lived in sunless tenements, far from the sight of any greenery. In 1906 the leaders of the settlement movement and municipal park proponents formed the Playground Association of Chicago to foster recreational spaces for city children. Three years later an offshoot of the association called the Saturday Afternoon Walks became the first organized group to explore the Indiana Dunes. Combining many of the elements involved in the budding American conservation movement, its members included adherents of the Thoreauvian tradition, who ascribed mystical, almost evangelical, renewing qualities to contact with nature; partisans of the social welfare movement, who believed that contact with open space and clean air could ameliorate the evil effects of city life for the urban working class; and devotees of outdoor recreation. The Saturday Afternoon Walks never attracted any of the poor about whom its founders—teachers, social workers, and churchmen—expressed such concern, but it did provide its middle-class professional members an opportunity to explore the natural areas around Chicago. Trips to the Indiana Dunes figured prominently in the schedule of activities.

The Saturday Afternoon Walks members rambled through the Dunes in ever-increasing numbers. They roamed its wilderness via the electric cars of the Chicago and Indiana Air Line Railway or the steam trains of the Michigan Central. Arriving at Gary, Miller, Baillytown, Mineral Springs, or Tremont, these outdoor enthusiasts spent the day tramping up and over dunes, cutting trails through marshes and bogs, and glorying in views of the lake. Back in the city by nightfall, they inevitably yearned to return. For the next three years, their all-day hikes, winter trips, and special excursions heightened the members' growing focus on the Dunes, so close to their city homes but so different in its unspoiled natural beauty.

JENS JENSEN

Few people today know of Jens Jensen, the first champion of Indiana Dunes preservation. Musty correspondence, forgotten speeches, and yellowed records provide evidence of this Danish immigrant's farsighted efforts. Without his papers, which burned in a disastrous fire, the full extent of his labors remains unknown. However, the surviving documents portray a dynamo. Through hard work and ability, Jensen became an internationally known landscape architect and a passionate conservationist.

Jensen's life resembled a Horatio Alger story. The eldest son of a Schleswig-Holstein family whose landholdings dated back 400 years, he rejected the life of the gentry. After conscription into the German Royal Guard, he could no longer tolerate living under Prussian rule, nor could he accept his family's disapproval of his intended bride. The couple came to America in 1884; Jensen parted so bitterly with his father that he never wrote to him again.

Two years after their arrival in the United States, poor, friendless, and with a cash reserve of ten cents, the Jensens came to Chicago. Here he landed a city job scraping mud off Chicago's Washington Boulevard. Unknown to the young laborer or his employer, the West Park District, he had begun working in the field of landscape architecture, a profession that suited his romantic-idealistic temperament and upon which he left his mark in midwestern parks, playgrounds, and estates. Within eight years he climbed to the post of superintendent of Humboldt Park and, in the subsequent decade, became a leading figure in Chicago. Jensen's Old World experience heightened his appreciation for the openness, freedom, and broad vision he found in his new home. Unlike Denmark, which cultivated every inch of its land, America gave hope and strength through the limitless flower-covered midwestern prairie, which then still touched Chicago's boundaries.

His landscape design reflected New World philosophic and aesthetic influences. Jensen became famous for pioneering the use of communities of native plants to create natural, free-form settings that flowed with the land. Rejecting the classic, formal Italianate style prevalent at the time, he devoted his unschooled talents to designing artistic compositions that emphasized relationships of open space to midwestern woods, qualities of light and shade, and linear movement. Frank Lloyd Wright called him a nature poet. For Jensen, a park career involved more than designing naturalistic environments. Equally important, parks served his humanitarian instincts. He profoundly believed in the redemptive power of nature. He saw parks as providing space for "the city bred that broadens out his vision and makes him better fitted for the struggle of existence."[8]

In 1900 Jensen lost his superintendency because he exposed corruption in park procurement. Freed from the constraints of a regular job, he plunged into conservation battles. He proposed a plan for a belt of forest preserves encircling Chicago based on his survey of lands beyond the city limits along the Des Plaines, Sac, and Calumet rivers. As a member of the Metropolitan Parks Commission he successfully advocated this project before the Illinois legislature. To develop public support he became an excellent "matinee speaker" wherever he could find an audience: men's clubs, women's clubs, lodges, and churches. This experience served him well in the next decade, when he returned to many of the same audiences on behalf of the Dunes. During this period Jensen also established a private practice in landscape architecture. In the next three decades he developed a clientele that included Henry Ford and the architects Wright and Louis Sullivan, as well as many of Chicago's richest families, the Ryersons, Rosenwalds, Florsheims, Armours, and Cudahys. His work for the wealthy gave him important contacts for the coming Dunes battle. He never kept more than a modest income; any surplus went to support his conservation activities.

A new group of reform-oriented West Park commissioners rehired Jensen in 1905, elevating him to superintendent of the entire district and chief landscape architect. He now had a secure post from which to promote preservation causes. Jensen enlarged his initial concern with urban parks to include advocacy of outer ring parks. Then, because he had seen the buffalo disappear from the plains, the plow turn over the last remnants of virgin prairie, and the beginnings of the end of the wilderness he so prized, he recognized the need to preserve the remaining natural areas around Chicago. Protection of the Dunes became his first goal.

With his breadth of interests and his proclivity for joining organizations, Jensen belonged to many notable Chicago intellectual groups: the City Club, Cliff Dwellers, Chicago Architectural Club, Art Institute, Municipal Art League, Chicago Academy of Science, and the Geographic Society. He served also as secretary of the State Arts Commission. His intense devotion to preserving the Dunes drew his friends and associates in all these assemblages—the rich

*and powerful in Chicago's business, civic, scientific, and artistic
circles—into the Dunes' cause.*

*Over six feet tall, with a ruddy complexion, striking blue eyes,
and erect carriage, Jensen presented a commanding figure. His im-
maculate grooming, magnificent head of white hair, and beauti-
fully trimmed mustache marked him as one of the most handsome
men in Chicago. Aristocratic in appearance and manner, he combined dignity with joyousness. Jensen wore rough tweeds along with
his trademark, a rich silk ascot drawn through a silver ring cast in
the form of a Danish sea wolf.*

*Indomitable and indefatigable, he pursued every possible and
improbable avenue to achieve his vision of creating a natural preserve in the sand dunes. Using photographs of Dunes flowers and
landscape compositions, he went on the lecture circuit in Chicago
and northwest Indiana. Through his whirlwind of activity he forged
a coalition of Illinois and Indiana organizations that backed his
dream.*

*Nevertheless, he failed. Indiana opposition to a Sand Dunes Na-
tional Park prevailed. After the war Chicago voters reelected "Big
Bill" Thompson, another of the city's machine bosses. Corruption
and patronage overran the Park District. Jensen, without political
support, lost his job and never again held a public position. His
final mission for the Dunes came in 1919, when he escorted Richard Lieber, director of the new Indiana state parks system, on a tour
of the Dunes. The all-day hike convinced Lieber that the state had
to preserve a portion of the Indiana Dunes for posterity. Though
Jensen's advocacy of wilderness preservation in the Dunes proved
unsuccessful in his time, he inspired another generation to take up
his fight. Justly, he became known as the "Apostle of the Dunes."*

By 1911 the Playground Association, burdened with the astonishing popularity of the Saturday Afternoon Walks, encouraged the formation of a new sponsoring organization, the Prairie Club. Its charter
outlined additional purposes: "Establishment and maintenance of
temporary and permanent camps, promotion of outdoor recreation,
encouragement of the love of nature . . . dissemination of knowledge
of the country . . . [and] the preservation of suitable areas in which
outdoor recreation may be pursued."[9] The Dunes rapidly became the
center of the club's recreational and conservation focus, in large part
because of the immense influence of Jensen, who helped found the
club, suggested its name, and served as one of the original directors.
Soon after its organization, the club established a temporary camp

site at Tremont, beginning there two decades of association with the Dunes. More than any other single group, the club made Chicago's intellectual and professional circles aware of the need for protection of the Dunes. By 1913 the club's Tremont camp featured a permanent beach house and associated rustic cabins and tenting platforms, enjoyed by an ever-growing colony of Chicagoans enchanted with the Dunes.

In 1913, to further its objectives, the club formed a Conservation Committee, headed by Jensen, "to seek to stimulate public opinion for the conservation of the natural features of the country about Chicago and the preservation of its original beauty; to obtain, if possible, such action by individual clubs or public bodies as may secure these natural features from encroachment or destruction; and for those ends to cooperate with other societies and movements."[10] Through the committee's work, the Prairie Club quickly emerged as Chicago's most important organization promoting preservation, particularly of the Dunes. Professor Henry Chandler Cowles, of the University of Chicago, served as one of its most influential members.

HENRY CHANDLER COWLES

In 1895 a twenty-four-year-old graduate student rode the Michigan Central en route to Chicago. He looked out the window, reading the landscape, a method he later perfected for examining a particular environment. Henry Chandler Cowles remembered the sand dunes of his native Connecticut shore and the Ohio woodlands surrounding his alma mater, Oberlin College. The Indiana Dunes landscape struck him as different and puzzling. With uncharacteristic impetuosity, he got off the train at Miller, the next stop. He hired a horse and buggy and returned to the locale that had piqued his scientific curiosity. Here Cowles found the setting for his later field investigations. Here he formulated his theories of dynamic plant succession, which established his international reputation as a pioneer in the field of plant ecology. Here he began forty years of championing preservation of the Indiana Dunes.

After examining the Dunes and vowing to return, Cowles continued on to the new University of Chicago to begin his graduate fellowship in geology. He could not have found a more stimulating or conducive milieu for his doctoral work. With the millions provided by John D. Rockefeller, the young university aspired to become the intellectual center of the Midwest. President William Rainey Harper chose his faculty from among the leading scholars of the nation.

He named John Coulter, former president of Indiana University and Lake Forest College, as the first chairman of the botany department, to which Cowles soon transferred. Coulter, a native of Indiana, had conducted probably the first scientific explorations of the Dunes in 1872. His knowledge of the region and its botanical wealth encouraged Cowles's later efforts.[11]

Traditional botany then emphasized taxonomic classification, but Cowles used the Indiana Dunes as a living laboratory, painstakingly observing the effects of geological formations upon various plant communities. He "formulated no rigid system with complex classification and formidable new terminology, preferring to use nontechnical language [to explain] ... the facts, processes and principles."[12] *Drawing upon his training both as a geologist and a botanist, Cowles recognized that nature had conducted a unique and momentous experiment in the Dunes, enabling accurate dating of the lands running southward from Lake Michigan. He realized that the oldest dunes, formed 10,000 years previously and now covered with forest and soil, initially had begun as barren foredunes adjacent to the lake. On the basis of two years of field studies he traced the succession of plant life from the vegetationless beach to the climax forests of maple and beech, demonstrating the increasing complexity of the plant communities. Here, in a small space, he found the botanic and geologic history of the North American continent since the Ice Age, history continuously repeating itself and available in its natural state to be read by those with the knowledge and desire to do so.*

In 1897, appointed an assistant in the botany department, Cowles began to teach a course in plant ecology, then a new branch of science. A stimulating instructor whose fascinating stories enlivened even the most ordinary subject, Cowles then started his lifelong practice of bringing classes to the Indiana Dunes for field observation. Generations of students remembered these trips as high points in their academic careers. Following the quick steps of the professor, they began their day walking back through history, tracing the stages of succession. Starting at a climax forest, they tramped northward through yellow birch and white pine to a cattail marsh and finally, undeterred by mosquitoes or blowing sand, to open water. Enthusiastic but never dogmatic, gentle and humorous, Cowles epitomized the rare teacher who "devoted himself mainly to his students, rejoicing in their progress and in their subsequent accomplishments."[13]

For his doctoral thesis Cowles developed his field observations into what later became a classical paper on "The Ecological Rela-

tions of the Vegetations of the Sand Dunes of Lake Michigan." Published serially in the Botanical Gazette, the dissertation read like a suspenseful, scientific thriller, describing how the Dunes unfolded from one age to the next.[14] Cowles employed a professional photographer, an unusual practice in those days, to illustrate his paper, and these pictures of a heretofore unknown environment added to the considerable interest his articles generated. The monograph quickly established his scientific reputation. Two years later he published "Physiographic Ecology of Chicago and Vicinity," applying the principles of dynamic vegetation, which he had discovered in the Dunes, to vegetation in general.[15] He presented the concepts of succession and climax so convincingly that they influenced scores of future researchers. Worldwide dissemination of his papers brought the Indiana Dunes and its unique characteristics to the attention of the international scientific community.

With graduate work completed and a lifelong association with the university's botany department begun, Cowles pursued a parallel career in conservation. His many field trips convinced him of the importance of preserving the natural environment in the Chicago region for further scientific research. Cowles became acquainted with the city's conservationists, and he formed a lifelong friendship with Jensen. Cowles taught Jensen about plant communities, and Jensen used this knowledge to good advantage in his naturalistic landscape architecture. In turn, he heightened Cowles's aesthetic appreciation of plant form and line. United in their interest in preservation, they formed a complementary team.

Promoted to full professor in 1911, he succeeded Coulter as chairman of the botany department in 1925. Cowles remained in that post until his retirement in 1934. He also served as editor of the prestigious Botanical Gazette. In 1913, as part of an International Botanical Congress, Cowles escorted a European delegation on a tour of the natural wonders of the United States, which they had chosen. They visited the Grand Canyon, Yosemite, Yellowstone, and, in recognition of Cowles's scientific interest, the Indiana Dunes. Regardless of the many professional organizations that he headed and the academic honors that he received, Cowles reserved his deepest enthusiasm for the Dunes and the creation of a Dunes National Park.

After Cowles's death in 1939, he became known as "America's first professional ecologist. The Dunes showed him the process of ecological succession at work and he in turn imposed that phenomenon vividly on the scientific imagination of his students."[16] Without the scientific documentation that Cowles and later generations *of investigators provided, the battle to preserve the Dunes might well have failed.*

On November 14, 1914, the Prairie Club called together all groups interested in Dunes preservation for a conference at the City Club. The participants included Mrs. Julius Rosenwald of Friends of Our Native Landscape; Cowles, speaking for the Geographic Society of Chicago; and representatives of the Horticultural Society, the Wildflower Preservation Society of America, the Outdoor League, the Audubon Society of Illinois, the Arche Club, the Municipal Art League of Chicago, the Ridge Woman's Club, the West End Woman's Club, and the Second District Woman's Club of the Illinois State Federation of Woman's Clubs. They formed the Conservation Council of Chicago, adopting the broad and lofty goal of perpetuating the beauties of the American landscape and protecting wildlife. Preservation of the Dunes became the council's first project. By forming the council, the Prairie Club forged a prestigious coalition and significantly enlarged the pro-Dunes constituency.

The land under consideration stretched twenty-five miles from Gary to Michigan City, and all of it belonged to private owners. For the next year or so, the Conservation Council struggled to find a midwestern benefactor for the conservation effort, hoping to emulate the method of acquiring park land used in other parts of the country. The group asked the University of Chicago to purchase three thousand acres for an outdoor nature laboratory. Though a faculty committee reported favorably on the plan, the university's board of trustees vetoed it. The Conservation Council solicited support from Julius Rosenwald for a school of horticulture in the Dunes, but the millionaire philanthropist refused, explaining that he was only interested in helping the poor. They turned to Henry Ford and asked him to buy five to six thousand acres of Duneland for an arboretum of native plants. Ford balked at the cost. They proposed a bistate park along the Calumet River from Wolf Lake to the Dunes, but the politicians ignored them. After these repeated failures members became convinced that only governmental purchase could ensure success.

The Prairie Club and its allies, no strangers to the concept of civic support for parks, drew upon methods used in their prior victorious campaigns for Chicago park expansion and the formation of the Cook County Forest Preserves. Yet for these Illinoisans to seek establishment of a Dunes park in Indiana presented a difficult political problem. On their home base they combined intellectual influence with political strength, but Indiana considered them interlopers. As city folk from across the border, their ideas seemed strange and offensive to their rural neighbors. Moreover, the Illinois conservationists had no political connections with Indiana's government. Unlike its sister state, Indiana had yet to embrace the notion of spending hard-earned tax dollars for state parks.

In spite of such an unpromising political milieu, the Prairie Club kept up a persistent publicity campaign to popularize its cause. Jensen gave an illustrated talk at the Art Institute. Chicago artist Earl Reed lectured at the City Club. The club presented plays in the Dunes, attracting thousands of Chicagoans to the productions. By 1916 the campaign for Dunes preservation had developed widespread public support in both Illinois and Indiana; but the means to achieve final victory remained elusive.

Then the first stirrings of enthusiasm for a state park system occurred in Indiana. The ever-active Conservation Committee corresponded with Enos Mills, a nationally known naturalist-author and a native of Indiana, who later successfully led the fight to establish the Rocky Mountain National Park in Colorado. To mark Indiana's centennial in 1916, Mills proposed a state park system, which would include a large portion of the Dunes. The state's Historical Commission, in charge of the forthcoming celebration, adopted the idea enthusiastically and appointed Lieber, an Indianapolis businessman, as chairman of its state park committee. Mills, however, cautiously advised the Prairie Club that public sentiment in Indiana had not grown sufficiently to assure a state park system.

At the same time Chicago conservationists pursued another avenue, that of national park status, to achieve a Dunes preserve. Their decision resulted, in no small part, from the appointment of Stephen Mather, a Prairie Club member, as assistant to the secretary of the interior. Now Dunes park promoters had a highly influential friend in the upper echelons of the federal government, the man in charge of national parks.

STEPHEN MATHER

Tourists sightseeing at Yellowstone, Yosemite, Grand Canyon, Rocky Mountain, or most other of the older national parks and monuments find a simple plaque near the visitor centers. The bronze memorial to Stephen Tyng Mather reads: "He laid the foundation of the national park system defining and establishing the policies under which its areas shall be developed and conserved unimpaired for future generations. There will never come an end to the good he has done."

Indiana Dunes National Lakeshore lacks a similar marker, but, rightfully, one belongs there, too, because Mather first recommended the establishment of a national park in the Dunes. Although his proposal for the Sand Dunes National Park failed to receive congressional attention, its existence provided the moral authority and historical underpinnings for a half century of efforts to establish a federal preserve in the Dunes. Mather's imprimatur clothed the concept of a national Dunes park with a nostalgic halo that future generations of conservationists used at every opportunity in their promotions.

Despite the popular myth of Mather's immersion in the project, in reality he gave the Sand Dunes Park effort no more than three to four months of his time. The need to organize his brand new agency, build congressional support, and promote the use of the already established national parks claimed his prodigious energy, enthusiasm, and interest. A native of Connecticut who spent his boyhood in California, Mather came from Chicago to Washington in 1915 for a year of public service. A self-made millionaire, bored with the borax business, Mather had written to Secretary Franklin Lane, castigating the failures of Yellowstone and Sequoia superintendents to prevent logging and grazing on park land and other park misuse. Lane wrote back to his fellow University of California alumnus and offered him the job of running the parks, then a far-flung string of individual, patronage-ridden fiefdoms.

Oblivious to the magnitude of the problems, optimistic to an extreme, and utterly naive in the ways of Washington, Mather confidently expected to correct all park deficiencies in a year. His monumental goals included persuading Congress to authorize a separate national parks bureau, a proposal rejected since 1910; convincing the legislators to appropriate vast sums for park operations and development; publicizing the parks to a nation generally ignorant of them; and last, but most significant, securing "national park integrity to the point where Congress would (a) add to the system all appropriate sites possible, (b) keep out inappropriate sites, (c) keep the established sites safe from invasion, (d) purge the established sites of private holdings."[17] No small agenda for a single year!

Immune to political pressure because of his wealth, Mather had a job that seemed tailored to his inborn promotional talents. Moreover, he truly believed in conservation and served as an active member of the Sierra Club and the American Civic Association. Mather's appointment overjoyed park supporters and drew praise from the business community.

Even though his frenzied pace of 1915 achieved some of his objectives, he failed to win congressional approval of a national park bureau. Unimpressed by his success but unwilling to accept failure, he reluctantly decided to stay on for another year.

During 1916 Mather's publicity campaign produced a heightened public consciousness of parks, and in August, swayed by Mather's barrage of the press, Congress finally approved the National Park Service Bureau.

Mather now had time to respond to the importunings of his Chicago friends to take up the Sand Dunes Park proposal. From his days on the Prairie Club's Conservation Committee he knew both the project and many of its promoters. Jensen headed the Conservation Committee during Mather's tenure. Both Cowles and Mather lived in Hyde Park. Mather had worked for Hull House and held office in the City Club. At forty-eight, with a strong, handsome face, notable blue eyes, and prematurely white hair, Mather had achieved great success. His activity made him well known and well liked in Chicago business, conservation, and social welfare circles. Both his wealth and his obvious desire to do good works had caused his perennial selection as committee chairman. Moreover, he had already come to know Indiana's Senator Thomas Taggart during the Senate Parks Committee's consideration of the National Park Service Bureau bill.

Mather served both as behind-the-scenes orchestrator and public conductor of the Sand Dunes Park hearing on Thursday, October 30, 1916, but his attention and concern were focused on the presidential election to be held the following Tuesday. He and his aides remained in Chicago after the hearing and his official inspection of the proposed Dunes park lands. They sat up all Tuesday night and Wednesday morning until the returns from California assured them that President Woodrow Wilson and Secretary Lane would remain in office, thereby ensuring their continued tenure.

Returning to the capital, Mather formulated his extensive and laudatory report on the desirability of the Dunes park. At the same time he completed arrangements for a national parks conference to be held in January 1917, where he intended to pursue the Dunes proposal. During the conference, and for the second time in his life, he suffered a mental breakdown. Eighteen months later, after a stay in the hospital and a period of recuperation he returned to the Park Service.

No longer naive and now more realistic in his goals, Mather concentrated his efforts on the possible, without giving up his idealism. His focus became state parks. He correctly believed that they would preserve scenic, pleasant, and locally important areas and also discourage Congress from authorizing national parks below his standards of size, wilderness, and uniqueness. He called another conference, in Des Moines, Iowa, in 1921, which resulted in the organization of the National Conference on State Parks. Richard Lieber, Indiana State Parks director, played an important role at the meeting. Jensen and Cowles also attended.

By this time Mather had decided the Dunes park project did not merit a battle. According to his chief aide, Horace Albright, then assistant director of the National Parks, industrial plans for expansion, together with the existence of industry already operating on the proposed park's boundaries, made the Dunes "unacceptable for National Park status."[18] More to the point, Mather concluded that the Dunes proposal had no possibility of success, primarily because it lacked political support in Indiana. As Albright explained, "Mr. Mather was just too busy to get back to the Dunes project and he gradually came to the conclusion that the only hope for them lay in the state park movement."[19] Mather left it to Lieber to push for a Dunes preserve, kept him active in the state parks conference, and turned to other, more promising, national park plans.

Mather's association with the Dunes convinced him that Congress would not appropriate funds for any park acquisition in the foreseeable future. His Indiana experience also taught Mather the importance of expanding the national parks system beyond its western base. The sectional concentration of the original parks hindered increased funding from Congress for any park purpose. His goal became finding rich contributors for eastern and southern parks. The Midwest would wait fifty years for its turn.

Despite the obstacles of precedent and politics, the Prairie Club forged ahead in its quest for national park status for the Dunes. In March 1916 Indiana Senator Taggart, who sympathized with the cause, arrived in Washington, and the Dunes's political prospects improved notably. Taggart's senatorial post came about in a rare moment when his party controlled both the governor's mansion and the White House. He had succumbed to the pleas of Governor Samuel Ralston and accepted appointment to the Senate, filling a vacancy caused by the death of Republican Bernard Shively. Taggart's term lasted eight months, during which he willingly sponsored a plethora of patronage bills. Nevertheless, Taggart, a nature lover, chose assignment on the Senate Parks Committee. He did not share Mather's doubts about congressional acceptance of a Dunes National Park. New to Washington politics but sure of his widespread contacts in a Democratic Congress and the Wilson administration, he responded to requests of the Prairie Club and the pleas of Calumet region Democratic party leaders. One trip to the Dunes convinced Taggart.

TOM TAGGART

Today one can get to French Lick only by car. The daily Monon trains, which used to clog the line between Chicago and the hotel-spa, have vanished. Now almost covered with asphalt and surrounded by parking lots, the spur alone, leading to the main entrance, remains.

Tom Taggart has gone, too. His once internationally prominent hostelry still retains the aura of a fashionable turn-of-the-century resort, in spite of the prefab housing the indoor tennis courts and the rows of mechanized golf carts parked adjacent to the rambling eight-story building, with its seemingly endless corridors, wings, and alcoves. But if one wanders the grounds of the French Lick Hotel, all 2,600 acres, as few guests now do, Taggart's penchant for the natural environment becomes apparent.

Wearing the large bow tie of the day, his handlebar mustache carefully trimmed, and his bushy eyebrows calling attention to piercing eyes, Taggart used to greet his guests by name, one by one, as they alighted from their private railroad cars or stepped off the public trains. A host par excellence, he entertained the rich and famous of society with sumptuous meals. His obsequious but shrewd "colored" waiters never failed to remember the names or seating preferences of repeat customers. The elite came from everywhere for "the cure." They stoically consumed unlimited quantities of Pluto water drawn from the mineral springs on the hotel grounds, spent hours in the baths, and pampered themselves with massages, cold mud packs, and hot steam treatments. His clients also frequented the gambling casinos in the tiny community. Attempts to link Taggart to the gaming operations failed in court.[20] Al Capone visited regularly; Bing Crosby came to play golf on the two championship courses. The guests rode around the Cumberland foothills in horse-drawn carriages or rocked peaceably on the wide, circling veranda. Close enough to Louisville to attract the horse-racing crowd, French Lick became the natural stopping-off place for Derby Week. Taggart silks frequently appeared on Kentucky tracks.

From his store of years in lesser known and less fashionable eateries and commercial hotels, Taggart fashioned French Lick as a pinnacle of pleasure, almost as central to his existence as politics, his first love. From the age of thirty until his death at seventy-three, he combined these two passions, using one to boost the other and, in turn, nurturing the second from the profits of the first.

To both he brought his Irish forebears' garrulity and shrewdness. His individual traits of "extraordinary business capacity, remarkably accurate judgment of men and faculty for dispatching work rapidly" distinguished the County Monagham immigrant boy of five from other equally puny, poor, and plucky arrivals.[21]

A national "Democratic kingpin," he did not let his Xenia, Ohio, common school education deter him. He mixed well and worked hard. He catapulted from his first job, at fourteen, as a railroad hotel and restaurant clerk to running the Union Station restaurant in Indianapolis at twenty-one. For the next half century, Indiana's capital city felt his presence and his power. Indiana never knew a political boss like him, before or since.

By twenty-five, he owned the Union Station restaurant and made it famous among railroad and traveling men. He pursued personal contact with his patrons and soon caught the attention of Marion County Democratic leaders, who slated him to run for county auditor in 1886. In the campaign his phenomenal organizational skills and willingness to contact voters day and night marked him not only a sure winner but also a rising star in state Democratic circles. He became county chairman within a year. At the end of his term he broke the usual custom and won reelection without opposition. In 1892 he took over as state Democratic chairman. By then, Taggart had moved up in the hotel business, too, having acquired the Indianapolis Grand Hotel and managed the New Denison.

While thriving commercially, Taggart continued his steady rise in politics, serving three terms as mayor of Indianapolis, from 1895 to 1901. There he revealed a quality that politics, success, and fame had so far overshadowed—a soft spot for nature. He decided to save some scenic beauty for his adopted city. In fiscally conservative Indiana, where spending money for nonproductive purposes ranked with heresy, he proposed and persuaded until his loyal Democratic city council adopted Indianapolis's first park plan. The city then acquired 970 acres, comprising a swath three-quarters of a mile on both sides of the White River.

When Taggart retired as mayor, he concentrated on elevating his hotel and political careers to national prominence and accomplished this feat within two years. He became a member of the

*Democratic National Committee, where he remained for sixteen
years, serving as chairman for four. And he purchased the Old Baden
Hotel, transforming it in size and stature to the French Lick Springs
Resort.*

*For fifteen years he disdained elective office, preferring to use his
considerable political influence to select governors, senators, vice-
presidents, and presidents. After serving as U.S. senator for eight
months, he never held elective office again, as Indiana voters denied his bid for a four-year term in 1916, electing conservative Republican James Watson instead. Charges, subsequently dismissed,
of election fraud in Indianapolis hurt Taggart's candidacy. Despite
his contributions as a politician and businessman, the preservation
of the Indiana Dunes remains Taggart's most enduring legacy.*

A new organization, the National Dunes Park Association, initiated by A. F. Knotts and his cousin, John O. Bowers, formalized Indiana's base of support for a national park in the Dunes. Their
motivation stemmed from disenchantment with the industrialization of Lake County and determination to preserve the adjoining
duneland in Porter County. Egged on by Jensen's behind-the-scenes
maneuvering, the leaders of the National Dunes Park Association
invited everyone interested in saving the Dunes to a meeting at Waverly Beach in July 1916. The meeting resulted in the selection of the
first board of directors, which included the ever-present team of Jensen and Cowles, Knotts, Bowers, and Bess Sheehan, a Gary club
woman.[22]

Meanwhile, Taggart tried to introduce a bill directing the federal
government to purchase the Dunes, but he discovered that Congress
would not act without hearings and a favorable report from the secretary of interior. Taggart next sponsored a resolution, which the
Senate passed on September 7, authorizing a study of "the advisability of the securing by purchase or otherwise, all that portion of
the counties of Lake, LaPorte, and Porter in the State of Indiana
bordering on Lake Michigan and commonly known as the 'sand
dunes' together with the cost of acquisition and maintenance."[23]
Mather was assigned to conduct the hearing. He paid a reconnaissance visit to Chicago shortly after the resolution's passage. At the
City Club Dunes promoters, including Jensen, discussed plans for
the hearing. Mather promised to set the hearing date as soon as he
could arrange a strong representative meeting. He also agreed to make
a personal inspection and asked the proponents to gather information about land ownership and prices.

All during October preparations for the hearing continued. The National Dunes Park Association collected financial data. The Prairie Club, in collaboration with the Conservation Council, secured impressive witnesses. Mather and Jensen, superpromoters working in tandem, looked for possible additional sources of support. Jensen worried about "the Gary Crowd," explaining that "politicians are mighty good assets but it takes the intellect of the country to bring matters of this kind to an issue." [24] Mather suggested enlisting the Indiana Society of Chicago.

THE FIRST DUNES HEARING

On October 30, 1916, Dunes etchings graced the walls of Judge C. C. Kohlsaat's courtroom in the federal building. A display of Dunes cactus faced the audience awaiting the start of the Department of Interior's public hearing on the merits of a national park in the Dunes. Few in the packed room recognized the extent of the careful planning that the day's meeting represented. Nothing had been left to chance. Many of Chicago's art, civic, literary, scientific, and business leaders had come, due to the combined contacts of the Dunes promoters. Even the use of this particular courtroom stemmed from Jensen's association with Judge Kohlsaat, his former West Park District employer.

Waiting for the 10:30 A.M. session to begin, some partisans basked in the day's favorable Chicago Tribune editorial. [25] Others recalled the previous laudatory Tribune editorial and the paper's feature of two Sundays ago. [26] As Mather appeared, guards closed the doors to prevent further overcrowding. Mather, speaking for the newly authorized National Park Service, began the hearing with a review of the national parks and their history. He reiterated the political reality facing the proponents of a Dunes park, that favorable action on the proposition before them would require Congress "going far afield" and, for the first time, spending public funds to purchase parkland. [27] He reminded the audience that he had worked long and hard to get a congressional appropriation of $50,000 to enlarge Sequoia National Park and had won the money only after personally obtaining an option on the land.

But the crowd promptly forgot Mather's speech and its portents of the political problems that lay ahead. A long parade of supporters testified. Recognizing the necessity of national backing, the organizers placed Dr. Abraham Flexner as the first speaker. Flexner, general secretary of the Rockefeller-endowed General Education

Board, just happened to be spending a night with his good and great friend and patron, Julius Rosenwald, president of Sears and Roebuck.

Mrs. John Dickinson Sherman, the Conservation Chairman of the General Federation of Woman's Clubs, pledged "the support of the two-and-one-half million clubwomen of the country to the . . . sand dunes national park."[28]

John W. O'Leary, president of the Chicago Association of Commerce, joined Chicago and Indiana labor groups in praising the proposal. The University of Chicago sent four faculty members, headed by Cowles, to explain the scientific and educational value of the Dunes. Cowles eloquently presented the scientific argument. "For 20 years, I have been studying the dunes more than anything else combined. In fact, that has been the chief reason for my existence, perhaps for those 20 years. . . . No other dunes than such as ours show such bewildering dune movement and struggle for existence, such labyrinths of motion, form and life; just because its uniqueness preserved Yellowstone . . . so should their uniqueness preserve our dunes for they are without parallel."[29] All the member organizations in the Conservation Council appeared. Every witness added his appeal to the record, but none could outdo Jensen, who declared, "If this wonderful dune country should be taken away from us and on it built cities like Gary, Indiana Harbor and others . . . it would show us to be in fact a people who only have dollars for eyes."[30]

The Indiana contingent included Will Davis, vice-president of the Indiana State Society; Tom and A. F. Knotts; and a representative of Michigan City's Mayor Martin Krueger, bringing a petition signed by 27,000 residents, including Congressman E. D. Crumpacker and pioneer settler J. G. Morgan. Chicago Board of Trade President Stanford White, who owned 3,000 acres of Porter County duneland, promised a reduced price for his holdings.

Nowhere in the hearing record did the arguments of the opponents appear. Their spokesman, A. J. Bowser, owner of the Chesterton *Tribune,* later claimed that he was not allowed to speak, although he had been invited to attend and had prepared a statement. He charged that A. F. Knotts had censored the program so that "no discordant note was sounded."[31] Some of the speakers rebutted the opposition's arguments as if to destroy them before their voices could reach Washington.

The only practical message came from President McFarland of the American Civic Association's representative, who quoted an unnamed congressman's remark that the federal legislature "is sin-

*gularly uninterested in national parks and there is no precedent for
buying land for such a purpose."*[32] *Mather quickly agreed with this
assessment. He again tried to inject a note of reality into the proceedings by describing the hearing as only a prelude to congressional deliberations. On one hand, he cautioned that the Department
of Interior could not promote the Dunes park officially, and, on the
other, he promised to bring up the issue of Dunes preservation at a
conference in January. Again, he suggested a fund-raising campaign
to whet congressional enthusiasm for a national park in the Dunes.*

*But in the afternoon session, the bird, flower, and wildlife enthu-
siasts proceeded as if Mather had not spoken. Even a Potawatomie
Indian, descendant of the original inhabitants of Dunes country,
eloquently added his voice to the cause.*

*When the hearing ended, the Dunes proponents believed they had
compiled an overwhelmingly impressive record. Two weeks later
the Chesterton* Tribune *accurately predicted the fate of the effort.
"With the present line-up of Congress, it seems improbable that Mr.
Mather's scheme of planning national parks all over these United
States will have a smooth sailing. Mr. Taggart will be a private citizen on December 4 and his resolution will be without a father."*[33]

As Mather prepared the required report to Congress, the conservationists carried on their promotional campaign, despite the loss of
their political mentor. Letters of support for the Sand Dunes National Park flowed from all parts of the country into the Interior
Department. The Chicago Association of Commerce devoted four
pages of its November house organ to a report on the hearing.[34]

All this time opponents of the Dunes park also had kept up a
steady barrage. Bowser had urged his readers to defeat Taggart and
thereby kill the park plan. The Chesterton editor had accused the
senator of supporting the park to disguise his involvement in another project. Bowser charged that Taggart wanted to locate a federal
armor plate factory in either Evansville or Jeffersonville, two Indiana cities close to Taggart's home base. Porter County and Bowser
also had wanted the plant. If the park plan went through, Bowser
contended, it would eliminate Porter County from consideration for
the factory.[35]

Bowser had also raised the issue of why Chicagoans wanted a park
in Indiana, asking, "What's in it for Indiana?" Porter County, he had
predicted, would become the playground of Chicagoans. "They would
gradually absorb our farmland and our souls would, like lo the poor
Indian, have to be kept in perpetual bondage to them."[36] A spokes-

man for the Valparaiso Chamber of Commerce had railed, "It would mean a loss of taxes and would deprive Porter County of every foot of beach on Lake Michigan."[37] The Chesterton *Tribune,* in another of its editorials on the Dunes park question, had offered the solution advocated by the national park opponents. "Indiana should adopt enabling legislation this winter that would solve the lake front problem. Part of the front should be set aside for park purposes and the rest should be reserved for industry."[38] Oblivious to the opponents' contentions, Mather prepared the department's report. He submitted it to Secretary Lane on December 20, less than a month after the hearing, proposing a scaled-down version of the park, consisting of a twenty-five-mile stretch of undeveloped land, one mile wide, between Miller and Michigan City. Disregarding precedent and his better judgment, Mather capitulated to the pleas of his friends and endorsed federal purchase of a maximum of 12,000 acres at a cost of $2.6 million.

Although Mather's recommendations fulfilled the fondest hopes of Illinois and Indiana Dunes adherents, it produced no legislative results. Dutifully filed by Secretary Lane, the report never even received congressional consideration. A new Congress concentrated on the needs of a nation at war. Taggart had gone. Mather also left the scene in 1917, with another of his recurring nervous breakdowns. No one remained in Washington to agitate for a Sand Dunes National Park.

Unwilling to recognize the events that had shattered their dream of national park status for the Dunes, the proponents continued their activities, wisely realizing that only sustained public attention would further their project.

THE GREAT PAGEANT

On Memorial Day, 1917, crowds descended on Waverly Beach in the Indiana Dunes, their somber war mood temporarily suspended. Neither the rain that pelted the first fourteen-car special train as it pulled out of the Randolph Street station in Chicago nor the sultry stickiness of the day dampened their enthusiasm. Soon to number 40,000, they looked forward to witnessing the largest outdoor pageant ever to be presented in the United States. In spite of the weather, the half-mile walk from the station at Port Chester and the weight of their wicker picnic baskets, the only complaints came from those arriving by automobile. Although the route printed in the Chicago Herald Examiner *guided Model A's and Overlands accurately through every twist and turn of the fifty-three-mile journey, the drivers found*

long lines of cars blocking all the roads leading to the great historical extravaganza. By noon 5,000 motor cars packed the parking
ground, leaving the occupants in hundreds of others unable to come
within sight of their destination in time for the three o'clock production.

The earliest arrivals finished their lunches and obediently refrained from picking the wild flowers and trampling the delicate,
unfamiliar vegetation. Some participated in guided walks to Mount
Tom and the Tamarack Grove, while others succumbed to the heat
of the early afternoon and napped. All marveled at the color and
variety of this little known country. Enjoying the uninterrupted expanse of lake, beach, and surrounding forest, they waited eagerly
for the festivities to begin.

Shortly before three, Thomas Wood Stevens, writer and director
of the pageant, paused from his frenzied, last-minute preparations
to exchange a word with Eames MacVeagh, chairman of the reception committee. Up to now too busy to notice the size of the crowd,
they surveyed the surrounding dunes. It appeared as though all the
world in these parts stood assembled before them. Four months of
tireless work would culminate in the day's performance, and both
men wondered about their readiness. They entered one of the city
of tents erected for the dressing and making up of the 500 actors
and began a final check, protected from the momentary emergence
of the sun.

MacVeagh went to receive honored guests in the reception tent as
limousines deposited some daring society folk within, for tea and
a word of welcome from the bustling ladies of the committee.

Stevens reviewed the other arrangements. Several hundred Boy
Scouts from Gary and Chicago had taken their posts hours earlier.
Their impatience at the prolonged inactivity now assuaged, the
ground patrols began to perform their often-rehearsed duties. Other
Scouts with field glasses and red semaphore flags perched on the
highest dunes and in the tops of trees prepared to receive messages
and pass them on. A little time remained before their part in the
production began. The full emergency hospital, installed by the Gary
Red Cross, stood ready, but the staff hoped for a quiet afternoon.
Pinkerton Guards, together with the local police, started to realize
that, for them, a very long day still awaited. The twenty-five uni-
formed Camp Fire Girls circulated among the crowds, soliciting
memberships in the National Dunes Park Association at a dollar
for each life membership.

The actors, following the instructions printed in the Gary Tribune *the preceding evening, had arrived at Port Chester on the 10:30 A.M. South Shore train carrying their costumes and lunches. From there they had proceeded directly to the dressing tent. Now, many hours later, they listened to the full orchestra starting to tune up. Groups of brightly costumed men, women, and children—Indians in feathers and blankets, soldiers of four nations, nymphs in gauze draperies, pioneers, explorers, and priests—scattered to their assigned portion of underbrush to await the whistle or bugle call, their cue to appear.*

Stevens stepped out of the tent, cast a skeptical eye at the green-black clouds gathering overhead and looked about to make sure he should start the spectacle. He barely noticed the thousands of spectators scattered over the slopes of the high dunes surrounding the blowout where the action would take place. The stage, marked off by an arrangement of shrubs and saplings, resembled an amphitheater scooped out of the sand from which the voices traveled one-third of a mile.

As the first notes of music sounded, the crowds became aware of Indians marching single file from the distant sand hills toward the stage. They watched in silent appreciation. Soon a new and louder sound interrupted the music. From the lake came the roar of wind and waves, and from the rapidly darkening sky the first rumbles of thunder threatened to disrupt the meticulous preparations. The actors gamely continued against a backdrop of wind-whipped trees and blowing sand. The crowd remained intent, unafraid of the noise and rain, until the torrents and thunder together blotted out all sight and sound.[39]

An uninterrupted performance of the pageant occurred the following Sunday under sunshine and blue skies. Both the aborted and complete renditions fulfilled the purposes of the sponsors: to achieve widespread publicity for their cause of a national park in the Dunes and to introduce thousands of visitors to the region's charms. The pageant followed an equally successful promotional effort in April, when, at the instigation of Bess Sheehan, the National Dunes Park Association secretary, there had occurred a wide dissemination of a four-page newspaper, the Gary *Dunes Park Post*. The issue had carried highlights of the testimony at the Mather hearing as well as Indiana Governor James Goodrich's endorsement of the national park concept and the Gary *Post*'s editorial backing.[40]

In spite of their valiant and successful efforts to win public support, the Dunes preservation proponents failed to accept the political reality of their situation. Their cause was doomed. No Indiana politician appeared to assume Taggart's mantle. The sharp change in public policy, which public purchase of private land necessitated, lacked a congressional sponsor of sufficient national stature. Mather contented himself with the proposition that only a state park in Indiana seemed politically feasible. While a bipartisan and bistate coalition of amazingly diverse groups had united for the Mather hearing, with Taggart's defeat they lost the key ingredient for legislative success—a durable political mentor. Without sufficient political influence in the national arena, Dunes conservationists doggedly continued to pursue their unrealizable goal, using Mather's report as written proof of the validity of their cause.

Moreover, Mather's influence on the future of Dunes preservation had another, more negative result. In the next half century his philosophy and policies imprinted the National Park Service he founded. His preference for large, pristine tracts, removed from population centers, became the service's standard measurement of a park's worth, even as such scenically spectacular areas became difficult to obtain in an increasingly urban America. In addition, since they most often existed far from population centers, parks became accessible mainly to the affluent. Nearly a half century after Mather's Sand Dunes National Park proposal, National Park Service leaders rejected the Indiana Dunes for a national park because it failed to meet agency criteria of size and isolation from man's imprint. This traditional point of view remained dominant in the service until John F. Kennedy's administration initiated a new national park policy.

NOTES

1. Theodore Roosevelt, *The New Nationalism* (New York: Smith, Peter, 1910), p. 50.

2. Alfred Runte, *National Parks: The American Experience* (Lincoln: University of Nebraska Press, 1979), p. 1.

3. Ibid., p. 188.

4. Ibid. Runte cites many examples in his book.

5. Helen L. Hurowitz, *Culture and the City: Cultural Philanthropy in Chicago from the 1880's to 1917* (Lexington: University of Kentucky Press, 1976).

6. John Moses, *The White City* (Chicago: World Book, 1893).

7. Lois Willie, *Forever Open, Clear and Free* (Chicago: Regnery, 1972).

8. Emma Doeserich, Mary Sherburne, and Anna B. Wey, comps., *Outdoors with the Prairie Club* (Chicago: Paquin, 1941).

9. Prairie Club Charter, Prairie Club Files, Chicago.

10. Doeserich, Sherburne, and Wey, comps., *Outdoors with the Prairie Club*, p. 19.

11. Andrew Denny Rogers III, *John Merle Coulter* (Princeton: Princeton University Press, 1949).

12. George D. Fuller, "Henry Chandler Cowles," *Science*, 90 (Oct. 20, 1939), 363.

13. Charles C. Adams and George D. Fuller, "Henry Chandler Cowles, Physiographic Plant Ecologist," *Annals of the Association of American Geographers*, 30 (Mar. 1940), 41.

14. Henry Chandler Cowles, "The Ecological Relations of the Vegetations of the Sand Dunes of Lake Michigan," *Botanical Gazette*, 27 (1899), 95–117, 167–202, 281–308, 361–91.

15. Henry Chandler Cowles, "The Physiographic Ecology of Chicago and Vicinity," *Botanical Gazette*, 31 (1901), 73–108, 145–82.

16. Donald Wooster, *Nature's Economy: The Roots of Ecology* (San Francisco: Sierra Club Books, 1977), pp. 207–8.

17. Robert Shankland, *Steve Mather of the National Parks* (New York: Knopf, 1951), p. 59.

18. Horace Albright to authors, July 21, 1977.

19. Ibid.

20. Clifton Phillips, *Indiana in Transition: The Emergence of an Industrial Commonwealth, 1880–1920* (Indianapolis: Indiana Historical Society, 1968), pp. 97–98.

21. Ibid., p. 125.

22. George S. Cottman, *Indiana Dunes State Park: A History and Description*, publication no. 97 (Indianapolis: Indiana Department of Conservation, 1930), p. 35.

23. Senate Resolution 268, 64th Congress, 1st. sess. (1916).

24. Jens Jensen to Stephen Mather, Sept. 21, 1916, Record Group 79, Records of the National Park Service, National Archives, Washington.

25. "For A Dunes Park," Chicago *Tribune*, Oct. 30, 1916, p. 8.

26. "A Real People's Playground," ibid., Oct. 3, 1916, p. 8; Jon DeLong, "Dune Country with Its Strange Beauty," ibid., Oct. 1, 1916, section 8, p. 10.

27. U.S. Department of the Interior, National Park Service, Stephen T. Mather, *Report of the Proposed Sand Dunes National Park Indiana* (Washington: Government Printing Office, 1916), p. 21, hereafter cited as Mather, *Sand Dunes Report*.

28. Ibid., p. 59.

29. Ibid., pp. 93–96.

30. Ibid., p. 26.

31. Untitled editorial, Chesterton *Tribune*, Nov. 2, 1916.

32. Mather, *Sand Dunes Report*, p. 77.

33. Chesterton *Tribune*, Nov. 16, 1916.

34. "At Federal Hearing Chicago Pleads That Indiana's Matchless Sand Dunes Be Created National Park," Chicago *Commerce*, Nov. 1916, pp. 9–12.

35. "Park Scheme Uncovered," Chesterton *Tribune,* Sept. 14, 1916, p. 1.

36. Ibid.

37. "Crumpacker Sounds Alarm," ibid., Feb. 22, 1917, p. 1.

38. Ibid., Oct. 11, 1916, p. 11.

39. Adapted from materials found in Dunes Scrapbooks, Gary Public Library.

40. Gary *Dune Park Post,* Apr. 16, 1917, pp. 1–4 (supplement to Gary *Evening Post*).

3 Port Skirmish

By 1900 America had realized, spectacularly, its nineteenth-century values of growth and development. Ironically, however, that achievement resulted in substantial erosion of the nation's cherished way of life. Rapid industrialization had produced a host of societal ills, among them, unrestrained corporate dominance, the alliance of industrial giants with potent political machines, inequitable taxation that benefited business property, urban slums, poverty, and exploitation of workers. Early in the twentieth century an aroused middle class compelled governmental enactment of social and economic reforms that sought to alleviate these problems. The advent of World War I turned the nation away from such trends, and interest in continued change did not resume after its conclusion. Indeed, Warren G. Harding's ascendance to the presidency in 1920 obliterated many of the early twentieth century's progressive reforms. As a candidate, Harding had pledged to eliminate the war's legacy of disruption and depression by returning the country to "normalcy." Upon election, he quickly made good his campaign slogan "less government in business and more business in government."

By 1923 Americans once again enjoyed prosperity. At the same time the national mood veered precipitously toward ultraconservatism. Government policy under Harding and his successors reversed earlier progressive reforms. Their administrations raised the tariff, instituted tax policies advantageous to industry, legislated continued business consolidation, and removed government regulations curbing corporate expansion.

Business leaders in northwest Indiana welcomed these policies. There the Republican programs represented a return to accepted practice rather than a reversal of widely approved reforms. No one in Lake or Porter counties mourned the loss of the progressive movement, which, in fact, had never reached the region in the first place. Prior to World War I, still rural Porter County had no conditions in need of reform, and industrialization of Lake County's cities had existed for too short a time to show the effects suffered by older urban-industrial centers. By 1919, when labor unrest resulted in prolonged strikes in Gary, Hammond, and East Chicago, the national reform movement already had lost its momentum. Northwest Indiana's proindustrialization attitudes precluded acceptance of reforms similar to those instituted elsewhere. In their zeal for development and progress, boosters in Lake and Porter counties imagined only endless benefits from industrialization. During the late 1800s they had encouraged, gladly and without question, industries that other areas no longer found acceptable; they had permitted activities that other cities had passed laws to prohibit. If they recognized potential problems from development, they did not allow the prospect of future trouble to interfere. Furthermore, the possibility of eventual dissolution of their highly revered way of life did not cross their minds.

After the war, however, disintegration of many nationally honored values caused rural Americans to distrust those threatening their nineteenth-century conception of the nation. They held tightly to their "historically rural, individualistic and anti-urban bias."[1] With indiscriminate equality they feared communists, foreigners, Catholics, Jews, blacks, and intellectuals and, at first, looked to government for protection from them. National legislation that set immigration quotas and made Prohibition a reality supported their attempt to return to the "code by which rural, small town, Anglo-Saxon America had lived."[2] It undid, willy nilly, the hopes and dreams of a more optimistic time.

A growing split between the urban and rural perspective, which the progressives had earlier attempted to narrow, became a chasm during the 1920s. "The city had at last eclipsed the country in population and above all as imaginative center of American life." To nonurbanites, "Babylons like New York and Chicago" represented all that seemed evil, lawless, and menacing. They deplored the Jazz Age and its bobbed hairstyles, short-skirted fashions, and "fast" dances like the Charleston. The rural mind set of the 1920s, therefore, provided appropriate conditions for the flowering of the Ku Klux Klan (KKK), which "appealed to relatively unprosperous and uncultivated native white Protestants who had in them a vein of misty but often quite sincere idealism."[3]

Northern Indiana provided particularly fertile ground for Klan activity. The industrialized cities of Gary, Hammond, Whiting, and East Chicago had large foreign-born populations, strong union groups, and enough Jews, Catholics, and blacks to arouse Klan antagonism. In 1921 the Gary *Post Tribune* estimated Lake County Klan membership at 2,500. In 1922 a Klan meeting in Hammond drew a crowd estimated as high as 12,000.[4] The KKK's involvement in politics paid off handsomely both in Lake County and in the state as a whole. Using the Republican party as a vehicle, the Klan candidates for most state and county offices won nomination in Lake County's 1924 Republican primary. The same year Klan choice Ed Jackson became Indiana's governor.

Porter County also had its share of Klan activity. Its rural complexion represented the kind of home base the Imperial Knights preferred, and its location provided an easy jumping off point for Lake County targets. In 1923 the KKK staged a rally at Valparaiso, the Porter County seat, that attracted an estimated 10,000 spectators. In the same year Klansmen unsuccessfully attempted to buy Valparaiso University for the purpose of teaching "Americanism" to the unenlightened.[5]

Both Lake and Porter counties embraced the nation's Republican resurgence during the 1920s. With few exceptions voters in Lake County's industrial cities and Porter County's rural communities always marked the Republican "X" for local, state, and national offices, until the Great Depression of the 1930s. The 1932 election moved Lake County and its unemployed masses into the Democratic camp, where it has remained. By contrast, in Porter County that same election left the Republicans in control, despite a sprinkling of Democrats who won close races. Over the years the Republicans frequently protected their control of Porter County by paying special attention to its boundaries in congressional redistricting. This tactic began with the 1931 reapportionment. The tenth congressional district became the second, carefully gerrymandered to give Republican Will R. Wood his congressional seat in the next election. The maneuver separated Lake and Porter counties, leaving Porter a Republican stronghold. Ironically, Wood lost the 1932 election and died, presumably of shock, four days after leaving the Congress.

Not even the Republicans, however, could prevent urban-industrial problems from reaching Lake County cities. By the mid-1920s these cities, too, suffered from atmospheric pollution, labor unrest, lawless defiance of Prohibition, and the difficulties of assimilating an immense foreign-born population. Nonetheless, these cities still represented a model of growth and development which all who desired progress envied and emulated.

Businessmen in Valparaiso still coveted Lake County's success. Though thoroughly imbued with small-town America's disdain for the urban experience, they would gladly have taken on metropolitan problems in exchange for a share of the industrialization that produced them. Two decades into the twentieth century they lamented the all-too-slow growth of their own town and county as compared with what they saw in adjacent Lake and LaPorte counties. By the late 1920s these men regarded "the wonderful industrial growth of the lake shore" in neighboring counties with the kind of intense, painful longing that only sustained envy can produce. They certainly believed that such progress "must eventually be felt in Valparaiso and that the available sites on the Porter County shore line of the lake [would] become throbbing with life and activity in the near future."[6] But "eventually" seemed too far away. As they compared their status with that of neighboring counties, their discouragement increased.

To the west, Lake County's population had zoomed from 37,892 in 1900 to 261,310 in 1930.[7] In Gary, U.S. Steel had invested upward of $150 million and employed 15,000 workers in round-the-clock shifts. American Sheet and Tin Plate, American Bridge, National Tube, and Universal Portland Cement workers numbered another 12,000 in U.S. Steel–affiliated industries. Other industries, such as Gary Screw and Bolt and Arex Ventilator, brought factory employment in Gary to over 30,000 and represented an annual payroll in 1926 of approximately $60 million. Existing plants planned a $30 million expansion for the coming year.

Other Lake County communities had similar success. Hammond boasted ninety-four industries employing from three to 3,000 workers. Their striking diversity, fully as impressive as their number, insured a stability not common in burgeoning industrial centers. East Chicago industries reported an assessed valuation of more than $100 million and an annual payroll exceeding $40 million. Like Hammond, East Chicago claimed diversity and stability, with oil, steel, and the manufacture of railroad equipment leading the way. Giant corporations controlled many East Chicago plants, having located there because of "the desirability from every standpoint of manufacturing and marketing . . . which assures permanency of industrial activities, . . . community stability, continuous growth and regularity of pay rolls."[8] Each Lake County city near Lake Michigan's shore trumpeted similar success. During the same period LaPorte County's population jumped from 38,386 to 60,490, with Michigan City capitalizing on its shoreline to develop a less spectacular but nonetheless substantial industrial base. Porter County's experience contrasted sharply with this pattern of growth. Its population remained relatively static, having increased by only 2,000 in thirty years.[9] Of the three Lake Michigan counties, Porter alone had failed to use its lakeshore resource and remained rural and underdeveloped. In 1927 the State of Indiana gobbled up three miles of Porter County lakefront for the Indiana Dunes State Park, removing them from the tax rolls and making them perpetually unavailable for industrialization. Small wonder that Valparaiso's businessmen felt cheated.[10]

By comparison with its successful neighbors, Valparaiso still resembled the bypassed backwater it had become after winning the contest for county seat in the mid-1800s. Although it had other compensating qualities, the center of Porter County had not yet emerged as a center of progress. In 1927 Valparaiso counted only nine industries, including the Chicago Mica Company, which had arrived in 1900 as the result of a $5,000 inducement paid by the town council.

Although the city fathers seemed unable to find an incantation capable of improving the prospects, a universal belief pertained: "It is almost a certainty that the hum of industry will in the not distant future be heard in the available industrial territory along the lake shore and thriving cities arise as the favorable conditions for the location of large industries in northern Porter County must soon be taken advantage of by great leaders in industry."[11] One of those "great leaders" showed up in Valparaiso in December 1930.

A WINNING COMBINATION

George A. Nelson certainly did not look like the man whose work would change the topography of Lake Michigan's shore and fulfill a hundred-year-old Hoosier dream. He came to Valparaiso in 1930 to interview with the chamber of commerce, in response to their advertisement for the job of secretary-manager. At twenty-four, George "felt he was ready to sprout new wings."[12] He sized up the interview committee positively: Lynn Whipple, owner and editor of the Vidette Messenger; *Justin Shauer, owner of the Premier Theater, one of Valparaiso's four movie houses; Frank Clifford, vice-president of Foster Lumber, and three others, American Legionnaires, pillars of the community. Seeking the first rung on the ladder of success, young George took the risk of tacking two years onto his age; he never hesitated to present himself in the most expedient light. Nelson felt ready to conquer new worlds. His course in accounting and business from the Indiana Business College in Lafayette completed and four years of experience as assistant manager for the Greater Lafayette Chamber of Commerce behind him, he looked forward to a new challenge. But the committee handed him more than he expected.*

Nelson thought he had checked Valparaiso thoroughly—a town of 8,079 people, all white and less than 1 percent foreign-born, noted for its "neat attractive homes with well-kept lawns, broad main thoroughfares and shady residential streets lined with beautiful trees"; healthful and clean; high standard of morality; good highways and railroad transportation; 115 retail businesses; two newspapers, and a flourishing university.[13] *New industry would need encouragement, of course, but the lure of such a promising environment, together with his know-how and drive, would induce even the most reluctant. Despite a Democratic mayor in 1916, Valparaiso even had the right politics: 70 percent Republican to 30 percent Democratic. (During the early 1940s Valparaiso would turn as anti-Roosevelt as any town in the country, and locals would often refer to the Republican triumvirate: Maine, Vermont, and Valparaiso.)*

The committee, however, painted quite a different picture, calling Valparaiso a "sick community." They provided copious examples, ranging from stagnation to scandal. Valparaiso University, then emerging from a decade of disarray (including an attempted purchase by the KKK in 1923), maintained only the poorest relations with town officials, creating a divided community. "Indiana's Cowpath," a local designation for the eastern section of state highway 2, joined several other poorly paved and potholed roads as the basis of Valparaiso's questionable highway network. Wooden boardwalks still served as sidewalks in downtown Valparaiso. Worse yet, the smell of corruption permeated the ranks of city officials.[14]

Had Nelson known how much worse things would get before they improved, he might have high-tailed it back to Lafayette. But he did not know. Therefore, regarding Valparaiso's offer as a big step up in the world, he solemnly elicited full cooperation from the chamber committee, promised know-how and energy in return, and grabbed the opportunity before anybody could think better of the whole idea.

Whatever sicknesses might have plagued Valparaiso at the moment of Nelson's employment, local old-timers had only one remedy to prescribe: industry. The cure-all potion, the fix-it-up elixir combined jobs, money, employment, and prosperity. Observation told them that without access to the one element common to all northwest Indiana's successful industrialization—a lakeshore committed to heavy industry—Porter County, and with it Valparaiso, would languish.

For a century towns and cities along Lake Michigan had depended on the construction of harbors for growth. In like manner each in-

dustry along the lake, from South Chicago east, required harbor facilities, whether publicly or privately financed, in order to function.
Valparaiso promoters, therefore, viewed construction of a public
harbor as the prerequisite to ending Porter County's underdevelopment and Valparaiso's fear of economic stagnation.

Before the grim days of the Great Depression, Pat Clifford, president of Farmer's State Bank, John Griffin, director of the Valparaiso
Chamber of Commerce, and other local boosters had revived the
fantasies of an earlier era. Like the eager investors of the 1830s, who
had platted Indiana City and Old City West, these modern vision-
aries dreamed of a channel that would link Porter County's rivers
to Lake Michigan, forming a great harbor where they converged. Then
they could relax and wait for a stampede of development.

Burns Ditch provided the vehicle for realizing their fantasy. In 1908
Randall W. Burns, a Chicagoan who owned 1,200 acres of Gary marsh,
had proposed rechanneling the Little Calumet River in order to prevent springtime flooding of the new city of Gary. The massive reclamation project promised widespread effects: drainage of 20,000 acres
in the immediate vicinity of Gary, with 1,200 acres within the city
limits; an overall drainage area of 806 square miles—455 in Indiana
and the rest in Illinois; an added $1 million in taxes to Gary; $10
million in taxable real estate to Porter County; $45 million to Indi-
ana taxes and $32 million to those of Illinois.[15]

Despite intense local interest in constructing the ditch, other forces
interfered. The Lake Shore and Michigan Southern Railroad Company filed suit demanding damages equal to the cost of constructing
the railroad bridges they would need to install. Other legal action
followed, including an injunction initiated by the Public Service
Company of Northern Illinois, which claimed that the ditch would
compromise the company's water supply, thereby decreasing its power
production.[16] In all, litigation delayed the project for fifteen years.

By 1926, however, engineers had finally diverted water from the
Little Calumet into Lake Michigan. In all they cut eight miles of
channel, one-and-one-eighth miles of which went through the high
Porter County dunes five-and-one-half miles west of what later became the Indiana Dunes State Park.[17] The completion of Burns Ditch
provided a concreteness to the dreams of Valparaiso businessmen,
but not long after its construction two unrelated events forced these
men to act rather than dream.

The first occurred late in 1928, when a local developer named
Nelson Reck petitioned the War Department for federal approval of
a "pleasure Yacht Harbor" at the mouth of Burns Ditch. The second, a long-awaited happening, provided a tangible focus for decades

of unrealized dreams: Midwest Steel, a subsidiary of National Steel, bought 750 acres of Porter County lakefront straddling Burns Ditch. Clifford, Griffin, and the others feared that, if approved, Reck's proposal would prevent lakefront industrialization. They protested to the Army Engineers. Griffin denounced the yacht harbor proposal, his language foreshadowing forty years of similarly worded fervor. He argued in part, "As this inlet called the Burns Ditch is the only Harbor available in Porter County, Indiana for Commercial purposes, as it adjoins three miles of Lake Michigan shore property which is being held for industrial usage; as the rail facilities together with labor market are available in such a desirable manner only near the Burns Ditch inlet; if the same is restricted to pleasure boat use, Porter County will be harmed tremendously and her industrial development in this natural strategic location will be forever foreclosed."[18] Griffin also contacted second district Congressman Wood, who put the congressional machinery for a preliminary commercial harbor survey into motion. By December 1931, without so much as a hearing by the War Department, Congress received an unfavorable report from the Army Engineers. The harbor effort died its first of many deaths. The report opposed spending federal funds for a harbor entirely surrounded by Midwest Steel property and, therefore, inaccessible to the public.

Meanwhile, Midwest Steel's fortuitous purchase stimulated activity of another sort. A year after Nelson started his new job, seventy-three-year-old Pat Clifford took young Nelson to the Consumer Sand property in north Porter County. As Nelson recalled this trip, "We went to the lakefront, where Pat pointing toward the water said, 'There she is—Lake Michigan—pointed down into the heartland of the USA like a great finger into the bread basket of America.' Then he turned to me and said, 'As surely as we stand here, a great public port will be built in this area. Maybe not in our time but let's see if we can make it happen.'"[19] Thus inspired, Nelson found his métier, beginning then a forty-year crusade for a public port at Burns Ditch.

Subsequently, Clifford and Nelson called on H. L. Gray, vice-president of Midwest Steel. They hoped to enlist Midwest's help in solving a basic dilemma: federal funds would not be expended for a harbor without sufficient industry to justify the cost; industry would not make a commitment without assurance of a funded harbor. Neither Clifford nor Nelson nor Gray articulated the alternative, that Midwest, like U.S. Steel and Inland Steel before it, would build a harbor of its own, which port proponents believed would foreclose public use, and with it the county's economic future. Probably in those depression days no one considered the cost of a private harbor feasible. In any case, at that time neither Clifford nor Nelson felt threatened by such an eventuality.

Encouraged by the spark of interest Gray demonstrated, they set about to organize. In short order the chamber of commerce formed the Burns Ditch Harbor Development Committee, chaired by Clifford and consisting of, among others, his nephew Frank Clifford, the *Vidette Messenger's* Whipple, a young electrical contractor and a merchant named John Van Ness, and, of course, Nelson.

Meanwhile, the depression brought hard times to Valparaiso. A run on the Valparaiso National Bank extended to the First State Bank and Clifford's Farmer's State Bank, forcing all three to close for a time. Merchants, businessmen, and the unemployed suffered together, united in mutual antipathy toward Franklin D. Roosevelt and the New Deal. Despite the depression, or perhaps because of it, the Burns Ditch Harbor Development Committee pursued Midwest Steel with great energy and persistence, trying to reach an agreement that would satisfy the objections raised by the Army Engineers' 1931 report. Then, in May 1935, Charlie Halleck went to the House of Representatives.

CHARLES A. HALLECK

In the congressional election of 1934 Frederick Landis defeated George R. Durgan as representative from Indiana's second district, ending two years of the only Democratic incumbency for the area during the twentieth century. Unfortunately, Landis died of pneumonia only nine days after the election without receiving his certificate of election. To replace him, Indiana's second district chose Charles A. Halleck. He went to Congress as the only Republican member in the entire Indiana delegation and held the seat for thirty-four consecutive years.

Hoosier conservatism ran through Halleck's veins. His family had practiced Republican politics for two generations, his father, Abraham, having served as state senator and his grandfather as Newton County commissioner.

Although both parents practiced law, Halleck's mother, Lura, attracted most of the clients and stimulated the success of their endeavor. She provided the role model for Charlie's interest in law and for his intense drive and ambition. Not finding her days sufficiently filled managing an eleven-room house and five children, Lura Halleck had learned the law from the books in her husband's office. Once admitted to the bar, she worked alongside him. The elder Hallecks embodied the Puritan ethic; they believed in ambition,

*hard work, industriousness, conservative principles, and sobriety.
Charlie Halleck practiced these virtues, for the most part, as a tested
means to becoming somebody.*

*He entered Indiana University, after his World War I service, in-
tending to carry forward the success he had known in high school
and in his community. His self-confidence soon suffered at the hands
of Indiana University's social codes. Two top fraternities turned
him down, and a third neglected to solicit his bid at all. He took
these rejections hard, seriously worrying about his personal appearance and his intelligence. These experiences demonstrated a
passionate need for social acceptance and personal power, which
thwarted and frustrated him throughout his long life.*

*Perhaps in compensation for the ostracism of the "in groups,"
Halleck resorted to the tried and true formula of his youth, hard
work and perseverance. He excelled in his studies, plunged himself
into extracurricular activities, and began to combine a rudimentary political talent with his proven oratorical skills to become a
campus leader. He made Phi Beta Kappa in college and graduated
first in his class in law school. He developed a folksy, rough-hewn,
casual style that never entirely disguised his drive, ambition, and
need for recognition and approval.*

*For ten years Halleck served as prosecutor of the Jasper-Newton
circuit, his campaigns for that office serving to polish his speech-
making prowess and hone his political style. No one could have
been more ready than he for the 1935 election. He won it by a plurality of 5,235 votes.[20] From that victory on, his district considered
him its undisputed darling and hero, despite the many ups and
downs of his long tenure in office. Halleck wooed his mostly rural
supporters with a calculated combination of bucolic imagery and
well-placed jabs at the outrages of the Roosevelt administration.
From the beginning his constituents approved of his performance.
The concerns of the port proponents exactly matched those of the
man who would become their mentor and successful spokesman.
Halleck recalled how he learned about the port project.*

> *In those early years, a delegation came down from Valpo—a
> bipartisan delegation—about getting going again to get a port
> in that area. . . . One of the biggest hurdles we had to get over
> was that it was referred to as the Burns Ditch, and that was no
> high sounding thing. . . . Watcha gonna do, build a harbor in a
> ditch?*

For Halleck, the taunting had an ironic ring.

> *My dad was top drainage ditch lawyer in this country, [yet] the*

*first guy to sign the ditch petition got the ditch named af-
ter him.*

*My principal concern all through the years was the efforts of
surrounding states to shut off all Indiana's possible opportunity for development. All we needed was a resolution from the
Rivers and Harbors Committee to get another survey and I got
that through. I think the first report . . . put us in a dilemma.
It developed that you had to have a steel mill or an absolute
promise of one before [the port] was economically feasible, but
if you had [a mill] in contemplation, with a firm commitment
to build, then the demagogues attacked you for building a port
just for one steel company. Well, National Steel had acquired
land there—obviously they didn't buy it for a wadin' pool—
they bought it for industrial development. They were far-sighted
people. By the time we saw the dilemma, I had become very
well acquainted with [E. T.] Weir, who founded National Steel.
I went to E. T. with [Homer] Capehart [Indiana's Senator, 1944–
62], and I got him to write a letter that was trying to hedge
between building a port for one steel mill or doing something
else.*[21]

As one of so few Republicans in the Congress in those years, Halleck could hardly have succeeded in getting the port through Congress. While he may not have had sufficient power to accomplish
such a feat at the time, his singular standing in the Congress contributed to the port's frequent consideration.

Halleck recognized that as one of a very small number of Republicans in the House he had a superb opportunity to rise rapidly in
the party ranks. He also knew that if he could hang onto the seat,
he could acquire the power and influence he badly wanted. A lone
Republican congressman could do little during the Roosevelt years
but try to keep the home folks happy, bide his time, and assemble,
carefully, the power base he coveted. Halleck did not miss an opportunity. He spoke to all who would listen. He appeared at Washington social functions. When party leaders needed someone for an
extra job, Halleck showed up. If the bosses did not produce additional assignments, Charlie requested them. He charmed the press,
wowed the home folks, and battered continuously at the New Deal.

Halleck's aggressive availability appealed to the Republican National Committee, which began to use him nationwide as a speech
maker. In June 1936 Halleck delivered the keynote address at the
Indiana State Republican Convention. His views on national affairs received statewide attention and approbation via the Republican press. He defied the Democratic sweep of 1936. Whereas the
Republicans totaled only eighty-eight members in the House that

year and lost all states but Maine and Vermont for the presidency,
"Halleck ran ahead of the Republican national ticket in every county
of the district and exceeded the vote totals of almost every Repub-
lican candidate running for public office." [22] *Again he went to Wash-*
ington as Indiana's only Republican.

After the 1936 election Halleck became, by default, a member of
many congressional committees requiring bipartisan membership.
Because the Democratic landslide had so depleted veteran Repub-
lican ranks, Halleck started close to the top in seniority on every
committee. To his credit, he continued to make a virtue and a vo-
cation out of being available, filling party needs with practiced or-
atory and an increasingly recognized face.

By 1938 Halleck seemed invincible. He defeated his hapless
Democratic opponent by a margin five times greater than in the
1936 race, garnering a plurality of 21,444 votes. [23] *Simultaneously,*
his seniority assured him important committee assignments, in-
cluding appointment to the House Rules Committee, in the next
session.

Though only a third-term congressman, Halleck had parlayed
fortuitous circumstances and unceasing work into the second-place
slot in the Republican hierarchy. Along with long-term Republican
leaders such as Joe Martin, he helped map policy and plan strategy.
Occasional rumors had him running for governor or seeking a Sen-
ate seat, but Halleck had worked too hard and had planned too
carefully to relinquish the power of his House seat voluntarily. He'd
stay put, thank you, and continue to build for his future.

The four years of quiet negotiations with Midwest Steel had produced a package of promises from the steel company. Now, with a
promising mentor in Congress, the Burns Ditch Harbor Development Committee felt ready to organize. Conditions seemed promising for success, and Halleck looked like the man to grease official
wheels. So the local committee expanded. Forming a coalition of
ten organizations, five chambers of commerce and five assorted civic
groups in Lake, Porter, and LaPorte counties, it emerged as the
Northern Indiana Industrial Development Association (NIIDA), a
united organization dedicated to preventing any use for the mouth
of Burns Ditch that "would eliminate forever the last possible location for a public commercial harbor, and rob this State for all time
of its last breathing point, an adequate outlet to the waters of the
Great Lakes and St. Lawrence and Mississippi waterways." [24]

Edward J. Freund, second district Republican chairman and a member of the Indiana Republican State Central Committee, volunteered to bring Halleck and the fledgling NIIDA together. He wrote to Halleck on June 20, 1935, explaining the current proposal for the Burns Ditch Harbor, outlining the project's history, including the month-old coalition, and reviewing the promises of Midwest Steel.

Confidentially, I have been informed by Mr. George Nelson, Secretary of the Valparaiso Chamber of Commerce, Mr. P. W. Clifford, President of the Harbor Organization, and Mr. Frank Morton, Democratic Chairman, that they have the assurance of Mr. Herbert Gray, Assistant to the President of the Midwest Steel Corporation, that the necessary land for the project will be available for the Government, and that the harbor can be, if constructed, a public harbor without objection from the Steel Company, and, furthermore, if the harbor project is approved, not less than four million dollars will be available and will be used for the construction of a steel plant adjacent to the harbor. In fact, if I remember correctly, Mr. Gray has indicated that this assurance will be given in writing, if necessary.[25]

While Freund pointed Halleck in the direction of federal approval for the port, the men of the chamber pursued other avenues. They did not allow their distaste for the New Deal to prevent them from trying to use its provisions. In 1934 the Valparaiso Chamber of Commerce passed a resolution recommending construction of Dune Harbor and Amusement Park in Dune Acres, a $2 million Public Works Administration (PWA) project promising jobs and the creation of a new lakefront industry.[26] Early in 1935 the chamber of commerce attempted to obtain PWA money for port construction, in order to eliminate the necessity for a favorable Army Engineers report. Neither of these plans succeeded. They then sought further amplification of Midwest's intention from Gray, requiring clarification about the type of plant Midwest proposed to construct. In a letter to P. W. Clifford, Gray spelled out the thinking behind Midwest's pledge to build a finishing mill, rather than a complete plant, coincident with the commitment of public funds for a breakwater and public harbor. The proposed facility, capable of employing 1,200 workers, fulfilled the stipulations of the National Recovery Act (NRA) steel code, whereas a complete steel-producing plant would violate them. The NRA code prohibited erection of new open hearths and blast furnaces without common consent of all producers but did not restrict finishing mills.

By the middle of July 1935, Halleck had gotten a resolution from the House Committee on Rivers and Harbors requesting a review of the 1931 report and calling for a public hearing on August 22. Ecstatic at such rapid action and convinced that Halleck indeed embodied the right man in the right place at the right time, Freund nonetheless cautioned a diplomatic approach.

> The best thing [is] to try to avoid publicity at this time, [the NIIDA] informed me that the Associated Press and the Gary papers had phoned but they had not given them any dope on it because of the fear that possibly the Michigan City crowd and the Gary Steel interests might throw a monkey wrench into the gear box. Furthermore, they're afraid that if too much publicity were given at this time, real estate promoters might get in there, which I understand they are already doing, and secure options and it might make it appear that this was a real estate promotion instead of a real, honest-to-goodness project for the purpose of providing for the development of a great district.[27]

The August 22nd hearing had all the ingredients of success. A notable assemblage of Indiana officials supported the project. Democratic Governor Paul McNutt, the Indiana State Planning Board, and John Van Ness, now director of the Valparaiso Chamber of Commerce, as well as a wide array of civic, business, labor, and banking organizations, testified in its favor. District Engineer Lt. Colonel Donald H. Connolly proved comfortable to work with and seemed favorably disposed toward the proposed harbor. However, he imposed three conditions for approval: first, active industry must be located at the site; second, the site must not be surrounded by Midwest Steel; and third, provision for a public terminal must exist. The negotiations with the steel corporation had successfully met all three conditions. Prospects looked so good that proponents did not concern themselves with a crucial restriction in Midwest's package—that funds to construct the public terminal must be secured within three years or the company would revoke its donation of land.

Caprice played its part in undoing the four years of painstaking planning that preceded the 1935 hearing. Unexpectedly and without explanation, Colonel Connolly withdrew from the project, to be replaced by Captain S. N. Karrick, an unknown quantity. In November Karrick recommended against funding the harbor, concurring with the findings of 1931 that the prospective public benefits would not justify the cost of improvements. As proof he cited current economic conditions, particularly the below-capacity production condition of existing steel plants.

An unbelieving State of Indiana appealed. The appeal hearing, held in Washington the following March, produced the big guns: Halleck, of course; Governor McNutt; Senators Frederick Van Nuys and Sherman Minton; Representatives William Schulte, Samuel B. Pettingill, and Virginia Jenckes; newspaper editors Harley Snyder of the Gary *Post*, Whipple of the *Vidette Messenger*, James Crane of the Chicago *South End Reporter*; engineers; lawyers; industrialists; and planners, all testifying that Karrick had displayed unsound reasoning and that the harbor, desirable and necessary for economic recovery and for the future of the state, would both benefit the public and justify the cost. To no avail. Again the Army Engineers rejected the port proposal.

> The board recognizes the probable future need for a suitable harbor for general commercial use on the lake shore of the State of Indiana, but is of the opinion that the selection of a site for such an improvement should be based on a comprehensive review of the whole available frontage rather than the consideration of the site at Burns Ditch alone. . . . The immediate beneficiary of the desired improvement at Burns Ditch would be the corporation holding an extensive tract of land at the site and the development would serve primarily to improve the competitive position of this corporation in the steel industry.[28]

Halleck's former professor, Governor McNutt, lost no time in making political hay over Indiana's failure to get its port in 1935. In the 1936 campaign McNutt charged that Halleck's vociferous criticisms of the New Deal had destroyed the proposal. Frank Clifford expressed Valparaiso's extreme pique to Halleck. "By this time most of us have gotten our feet back on the ground after getting the jolt which we did from the Army Engineering Board, but none of us can conceive how these people arrived at this decision. . . . In my opinion, the statement about a comprehensive review of the available frontage, etc. is a lot of 'hooey' . . . the paramount fear before the Board . . . was that they might do something which would strengthen [National Steel's] position in the industry."[29] In Clifford's view, Midwest had become a liability rather than a necessity, and the idea of a comprehensive survey had become a potential wedge in the solidarity of the NIIDA. Clifford's prophecy held true two years later, when Lake County Congressman Schulte withdrew support for the Burns Ditch site in favor of one in Lake County.

Halleck did not simply accept the decision. On the day the Army Engineers issued their report he introduced a bill authorizing the comprehensive shoreline review recommended by the report. His bill passed a year later, following which the Army Engineers held still another hearing, this time in Chicago, to determine the advisability of a shoreline survey. It rehashed the arguments of prior hearings with the same cast of characters and provided little new data, save the designation of the project as "meritorious" by the National Rivers and Harbor's Congress at its 32nd annual convention. Karrick still needed convincing. He required hard figures on projected use and tonnage of shipments through the proposed harbor, which proponents thus far had been unable to provide. Karrick gave them until March 1 to produce this information.

By March 4 Nelson still lacked the necessary data. His long detailed letter to Halleck made no attempt to disguise his frustration.

> The truth of the matter is, Charlie, that it is just impossible to secure the kind of information which Karrick has requested previously and which apparently we need to complete our case. . . . I within the past few days filed with Captain Karrick copies of the evidence submitted at the hearing in Washington on March 16, 1936, without, of course, the copy of the record of verbal statements and at that time Karrick made this remark to me, "that if on receipt of the data from the Indiana State Chamber of Commerce concerning tonnage that it did not appear to be what it should be, not to file it." . . . [I have] secured an extension of time until March 8th. It appears that we will not be able to file any information with him further than stating, of course, the steel corporation's tonnage is still a possibility . . . we would best make a closing statement to Karrick so that he can send in his report. He is anxious to do that as he says it is embarrassing to hold it up much longer. . . . It is evident that existing manufacturers, while they need the [harbor] facilities, will not go on record publicly because they fear antagonizing the transportation utilities now serving them. I am willing to do anything that I can and give all of the time that I can, necessary to securing any needed information, but I do not know at this time which way to turn.[30]

Besides being unable to obtain tonnage figures from prospective harbor users, Nelson had misjudged Midwest Steel. When the three years that the company had allowed for harbor funding in its 1935 agreement ran out, Midwest's parent company took the $27 million that it had planned to use in Indiana and spent it in Detroit instead. Consequently, since port proponents could provide no economic justification for construction of a harbor, the Army Engineers reported on July 6, 1938, that they could see no necessity for a survey of lake frontage.

Stymied by federal concern with cost justification, Nelson recalled a suggestion Halleck had made early in the preceding year. "I have learned," Halleck had written, "that a great many harbor improvements have been constructed by cooperation between the states and the Federal Government. . . . I am clearly of the opinion that if the state of Indiana should make some definite move looking to assistance in carrying out this project, our position would be materially strengthened. So if the local people interested in the Legislature can do something in the matter of an appropriation for this project, I think such action should be encouraged."[31] Port proponents now turned in this direction.

JOHN VAN NESS

In September 1938, after the death of state Senator Will Brown of Hebron, John Van Ness defeated three rivals to win endorsement by the Porter County Republican organization for the State Senate. In agreeing to run he even surprised himself, for he never previously had claimed political aspiration. But Guy Stinchfield, Republican County chairman, recognized a good man and counted on Valparaiso to back a native son with enthusiasm.

Everyone in town knew the Van Ness family. John's father, Elliott, who came from Michigan to study at Valparaiso University, met and married Rachel Wilson, a local girl and never left Indiana. In 1900 the elder Van Ness and some of his in-laws went into the electrical business, a profitable and successful venture that remained in the family for over fifty years. At the age of twenty, John joined his father in the firm, leaving only to serve in the Navy during World War I. His port of call became the Massachusetts Institute of Technology, where he put in his military time. In 1919 Van Ness returned to Valparaiso and the electrical business. He returned to begin his adult life as a full community member, joining the chamber of commerce, the merchants' bureau, the credit bureau, the American Legion, the Kiwanis Club, the YMCA, and the Free and Accepted Masons. By the early 1930s fellow businessmen respected John's willing participation in matters of mutual concern, his unfailing interest in the good of the community, and the quiet, methodical, almost plodding manner with which he accomplished his goals.

Valparaiso, like the rest of the nation, suffered greatly from the depression; few had an easy time. The 1932 bank failures, the sluggish business conditions and scarcity of jobs, the problems of "trying to live with nationally promoted Roosevelt 'give away' programs" all played a role in Van Ness's creeping dissatisfaction.[32] He felt increasingly critical of governmental interference in general and the *state tax situation in particular. As director of the Valparaiso Chamber of Commerce, in 1935 he worked closely with Nelson to minimize the burden of the newly enacted Indiana gross income tax on local retailers.*

Van Ness made an unlikely rabble-rouser and, in all probability, found his role as goad extremely uncomfortable. So when Stinchfield tapped him to run for the Republican vacancy, he saw the offer as an opportunity to "put up or shut up," a philosophy he believed in wholeheartedly and usually accomplished very well. Chairman Stinchfield convinced him to run and guided his first campaign. Stinchfield only had to play the mentor once, however, for Van Ness approached politics with the same thorough, businesslike efficiency that he brought to his commercial, community, and family life.

Politics proved to be unlike anything in John's experience, and he thrived on it. He could tell a political campaign story like a veteran—salty enough to keep his Hoosier audience interested, clean enough to get elected. Phrases like "I'll do my best in this great cause" or "these uncertain, unsatisfactory, chaotic times" rang with the sincerity of instant invention when he uttered them. His earnestness and desire to do the right thing changed the most time-worn cliches into inspired, rhetorical, original phrases. He met people easily, projecting honesty, competence, ability, and promise.

So the people elected Van Ness to the Indiana Senate in 1938; they continued to elect him for eighteen years. He served under nine governors, led the Republican Senate as president pro tem from 1944 to 1957, and became the Indiana representative on the Council of State Governments between 1944 and 1962. On the eve of his retirement, in the final hours of the 90th General Assembly, fellow legislators singled him out for "his wise, temperate statesmanship, his equable contention, and his warm friendliness," designating him President Pro Tem Emeritus of the Indiana Senate, an honor uniquely his.[33]

At the beginning of his political career, the future "Honest John" represented Porter, Newton, Jasper, and Pulaski counties, a gigantic district that ran one hundred miles from corner to corner. During the biennial session Van Ness lived in an Indianapolis hotel, which cost him $3.85 a day. On the weekends he journeyed home to Valparaiso where, in his absence, his wife Harriet had tended John's mother, their three children, and the thriving electrical business. When he could, he traveled his huge district, often by train, to learn firsthand the opinions of his constituents. And he did all this for a *salary of $10 per day. William E. Jenner, then minority leader of the State Senate and later U.S. senator from Indiana, became Van Ness's tutor and mentor during his freshman term. Of the sixteen Republicans then seated, Jenner most completely represented the views that Van Ness held.*

Early in his first term, former colleagues from the Valparaiso Chamber of Commerce approached their new senator about sponsoring legislation to authorize and fund the Port of Indiana. In 1935, as director of the chamber, Van Ness and other chamber of commerce directors had met with Governor McNutt about the project, and as a member of Valparaiso's Harbor Development Committee he had accompanied them to testify at the Army Engineers hearing. He never lost his enthusiasm for the proposed harbor. Indeed, from his first election to the Senate in 1938 to his departure in 1957, he introduced and sponsored all legislation dealing with Indiana's port.[34] Motivated by a desire to benefit all the people of Indiana, Van Ness believed that the Burns Ditch Harbor would promote the cheapest means of exporting the products of Indiana's farms, industries, and mines and also provide the most economical route for necessary imports. He assessed the significance of his 1939 legislation perhaps too modestly.

There was a great deal of interest in the project but because it was an entirely new idea there was no possibility of getting a major appropriation . . . we were successful in having a conditional appropriation of $50,000 added to the budget bill which was to be used to convince the Army Engineers to proceed with the study. Then if two or more industries were willing to locate at the site of the harbor, the money would be used to further the port project. At the same time, another piece of legislation I sponsored set up the Board of Harbors and Terminals which was to use these funds. But World War II came along and put a damper on this activity for some little time.[35]

Although the war temporarily scuttled the project, Van Ness did not waste the time. By 1944 Republicans had a majority in the State Senate, and both Jenner and his successor to the party leadership had joined the military. Van Ness followed as president pro tem, serving in that capacity for thirteen years, the longest such service in Indiana history.

After the war the Chicago District Army Engineer recommended still another survey of the Burns Waterway. This gave Van Ness new impetus to further the cause of the port. The senator's last five years in the legislature produced substantial advances toward port con-

*struction after years of discouragement. In 1957 the Indiana legis-
lature finally passed his bill allowing the state to construct the port
without federal participation and appropriated $2 million to begin
the process.*

*Retirement from the Senate did not remove Van Ness from public
service or proximity to the harbor project. In 1957 Governor Harold
Handley appointed him to the Great Lakes Commission, a non-
federally funded advisory group from the eight Great Lakes states.
But in 1959 Van Ness removed himself from state government entirely when he became an assistant to Albert Berdis, president of
Midwest Steel.*

*In retrospect, Van Ness took most pride in his role as a small
businessman, active as such in Valparaiso for forty-seven years. He
took pride also as a public servant who gave the people a good administration. The Port of Indiana represented his most satisfying
public achievement. Yet in the rosy glow of hindsight he would say
of it: "From a personal point of view I hoped they'd never build a
port there, but as a good citizen of Indiana and an elected representative of four counties, I would do less than my duty if I didn't do
everything I could to push for that port."*[36]

Early in 1939 Nelson began to urge state officials to consider
spending $1 million on the Burns Ditch Harbor. He believed this
sum would start the project and convince the federal government
that Indiana would do its share. In addition, he felt strongly that a
million-dollar appropriation would convince Midwest to cooperate
and "put the officials of the state in a position to horse trade with
the steel corporation."[37] Nelson successfully petitioned to delay the
appeal of the 1938 Chicago hearing until after the close of the 1939
session of the Indiana legislature. His optimism extended even to
anticipating support from the Democrats. "Unless we have been
kidded greatly, the Democratic officials of the state and the Indiana
senators have been willing to do everything they could for the project and are still willing to do so."[38] Senator John Van Ness agreed to
meet with the Republican leaders and "lay all the cards on the table
with them with the idea of selling this project to them and getting
their support to the extent that we would be able to go into this
session of the Indiana General Assembly and get a bill through for
the expenditure of one million dollars on the part of the state."[39]
Success of this plan, he felt, would insure the strongest possible stance
for the appeal. Its failure, however, might cause a sizable backfire.

Nelson considered the matter very urgent. A look into the near future convinced him that business conditions would soon return to normal and that when they did Midwest would assess its competitive position and push ahead with its midwestern expansion program. "It goes without saying, that if they have to make a development there themselves and if they ever expend a material sum of money on the construction of a harbor themselves, that the state of Indiana or any other public or private agency will have to pay dearly for the privilege of the use of their facilities."[40]

The meeting with the Republican leadership took place on January 12. Pat and Frank Clifford, Henry B. and Ralph Snyder from Gary, as well as Gary's mayor, Dr. E. L. Schaible, came to Indianapolis for the strategy session and private lobbying. The legislators responded favorably to the idea of a million-dollar state appropriation, contingent both on federal approval and on completion of the harbor by the federal government. As a result, Van Ness contacted Governor M. Clifford Townsend and secured his support. Nelson, meanwhile, met again with H. L. Gray to determine Midwest's intentions. Nelson reported that Gray exuded encouragement.

> Mr. Gray told me on the phone when I made the appointment, that while he did not want me to disclose the fact to the committee at that time, he felt there was a good possibility of securing renewal of the pledges. On meeting with him, he gave John Van Ness encouragement along that line also, and while we were there, called E. T. Weir and made an appointment with him for Sunday the 29th in Chicago, at which time he will be on his way to the west coast to sail for Hawaii. I have no doubt that he will take the matter up with him long before the 29th and that by Monday, we will have an answer or at least will know where we stand on the renewal of these pledges.[41]

However, the steel corporation played coquette. Weir would neither renew the pledges of 1935 nor commit Midwest to any course of action in the foreseeable future.

Thus Nelson came to Indianapolis for the 1939 session of the legislature lacking one of the necessary aspects of his plan. He and Van Ness collaborated in writing legislation to obtain the million-dollar appropriation. In addition, Van Ness introduced another bill creating a Board of Harbors and Terminals. This bill sailed through both houses without incident—but not so the appropriations measure. When the speaker of the house refused to hand the bill down for house consideration, Van Ness, in a surprise move, tacked $200,000 onto the Senate budget bill. A conference committee finally settled the issue, allowing a paltry $50,000 appropriation. This meager but safe sum had a big advantage—it would not revert to the general fund if unused by the end of the session. Van Ness regarded the $50,000 as a symbol of Indiana's support for the Burns Ditch Harbor and as available money for the start of construction when the time came. Equally important, the establishment of the Board of Harbors and Terminals meant that Nelson would no longer have to struggle to unearth the necessary economic data alone. He and the new agency together could proceed in orderly and official fashion to gather statistics to insure that, come spring, they would be ready for the appeal.

Unfortunately, continued pursuit of Midwest produced nothing. Although Nelson hounded Gray, the steel company would not renew any promises. Even Halleck, who contacted Weir at Nelson's urging, met with scant success. National Steel's Burns Ditch holdings would be developed next, Weir said, but he would not indicate just when "next" might be. Then, before plans for the appeal hearing could be completed, the United States declared a national emergency and suspended all nonmilitary activities by the Army Engineers. America would fight and win World War II before port proponents raised the Burns Ditch Harbor issue again.

The federal government's response to the Great Depression profoundly altered the values by which Americans previously had lived. Roosevelt's New Deal, which began where progressivism left off, soon went beyond the scope of earlier reforms. In the interests of recovery most Americans adjusted to the notion of federal responsibility for the nation's social and economic welfare. The port proponents and their political mentors, however, clung to the individualistic values of an earlier time. Though they decried the government's interference, they nonetheless pursued federal approval and federal money as the means of promoting growth, development, and prosperity for Porter County.

These men considered Porter County's industrialization a personal mission as well as a public duty. They did not allow the social, economic, environmental, and political consequences, observable in other industrial centers, to affect their judgment or alter their strategy. They wanted changes for the better and thought the port would bring progress and prosperity without concomitant change in any other aspect of life.

NOTES

1. "United States of America," *Encyclopedia Britannica* (1974), 18: 920.
2. Richard Hofstadter, *The Age of Reform* (New York: Vintage Books, 1955), p. 294.

3. Ibid.

4. Moore, *Calumet Region*, pp. 555, 556.

5. Ibid., p. 470.

6. Cannon, Loring, and Robb, eds., *Lake and Calumet Region*, 1:703.

7. Indiana State Planning Services Agency, *Indiana Fact Book* (Indianapolis, 1979), p. 17.

8. Cannon, Loring, and Robb, eds., *Lake and Calumet Region*, 1:804.

9. *Indiana Fact Book*, p. 17.

10. Cannon, Loring, and Robb, eds., *Lake and Calumet Region*, 1:770–826.

11. Ibid., p. 831.

12. George A. Nelson, "Chamber Job Got Nelson Here, Port Benefits All County Residents," Valparaiso *Vidette Messenger*, Nov. 4, 1976.

13. Cannon, Loring, and Robb, eds., *Lake and Calumet Region*, 1:703–4.

14. Nelson, "Chamber Job."

15. "Would Add $77,000,000 to Tax Valuation," Gary *Post*, Oct. 21, 1922.

16. Ibid.

17. Moore, *Calumet Region*, p. 13.

18. John Griffin, president of the Valparaiso Chamber of Commerce, to U.S. War Department, Jan. 26, 1929, quoted in "Early History of Port of Indiana prior to 1929," Valparaiso Chamber of Commerce, Save the Dunes Council File. Later the Army Corps of Engineers, Department of the Army, took over the War Department's function.

19. Nelson, "Chamber Job."

20. Henry Z. Scheele, *Charlie Halleck: A Political Biography* (New York: Exposition Press, 1966), appendix D.

21. Authors' interview with Charles A. Halleck, Rensselaer, Ind., 1977.

22. Scheele, *Charlie Halleck*, p. 87.

23. Ibid.

24. Northern Indiana Industrial Development Association, "Paper presented by the Northern Indiana Industrial Development Association" (undated), Save the Dunes Council Files.

25. Edward J. Freund to Charles Halleck, June 20, 1935, Halleck Papers, Lilly Library, Indiana University, Bloomington.

26. Minutes of Meeting, Feb. 27, 1934, Valparaiso Chamber of Commerce.

27. Freund to Halleck, July 17, 1935, Halleck Papers.

28. Quoted in "Development Association Paper," pp. 11–12.

29. Frank Clifford to Halleck, Apr. 7, 1936, Halleck Papers.

30. Nelson to Halleck, Mar. 4, 1938, Halleck Papers.

31. Halleck to Nelson, Jan. 20, 1937, Halleck Papers.

32. John Van Ness, "Van Ness Recalls Political Life," Valparaiso *Vidette Messenger*, Nov. 4, 1976.

33. "Van Ness Retirement Honored by Senators," Indianapolis *Star*, Mar. 12, 1957, p. 3.

34. Authors' interview with John Van Ness, Valparaiso, 1977.

35. Ibid.
36. Ibid.
37. Nelson to Halleck, Jan. 5, 1939, Halleck Papers.
38. Ibid.
39. Ibid.
40. Ibid.
41. Nelson to Halleck, Jan. 25, 1939, Halleck Papers.

A. J. Bowser, owner of the Chesterton *Trib-une* and outspoken advocate of industrial development in the early 1900s.

Tom Knotts, Gary's first mayor. Dismayed at the leveling of the Lake County Dunes, he worked for the preservation of the remaining sand hills.

Stephen Mather, first director of the National Park Service, whose 1916 public hearing on a Sand Dunes National Park started a fifty-year battle for preservation.

Henry Chandler Cowles, the father of North American plant ecology, conducted his pioneering research in the Dunes.

Jens Jensen worked unceasingly as the first champion of Dunes preservation at the beginning of the twentieth century.

Tom Taggart, political boss of Indiana's Democratic party, introduced, as a U.S. Senator, the first federal Dunes legislation in 1916.

At the 1917 Pageant: The dance of the waves from "The Dunes under Four Flags," performed at Waverly Beach.

Richard Lieber, a German-born immigrant, brought a Department of Conservation to Indiana and paved the way for the establishment of the Indiana Dunes State Park.

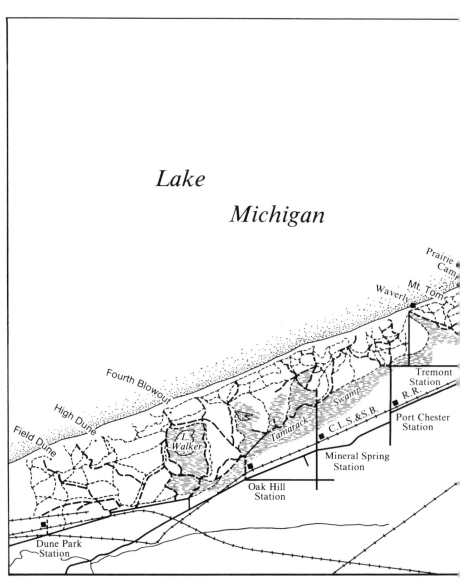

The Porter County Dunes in 1920.

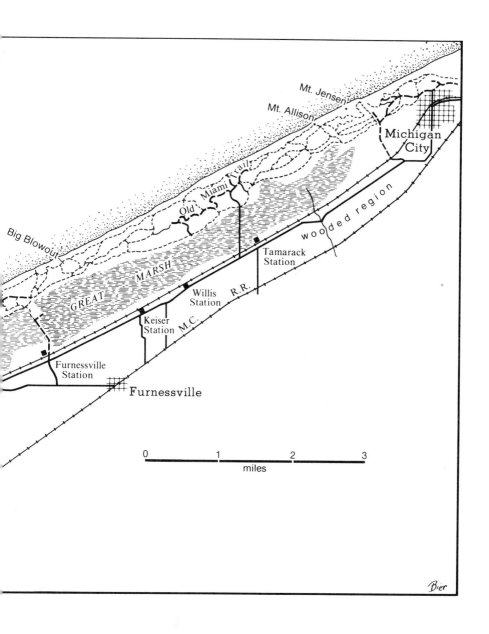

Mt. Jensen

Mt. Allison

Michigan
City

Old Miami Trail

wooded region

Big Blowout

Tamarack
Station

GREAT   MARSH

Willis
Station

R.R.

Keiser
Station

M.C.

Furnessville
Station

Furnessville

0   1   2   3
miles

Bier

Bess Sheehan, a Gary clubwoman, led the successful
campaign for the Indiana Dunes State Park.

George A. Nelson, secretary-manager for the Valparaiso Chamber of Commerce beginning in 1930, was a crusader for the Port of Indiana between 1930 and 1970.

John Van Ness, as an Indiana state senator from 1938–62, was the chief author of all port legislation in the Indiana Senate.

Charles A. Halleck, "Mr. Republican," represented Porter County in the House of Representatives and fought for the Port of Indiana between 1934 and 1968.

A Dunes cottonwood tree. The roots extending from the trunk indicate that the dune once covered the trunk to that height.

Lake, beach, and foredune covered with marram grass—the beginning stages in Cowles's theory of plant succession.

CHAPTER 4 State Rescue Operation

Congressional indifference to National Park Service
Director Stephen Mather's 1916 report supporting a Sand Dunes National Park spelled the end of federal involvement in the Indiana
Dunes for nearly half a century. At the time most Dunes advocates
refused to understand the message. Mather himself, however, saw
the real prospects, recognizing that the necessary ingredients for the
establishment of a national park—united local interest, congressional backing, and federal domain—did not exist. He concluded
almost immediately that "the only hope for the Dunes lay in the
state park movement."[1]

Fortuitously for the Dunes, the state park movement had just begun in Indiana as part of the state centennial observance. In 1916,
the same year as Mather's Sand Dunes hearing, Hoosiers marked
the one hundredth birthday of the state. Pageants in Bloomington,
Corydon, and Indianapolis suitably commemorated the anniversary.
As part of the observance, the establishment of the State Park Memorial Committee started a chain of events that would lead to the
initial preservation of the Dunes. The committee's success in pro-
curing donations of money and land to begin Indiana's park system
resulted in the development of a statewide appreciation for open space.
Location of the initial parks in southern Indiana increased pressure
for northern Indiana representation in the system.

Without the initial drive to establish a Sand Dunes National Park,
however, the state park campaign could not have succeeded. The
movement for a Dunes national park had generated massive publicity, had developed a network of loyal supporters, and had attracted
wealthy backers. Without the climate and constituency that this
earlier, doomed effort had created, Indiana would never have preserved a portion of the Dunes. Even the most ardent opponents of a
federal Dunes preserve had come to accept the inevitability of some
sort of a Dunes park in order to quell the preservationist forces. To
ensure reservation of most, if not all, of the Porter County shoreline

for other uses, a state park rather than a federal enclave seemed preferable to advocates of industrial development.

Happily for the Dunes, Indiana as a state embraced the concept of scenic preservation after Congress turned its back on a national park in the sand hills. In an earlier era Indiana would not have set aside three-and-one-quarter miles of lakefront and 2,000 acres that included Mount Tom, Mount Holden, and Mount Jackson, the "Monarchs of the Dunes."[2] Establishment of the state park came with relative ease, although proponents, in the midst of legislative maneuverings, despaired of the outcome.[3] A bill to authorize the Indiana Dunes State Park, introduced in the 1923 legislative session, passed in the closing days. No similar speedy legislative consideration would ever again happen to the Dunes.

That Indiana, a state as committed to economic materialism as any in the nation, adopted scenic preservation as public policy stemmed from the leadership of one man, Richard Lieber. His acumen in adapting scenic preservation to Indiana's values saved part of the Dunes and laid the groundwork for a renewed national effort thirty years later.

RICHARD LIEBER

In 1901 a twenty-one-year-old Rhinelander, Richard Lieber, arrived in Indianapolis. Six feet tall, slim, dignified, and well-groomed, the newcomer came from an aristocratic family. The son of a high-ranking imperial engineer, he had spent the previous year in London. His parents, frightened of his growing "liberal" views, decided to send him to visit his uncles, Herman and Albert Lieber, and their families, who lived prosperously in Indiana's capital city.

Lieber himself later described his Prussian attitude, which his English visit modified and which life in the United States would end.

> *My exposure to the milieu ran something like this. I have to be thankful to fate that I am a German and not a degenerate Frenchman, shopkeeping English etc., etc. Secondly, I am to be grateful that among the Germans, I am not an uncouth Bavarian, sloppy Suebian etc., etc., etc., but a Prussian, although not in the strictest sense, for I came into life in the Saar Valley. Thirdly, it is something to be proud that among the Prussians, I was the son of an Imperial Officer and not the hapless offspring of a banker, manufacturer or shopkeeper. Lastly, it is a happy fact that I am a Protestant and not a (epithet to be supplied ad lib) Catholic or Jew.[4]*

Happily at home among Indianapolis's large German population, where his great charm, generosity, and natural knack of meeting people made him immediately well liked, Lieber promptly adapted to American values. He initially found employment as a clerk in a hardware store, precisely the type of work abhorrent to his upper-class upbringing. His friendliness, keen sense of humor, general amiability, and native ability soon won his promotion to collector of accounts.

Lieber then fell in love with Emma Rappeport, daughter of the publisher of the Indianapolis Tribune. His marriage ended any thought of returning to Germany, and he plunged into a commercial career at the Western Chemical Company. After a disastrous series of fires at the company, Lieber withdrew to enter a calling more suited to his cultured background. A born musician who never had a lesson, Lieber could play the trumpet and piano by the hour. His avid reading of history, his natural linguistic ability, his knowledge of Latin, Greek, French, and Hebrew, and his understanding of science, literature, and art resulted in his becoming the art and music critic of the Indianapolis Journal and later reporter and city editor of the Tribune. His writing talent brought about an enjoyable journalistic career. Through his newspaper work Lieber learned the value of enlisting public support, which he practiced adeptly in his conservation years. His first contact with Chicago intellectual circles, early advocates of Dunes preservation, came during this period. As a result of his critical reviews he received numerous invitations to lecture on art and music before Indiana organizations. He also attended lectures given by members of the University of Chicago faculty and, using his newspaper's railroad pass, traveled to the Hyde Park campus, where he became further acquainted with the Chicago professors. Impressed by his erudition and teaching ability, President William Rainey Harper offered Lieber the opportunity to attend the university for a year, obtain his Ph.D. in Greek, Latin, or history, and then join the university faculty. But the demands of his growing family made Lieber reject the offer.[5] His need for additional income also led to his departure from the newspaper business. Backed by his uncle's money, he started the Richard Lieber Company, which manufactured soft drinks and soda water. Soon the firm added wines and whiskies to their line. Lieber's gift of storytelling, his lack of intellectual pretensions, and his geniality brought him success in selling to saloons and hotels.[6] But he disliked business and possessed not the slightest interest in accumulating wealth. Fortunately for him and for conservation, a larger and better organized wholesale company bought his firm in 1905. Lieber, freed from business and monetary responsibilities, now could devote his energy and intellect to social causes.

Initially municipal reform claimed his attention. Haunted by the memory of the Western Chemical Company fires, he worked for improvement in the city's fire protection system. Lieber's leadership in this campaign, which attracted the support of the business community, produced tangible and long-lasting results: better fire equipment, lower fire insurance rates, and establishment of the office of State Fire Marshal. Lieber then became president of the Merchants and Manufacturers Insurance Bureau, a post he held for thirty-seven years. He also spearheaded a drive to found the chamber of commerce and fought for a municipal civil service system. In all his civic work Lieber preached the tenets of efficiency and economy in government. He argued for application of business principles in public affairs and the importance of nonpartisan employment of governmental workers. Similar themes would mark his conservation efforts.[7] These positions reflected the philosophy of the progressive movement, then in vogue in the nation, as well as the beliefs of practical conservation. Like Lieber, the utilitarian conservationists believed that partisan politics interfered with government's proper role: maximizing the nation's long-term economic health through the elimination of waste and duplication, the application of scientific principles, and the rational use of people, machinery, and natural resources. Instead of the spoils system they advocated a trained bureaucracy.

By 1912 Lieber had become a well-known and well-respected business leader. He knew, both socially and politically, many of the city, state, and national Republican leaders. When the Fourth Conservation Congress, a national meeting of utilitarian-oriented conservation leaders, met in Indianapolis that year, Lieber served as chairman of the Local Board of Managers.

The Indianapolis News praised his appointment, citing his accomplishments in fire protection reform as exemplifying conservation principles. Lieber's remarks in the same issue clearly revealed his utilitarian convictions.

> Waste of a grand scale is a typical American vice. It is immense, gigantic, like the country itself.
> The buffalo and wild pigeons are gone, the game of the woods and the streams nearly so. Our forests have been cut or burned down, while the floods have come. Measured on a European scale, we have wasted away whole principalities by place mining. Natural gas was discovered to be wasted. The thick black

smoke hovering over our cities is an ever present witness of the continued waste. The city's sewerage is emptied into a river, valuable fertilizing material is not only thrown away, but becoming by our recklessness, a grave danger to the health of others. . . . The cure lies not in a superficial treatment of symptoms, but in prevention and conservation.[8]

The speech of Indiana's representative at the opening session of the congress also enunciated the practical conservationist's point of view. He proposed "a State Conservation Board with supervisory power over all subjects of conservation now committed to separate and independent boards or commissions, so as to more effectively coordinate their efforts in a scientific manner, avoiding duplication and intensifying the work."[9] This proposal won Lieber's wholehearted endorsement, and he pursued this objective until its enactment in 1918.

Lieber, however, also had a prior, long-standing, and deep attachment to aesthetic conservation's concern with scenic and historic preservation. His father's work as a landscape and building architect influenced his aesthetic appreciation.[10] His avid reading of history and his continual travels in the United States and abroad, together with his instant recall of every place he visited, fueled his preservationist tendencies.[11] Lieber first became impressed with the scenic beauty of his adopted country when he visited Yellowstone Park and was disturbed by its commercialization. Later, a forty-five-day hunting trip to Idaho and Montana crystallized his concern with the problems of wilderness preservation. Contacts with preservationists also strengthened Lieber's attachment to their cause. Through his Uncle Albert, president of the State Board of Forestry, he met a Purdue University dean, Stanley Coulter, also a member of the Forestry Board. Coulter introduced Lieber to his brother John, then chairman of the botany department at the University of Chicago. In turn, John Coulter brought his protege, Henry Chandler Cowles, and Lieber together. They became allies in the coming effort to preserve the Dunes.

Historic preservation clearly pervaded Lieber's thoughts when he wrote an article for the Indianapolis News in 1908 suggesting that the state protect memorials of its past as part of the centennial celebration eight years hence.[12] But it was not until Lieber's first visit to Brown County in 1910 that he saw the need for preserving Indiana's scenic beauty. He decided, "This whole county ought to be bought up by the state and then made into a State Park so that all the people of Indiana could enjoy this beautiful spot."[13]

His newspaper article, his record of civic achievements, his rep-

utation for giving time to worthy causes, and his contacts in business and political circles all contributed to Lieber's appointment to the State Park Memorial Committee in 1916. Thereupon, Lieber found a cause to which he contributed the rest of his years, first to the success of the committee, then to its absorption into the new Department of Conservation, which he formed, founded, and then headed for fourteen years. To his state conservation work Lieber brought his attachments to both utilitarian and aesthetic conservation. He used the former's arguments to boost the latter and saw no contradiction in his position. State parks preserved open space for the enjoyment of future generations and paid for themselves through user fees and the recreational benefits they provided. The agencies within his Department of Conservation clearly aided the state's economy and shone as examples of lean, efficient governmental operations.

Lieber became the Stephen Mather of Indiana, guiding the growth and success of a model state park system and a respected Department of Conservation. His scope and influence broadened beyond the state's borders. Lieber helped organize the first State Park Conference, called by Mather in 1921. He became a leading figure in the National Conference on State Parks, the organization that resulted from this meeting, a principal spokesman for the state park movement, and a national conservation leader.

Although forced out as director of the Indiana Department of Conservation in 1932 with the return of the Democratic party to power, Lieber did not retire from conservation work. Typically he spent seven days a week as an unpaid consultant to the National Park Service and served as a member of its advisory board. Traveling throughout the country, he inspected proposals for additions to the nation's parks until his death in 1944. A boulder from the Indiana Dunes marks his grave at Turkey Run State Park. Because of his vision, drive, and talent, Indiana became a leader in melding aesthetic and utilitarian principles of conservation, and the Indiana Dunes achieved partial preservation.

A conservation ethic grew in Indiana for the same reasons that it evolved in the nation as a whole. To the state's pioneers, Indiana's natural resources seemed unending and inexhaustible. Consequently, citizens used the rich soil, large forests, vast supplies of fish and game, and large deposits of mineral wealth as the raw materials from which to fashion profitable livelihoods. After fifty years the unlimited exploitation of natural resources resulted in virtual depletion of fish and wildlife. No longer did flocks of birds darken the sky above Indiana's prairies. The near extinction of those animals, which once furnished pioneers with a large part of their food supply—deer, wild turkey, quail, ruffed grouse, and prairie chicken—led to a closed hunting season. By 1867 the legislature outlawed trapping, shooting, or seining fish in Indiana waters. A prohibition on fish spearing followed in 1871. A decade later the enforcement of game and fish laws began. Where once the pioneer had loaded his flintlock, stepped outside his door, and unmindfully shot any animal, he now needed state approval. By 1907 regulations even governed the right to hunt rabbits.[14]

Indiana's native timber was similarly destroyed. In 1880 the state ranked sixth in the nation in the production of hardwood lumber. Within five years Indiana began importing timber. In 1889 hardwood lumber production peaked at 1,036,999 feet. By 1919 it had declined to 282,487 feet. The continued clearing of forested land for agricultural cultivation and grazing and the cutting of hardwoods to meet demands for furniture, farm implements, and other manufactured wood products contributed to Indiana's timber reserve depletion. Demands for forestry conservation, fiercely resisted by Hoosier farmers, led to the establishment of the first State Forest in 1903.[15]

Widespread development of Indiana's mineral reserves started in the 1880s with the mining of bituminous coal in the western and southwestern sections of the state. By 1919 a report labeled mining methods in the state less efficient than elsewhere in the nation and called for means to "halt this reckless, useless waste . . . before it is too late."[16]

Perhaps the burning of great flaming torches, or flambeaux, which day and night lit up the skies of the Gas Belt of east central Indiana best typified Indiana's traditional, wanton disregard for the conservation of natural resources. Believing an inexhaustible supply of natural gas existed, no one attempted to regulate the flow and instead wasted much of the supply. In the 1890s Indiana had the largest known natural gas field in the world. As early as 1893, however, the estimated waste in production amounted to 100 million cubic feet per day. Within two decades, natural gas supplies dried up, and by 1913 West Virginia gas filled Indiana's needs.[17] Similar depletion of Indiana's oil fields and fish population occurred. Sentiment for state control of natural resources grew in many quarters, from sportsmen interested in protecting fish and game supplies as well as their habitats; from scientists who called public attention to the effects of deforestation on erosion and flooding; from bird lovers and other naturalists who worried about the changing landscape and the lack of natural cover; and from business interests alarmed at the growing scarcity of Indiana's raw materials.

State interest in natural resource conservation had evolved sporadically and with little attempt at coordination. Soon after the advent of statehood the legislature had created the post of state geologist. In 1837 David Dale Owen, whose father had founded the utopian community of New Harmony, occupied the position with directions to make the state's first geologic reconnaissance.[18] After two years of work Owen failed to win reappointment from an economy-minded legislature. State-supported geologic studies resumed in 1853 with the issuance of a report on Indiana's mineral resources. Off and on, geologic services continued until 1869, when the legislature created a Department of Geology and Natural Sciences. From 1890 until 1919 Indiana had the only elected state geologist in the country. Whether appointive or elective, the state geologist kept track of Indiana's natural resources; his reports furthered the state's economy by disseminating information on their commercial and industrial uses.[19]

Indiana's conservation agencies developed to meet specific resource problems. Establishment of the Office of Commissioner of Fisheries in 1881 resulted from the depopulation and pollution of fishing waters. In 1899 due to a growing call for the enforcement of hunting laws, the agency's scope expanded to include game. The State Board of Forestry, authorized in 1901, answered the demand for forestry conservation.[20] In every case these agencies reflected the utilitarian conservation approach espoused by Gifford Pinchot: conserve natural resources in order to make them available for future generations. The economic argument underpinning this approach made sense to thrifty, hardworking Hoosiers. The only opposition came from those who rejected any governmental intervention in what they considered their exclusive right, as property owners, to use or abuse their land. A succession of Indiana governors and General Assemblies overruled the latter position in favor of limited government controls that would protect at least some of the state's resource-based economy.

Indiana's interest in scenic preservation initially resulted from a call for government-owned recreational open space. Unlike other cities and towns in the East and Midwest, Indiana's municipalities had no constitutional authority to establish parks until 1899. From the 1880s on the state's urbanization and industrialization led the rich and fashionable to take up outdoor recreation. They traveled to the resort towns of French Lick and West Baden to enjoy mineral springs and popular hotels set amid park-like settings; or they vacationed at water resorts like Lake Wauwauasee and Bass Lake in the northern part of the state.[21] They also organized new groups like the Indiana Fish, Game and Forest League to press for government intervention in habitat preservation.

In the first two decades of the twentieth century, as the use of automobiles increased, outdoor recreation became important to the growing urban population, both middle class and poor. Recreational use of the land became increasingly important, especially as tourist receipts in Indiana began to have an impact on the economy. However, the interests of these forces did not yet match the influence of predominantly rural Indianans, who looked upon fallow land, no matter what its aesthetic merit, as wasteful.[22]

Against this backdrop of subtly developing trends for nonutilitarian land preservation, the state's centennial provided the moment to initiate a state park system in Indiana. (One-third of the states already had such parks.) To plan for the centennial observation, the legislature in March 1915 authorized Governor Samuel Ralston to appoint an Indiana Historical Commission. In April the governor named another body to preserve Turkey Run, "a tract of virgin wilderness containing great, rocky canyons almost hidden by dense foliage."[23] In January 1916 Lieber asked for and received a seat on the Turkey Run Commission. Under his influence the Historical Commission adopted a state park platform as a suitable centennial activity. Two months later the Historical Commission incorporated the Turkey Run Commission into the State Park Memorial Committee with Lieber as chairman. His organizational genius quickly went to work. He convinced the Indiana Federation of Woman's Clubs, the Daughters of the American Revolution, and the Hoosier State Motor Club to appoint their own state park committees, and he added representatives of the chamber of commerce and the Trade Association to the State Park Committee. He received endorsements for the state park movement from prominent public figures, including President Woodrow Wilson, Theodore Roosevelt, Vice-President Thomas Marshall, and Interior Secretary Franklin Lane, Indiana's senators and congressmen, and such famous Hoosier writers as James Whitcomb Riley, Meredith Thompson, George Ade, and Booth Tarkington.[24]

Like Mather, Lieber knew the value of public relations. He enlisted the support of one hundred newspapers around the state and through them organized county committees to solicit public subscriptions for state parks. Governor Ralston declared the week of April 21 as Park Contribution Week. These popular fund-raising efforts did not bring in enough money to meet Lieber's objective of acquiring three parks in the centennial year. He learned that small private donations would not raise enough money to acquire land for the parks. Lieber instead raised much of the needed funds from his wealthy Republican friends; even Democrat Senator Thomas Taggart contributed $1,000.[25] After much trial and travail, Lieber solicited enough contributions to purchase two parks, Turkey Run and McCormack Creek, as centennial memorials, thus preserving a "bit of the land which her [Indiana] pioneers had seen when first they gazed upon her prairies, hills, forests and lakes."[26] The third centennial park, Indiana Dunes, had to wait seven more years for preservation.

Lieber now had realized two state parks but no permanent governmental agency to oversee them. To secure its establishment and operation he devised a plan that reflected national Republican political interest in governmental reorganization. During the twentieth century's second decade, Republican political leaders in Indiana, along with their counterparts elsewhere in the nation, adopted the progressive movement's interest in streamlining governmental operations. A partisan battle erupted in the legislature. The Republican plans brought business principles to state government, but the Democrats opposed establishing a bigger bureaucracy resulting in higher taxes, and they vehemently objected to removing any office from the choice of the electorate.

The inauguration of Governor James Goodrich in 1917 placed a strong advocate of centralizing and expanding the executive branch in the statehouse. Lieber, a good friend and political confidant of the new governor, saw an ideal opportunity to promote a Department of Conservation. His plan had the merit of providing not only for the coordination of state conservation activities but also for institutionalizing scenic preservation.

Lieber first sketched his idea to the governor-elect in 1916, before Goodrich took office. Though no conservationist, Goodrich saw the advantages of efficiency, economy, reduction of unnecessary duplication, and integrated planning that Lieber eloquently propounded for the department. A lawyer and a conservative, successful businessman, Goodrich assented to the plan.[27] His scheme proposed five divisions for the department: geology, entomology, forestry, parks and waters, and game and animal protection. The governor arranged the introduction of enabling legislation in both the house and senate on January 16, 1917. The bills died because of the combined opposition of incumbent officeholders and Democratic legislators, who saw the organization of a new department as a Republican grab for power. Their Republican confreres refused to accede to provisions for a nonpartisan agency. Undaunted, Goodrich appointed Lieber state forester in March 1917. The Indianapolis *Star* editorialized approvingly: "A conservationist who can present his reasons intelligently and convincingly, he will have in his official position an opportunity to make friends for the conservation program which failed in the last Legislature because of the ignorance and blind opposition of a small coterie of office holders and politicians."[28]

Lieber did indeed use his new post to press for the establishment of the Department of Conservation. He wooed the governor with tours of the new state parks and won the endorsement of the Republican State Committee for his plan. New legislation to authorize the Department of Conservation came off the press in December 1918, and all members of a heavily Republican General Assembly received copies.[29]

In the two years since the first defeat of the Department of Conservation legislation, many Hoosiers had visited Turkey Run and McCormack's Creek and reported enthusiastic impressions to their legislators.[30] The nation still lingered in postwar euphoria, and good causes had popular support. Lieber wrote an eighteen-page pamphlet summarizing all the arguments in favor of the Conservation Department. The rhetoric, clothed in patriotic language of the times, contained sentiments such as "our times will be noted for the beginning of that movement which is destined to protect our natural wealth and build up a true appreciation of national values."[31] On March 8 the bill became law. To no one's surprise, the post of director of the Department of Conservation went to Lieber. He was also chosen to serve as superintendent of Lands and Waters, the division which included state parks.

Lieber's strategy copied a similar national tailoring of scenic preservation purposes. The original concept of federal protection called for the preservation of the natural "wonders" of the United States, "in trust for all the people for all time," instead of their ownership by a few profiteers. Aesthetic conservationists added new rationales to counter the rising tide of the utilitarians. They emphasized the commercial value of parks for tourism, underscored the importance of outdoor recreation for an urban-industrial society, and appealed to nationalistic pride to protect the remaining unspoiled examples of the country's historical and prehistorical past.[32] In like fashion Lieber propounded the values of an Indiana state park system: to memorialize the Hoosier pioneer past; to offer "a great public lesson in conservation, and . . . the folly of prodigal waste of Indiana's superb natural resources"; and to "refresh and renew tired people and fit them for the common round of daily life."³³

Shrewdly, Lieber never attempted to secure a separate legislative mandate for state parks, preferring to include scenic preservation as part of the mission of the new Department of Conservation. In spite of the popularity of state parks in Indiana during their brief, administratively authorized, and legislatively funded existence, Lieber sought an established bureaucratic haven for the State Park Memorial Committee. He believed the committee's continuing success depended both upon placement within a legislatively approved structure and upon emphasis on business management. Proclaiming that scenery had a cash value, he quickly established policies for the parks that appealed to the economy-minded. He decided that an admission charge should be paid by every park visitor. Not only did this income make the parks less dependent on legislative whim, but it also made park operations seem more businesslike. Together with concessionaire fees, user charges enabled Indiana's parks to function without governmental operating support for many years.

Near the end of his life, Lieber wrote *America's Natural Wealth*, summarizing his lifelong conservation philosophy. He saw three values in parks: inspirational, social, and economic. "Parks are the dietetics of the soul," he wrote. He believed the "spell of nature" could effect character transformation. Natural beauty and wilderness offer "surcease from the pace of an increasingly mechanized existence and . . . restore balance in soul and body." Parks, Lieber believed, also fulfill a "great patriotic purpose" for they serve as memorials of American history. He appealed to civic pride to preserve its pioneer past. "Nowhere can [citizens] gain a greater understanding of what it cost our forefathers of '76 to found the nation in which we live with such ease and prosperity." Lieber looked upon parks as showcases of conservation in which to demonstrate wise land use principles. He also decried the dependency of parks on governmental appropriations and attendant political influence. Rather, parks should be self-supporting, so that "park visitors are citizens who pridefully consider themselves stockholders in a growing concern, not supplicants of charity or political favor."³⁴ Lieber pointed out that increased tourism to parks could generate jobs and other benefits.

Though he embraced wholeheartedly the concept of scenic preservation and he wrote and spoke glowingly about the value of wilderness protection, Lieber downplayed aesthetic considerations in his book and emphasized social and economic benefits. After twenty-five years as a conservation leader, Lieber extended his economic prescription to the national parks, arguing that they, too, should charge an admission fee. He called also for the application of modern busi- ness methods to the National Park Service and for the creation of a federal Department of Conservation, similar to the Indiana model.

During the years 1916 to 1919, while Lieber pursued the founding of the Indiana state parks and the establishment of the Conservation Department, Illinois and Indiana Dunes preservationists continued to promote their dream of a national park. Though mindful and sup- portive of Lieber's efforts for conservation, in Indiana they pursued their vision undeterred by the political realities that barred fruition. After the high point of Illinois involvement in the June 1917 pageant at Waverly Beach, leadership of the struggle passed to the "Gary crowd." Though the National Dunes Park Association's board of di- rectors included representation from Illinois, including such stal- warts as Cowles, Julius Rosenwald, and two representatives from the Prairie Club, all of its officers came from Indiana, and its political strength lay with Lieber, Knotts, W. P. Gleason, superintendent of the Gary Works and president of the association, and Bess Sheehan, the association's secretary.

BESS SHEEHAN

No one worked harder or more effectively to preserve the Dunes than Bess Sheehan. With dogged attachment to an ideal, she per- sisted for over a decade, stretching proven abilities in uncontem- plated directions and justly earning the title "Lady of the Dunes." Though dainty and small in stature, she possessed a spine of steel. Most of her contemporaries found her "a woman of charming per- sonality and keen intellectual ability." Not everyone agreed. Some felt that "although she was active enough, she was a woman, who liked to glean all the credit for herself, which wasn't right, because she relied on some of the other people for many of the things that were accomplished."[35]

Born near Jackson, Michigan, in 1882, Bess Vrooman completed her public schooling in southwestern Michigan, at Dowgiac High School. At the time of her graduation she had already demon- strated high intelligence and unusual ambition. She enrolled in the University of Michigan, graduating in 1904 with an A.B. in history. In 1905 she won a scholarship in American history from the Detroit chapter of the Colonial Dames and earned her M.A. from the same university, an unusual accomplishment for a woman in that period. For the next two years she taught history in Big Rapids, Michigan. In 1908 she left her native state to take a position as a history teacher at Gary's brand new high school. Bess considered herself "one of the Gary pioneers . . . having come to this city of more than 100,000 when it was only two years old, before there were sidewalks or city water, and most of the children were in portable schools. I saw the first class of three students graduate from High School in the spring of 1909. Those days were largely concerned with sand fleas and keeping sand out of our shoes and food."[36] Bess taught history in Gary for four years, reluctantly abandoning her career to marry Frank J. Sheehan, a lawyer and future judge of the juvenile court of Lake County. Nonetheless, she retained her interest in history, writing such diverse works as Gary in the World War, The Northern Boundary of Indiana, and History of Indiana Federation of Clubs.

Soon after her marriage, Bess became a clubwoman, rising quickly to positions of leadership. From local membership in the Pioneer Society of Gary, Woman's Club, YMCA, Historical Society, and College Club, she climbed, after four years, to chair the State Federation of Woman's Club's Committee on Forestry and Waterways in 1916.[37] Here she met Richard Lieber and for the first time came into contact with the burgeoning Indiana conservation movement. Up to this point, Bess, though an "old-time" Gary resident, had shown little interest in the inaccessible Dune wilderness surrounding her adopted home. Aware, certainly, of the ubiquitous sand and the ever-present fleas, she became increasingly impressed by the natural world around her. Stimulated by her exposure, she joined the local effort of the newly incorporated National Dunes Park Association. Promptly elected secretary, she now found a single focus for her myriad activities.

Between 1916 and 1923, Bess, as chairman of the State Federated Woman's Club's Dunes Park Committee, rallied the women of Indiana, first for a national and then for a state park in the Dunes.[38] She did it superlatively, unceasingly, and uncompromisingly. On March 6, 1923, when Governor Warren T. McCray signed the bill authorizing the Indiana Dunes State Park, he offered the gold pen to Bess Sheehan, thus acknowledging her crucial role.

For her accomplishment Bess also earned many official honors and recognition. The Chicago Geographic Society elected her an honorary life member, the first and at that time the only woman to be so rewarded. The National Conference on State Parks chose her as treasurer.

With as much of the Dunes preserved as then seemed politically feasible, Bess set aside her conservation work and turned again to club work. In 1925 she became president of the Indiana Federation of Woman's Clubs and in 1928, the Indiana director of the General

Federation of Woman's Clubs. In 1930 she took on the chairman-
ship of the federation's Library Extension Committee and also became president of the Indiana Historical Board. Bess, of course,
followed the progress of the Indiana Dunes State Park, finding her
role in its existence a source of continued gratification; but she had
more than enough to keep her busy and no interest in or inclination
toward reopening the Dunes preservation movement.

Almost two decades after that triumphal day in Governor Mc-
Cray's office Dorothy Buell, a worried, elderly lady, contacted Bess
Sheehan about starting a new organization to save the Dunes. Bess
attended the group's first meeting but discouraged prospects for
success. She declined any effort to involve herself, leaving the struggle
for newer, if not younger, women. In 1956 the Sheehans moved to
Winter Park, Florida, with Bess's appetite for public service and private achievement perhaps satiated. Despite the vast range of her
civic effort, for which one biographer titled her "the best known
woman in Indiana," she considered the Dunes her first love and the
Indiana Dunes State Park her most valued accomplishment.[39]

From 1916 to 1920, Dunes preservationists in Indiana vacillated
between clinging to the concept of a national park or accepting the
idea of a smaller state park. The maneuverings during these years
reflected a lack of coherent direction. National Dunes Park Association (NDPA) in January 1917 began a long series of moves and coun-
termoves by securing the introduction of a bill to permit "the
incorporation of associations which should have the power to acquire by purchase, gift, donation, devise, bequest and the right of
eminent domain, real estate and personal property for public or forest preserve purposes or both."[40] A. J. Bowser, continuing his role as
the self-appointed spokesman for the opposition, minced no words.
"House Bill 257 . . . is . . . for the purpose of gaining control of Indiana's Lakefront, taking it out of the jurisdiction of the State of Indiana and off the tax list. It is the most vicious bill ever offered the
legislature of this state. Ostensibly its object is to establish a national park in Porter and LaPorte Counties, but in reality it is a bill
to give the United States Steel Corporation the complete monopoly
in the future of Lake Michigan."[41] Although the legislation failed to
pass, Bowser's position remained the cornerstone of the opposition
for the next half century. The Valparaiso Chamber of Commerce
spoke up, too, arguing that the bill attempted to deprive Porter County
of all beachfront on Lake Michigan, a theme that would echo repeatedly over the coming fifty years.

Undaunted, the NDPA persevered, attempting to sustain public
interest in the preservation of the Dunes. The organization formed
a speakers' bureau to interest other clubs and groups in the cause,
issued a series of exquisite Dunes posterettes, carrying the message
"Save the Dunes for a National Park," sponsored an exhibition of
Dunes paintings by Frank Dudley at the Chicago Art Institute, established an impressive advisory board, and published articles ex-
tolling the Dunes.

Although considerable sentiment for a national park in the Dunes
still remained, by 1919 many forces urged the creation of a state
park instead. The NDPA tried to secure legislation enabling associations to obtain land for parks, and Sheehan managed a great coup.
Together with her fellow Dunes afficianado, Mrs. John D. Sherman
of Chicago, chairman of Conservation for the General Federation of
Woman's Clubs, she persuaded that nationwide women's group to
designate November 1919 as "Save the Dunes Month." She asked
each club president throughout the land to devote one program "to
a study of the Dunes Country of Indiana and its possibilities as a
National Park. This project has received the endorsement of the Director of the National Park Service, Stephen T. Mather." She appealed eloquently and directly, "Women of the East, let us join
together to secure the first National Park east of the Mississippi
River! Women of the West, who realize the advantages of the preservation of Natural Scenery, help us to save the finest specimens of
Dune formation in the world!"[42] In addition, Governor Goodrich, a
Dunes national park supporter, sent Lieber to the Dunes in June
1919 to investigate the possibilities. Jens Jensen escorted Lieber on
his inspection tour, convincing him of the need for the preservation
of the Dunes. Jensen, however, could not change Lieber's conviction
that Congress would not appropriate funds for the purchase of Dunes
land. In addition, Lieber opposed spending public funds for purchase
of park land without a corresponding contribution from the citizenry, especially the wealthy. No immediate substantive results materialized from Lieber's visit to the Dunes. Two years later, however,
he led the campaign for a Dunes state park, incorporating his idee
fixee that part of the cost must be borne by Chicago and Calumet
industrialists.

In 1919 interest in a Dunes state park quickened. The state legislature, besides authorizing the Department of Conservation, received a bill to establish the Indiana Dunes State Park from Gary
Representative J. Glenn Harris. Agitation for state park status for the
Dunes went back many years. From 1910 to 1916 the state geologist,

Edward Barrett, advocated the Sand Dunes "as one of the regions of picturesque natural scenery for State Park purposes."[43] In his 1916 annual report he included a sixteen-page report written by tireless A. F. Knotts and entitled "The Dunes of Northwest Indiana." A year earlier Enos Mills had issued a call for an Indiana state park system, which included the Dunes. The death knell for a federal preserve in the Dunes occurred in 1919, when some of the land that Mather had proposed for the Sand Dunes National Park passed into industrial ownership. Inland Steel purchased 1,300 acres, including one mile of shoreline in western Porter County abutting Lake County. NDPA members became anxious. They lived close enough to recognize this new threatening thrust of industrial expansion; it shook their devotion to the ideal of a national park in the Dunes. Inland's presence also meant the end of any hope of linking the Porter County dunes with a new Gary park established by the recent U.S. Steel Company donation of 120 acres, including three-quarters of a mile of Lake Michigan shoreline.

The NDPA's devotion to creation of a national park wavered more in September 1919. Their archenemy, A. J. Bowser, appeared at their September 5th meeting waving an olive branch. Bowser stated, "The people of Porter County were almost universally in favor of the creation of a Dunes Park; [that] they would be unwilling to consider a National Park, and would insist that the jurisdiction be kept within the State of Indiana . . . [that] they were prepared to surrender all territory from Burns ditch to LaPorte County."[44] The ex-senator even accepted a seat on the NDPA board, believing he could best protect industrialization of the Porter County dunes westward from Burns Ditch to the Lake County border by strategically hobnobbing with his former foes.

The next year saw another competing land use emerge in the Porter County Dunes. The postwar land boom, which gripped the Midwest, finally found its way to the still virginal Dunes. F. Randolph Chandler of Chicago proposed to purchase and subdivide 20,000 acres for a midwestern lakeside Atlantic City. His ten-square mile Dune City, replete with five miles of bathing beaches and steamship pier, never passed out of the announcement stage. NDPA adherents, however, saw still another harbinger of the future. They realized that construction of the Dunes highway, begun that year, would destroy the inaccessibility that heretofore had protected the Dunes from development. Lieber informed them that even Governor Goodrich leaned toward the state preserve idea. National legislation seemed as illusive as ever. Finally, beset by growing threats to the Dunes environment and, by this time, almost convinced of the federal government's disinterest, at their third annual meeting on April 3, 1920, NDPA members reluctantly supported a Dunes state park.

Still, doubts continued about the best course to follow. In one of many unanswered letters to Mather, Sheehan delineated some of the misgivings. "I have heard Mr. Lieber state that he would work equally as hard for a National as for a State Park, if that seemed the wisest course of procedure. I feel that the sentiment at present tends toward a State Park as following the lines of least resistance, although most of us are loathe to give up the National Park idea. Of course it could be created now and later tendered to the Nation, but I fear that when it is once part of the Indiana Park System, it may prove difficult to make a change."[45] After repeated appeals to Mather for encouragement proved fruitless, the NDPA accepted the line of least resistance.

On January 1, 1921, Governor Goodrich, in his final message to the legislature, strongly endorsed a Dunes state park. His successor, Governor Warren McCray, advocated the project in his inaugural address.[46] McCray proposed a plan that reflected Lieber's potent influence. If Chicago and Calumet industrialists would raise $1 million, he would ask the legislature to appropriate a matching million at the rate of $100,000 for the next ten years. A legislative committee visited the Dunes and came away impressed. Introduction of a bill to enact McCray's proposal followed.

Lieber campaigned for passage of the bill with all his conviction, knowledge, and expertise. He now believed that it became "the privilege and duty of Indiana, with private assistance, to preserve this heritage and God-given spot."[47] For the next three years he marshalled every argument—scientific, historical, inspirational, social, and demographic—ever uttered on behalf of the Dunes. He directed a skillful campaign to win the necessary votes; he sought endorsements of the Dunes state park proposal. Mills again championed the project, declaring, "The Indiana dunes ranked with Yellowstone and Niagara Falls among the natural wonders of the continent."[48] Lieber wrote to Mather for an endorsement letter, "which we may use for publicity in connection with the campaign before the legislature."[49]

Problems developed. Porter County opponents swiftly let their Republican governor know that they adamantly objected to his proposal, unless it provided for only a three-mile frontage on Lake Michigan instead of the nine miles suggested by the NDPA. Nor did the Chicago interests raise their million-dollar share, seemingly content to let Indiana finance its own state park. The authorization bill did not pass, but Governor McCray announced, "The Dunes are not forgotten, only postponed." Such a pronouncement further worried Valparaiso park opponents. When McCray visited the Dunes in August, the Valparaiso *Messenger* charged that tour leaders had excluded Porter County representatives from the tour. The Gary *Post* August 7, 1921, thundered back in a front page editorial headlined, "Shall Selfishness Despoil Our Finest National Phenomena?"

Lieber knew the importance of keeping up momentum for a project between legislative sessions. With McCray's support he planned for the 1923 meeting of the General Assembly. In July 1921 the Conservation Department acted as host for an outing of one hundred editors from around the state. The journalists hiked through the proposed park site and heard Lieber outline the importance of the project.

Lieber devoted 1922 to "building up the cause for the Dunes purchase and educating the public and its political representatives to the immediate need for saving the area."[50] That immediate need resulted from the further residential incursions into the Dunes of Dune Acres and Ogden Dunes. The latter occupied a large acreage adjoining Inland Steel's property; developers touted the former as a rival to Chicago's North Shore. The unspoiled Dunes seemed destined to disappear quickly before any park could emerge.

Sheehan did her part. Her Dunes Park Committee sponsored a Dunes summer camp during two June weeks at the Prairie Club Beach House. With the Indiana Academy of Science, Audubon Society, State Historical Commission, Nature Study Club, Indiana Fish, Game and Forest League, Association of Park Departments, and NDPA as cosponsors, the nature school had a distinguished faculty composed of Henry Cowles, Stanley Coulter of Purdue, and George Fuller of the University of Chicago. Earlier, Cowles and Orpheus Schantz of the Illinois Audubon Society had resurrected a prior plan for an interstate park in "Duneland."

Mather, kept abreast of developments by Lieber, wrote to an Indiana correspondent, "I think we can definitely put aside any possibility in the near future of the Sand Dunes area being created into a national park. . . . I think far more can be accomplished if the plan of creating this area into a state park is followed up vigorously, particularly by residents of Indiana like yourself who are keenly alive to the necessity of preserving this beautiful area."[51]

In 1923 conditions seemed propitious for passing the Dunes park legislation. Ten percent of the General Assembly, consisting of the delegations from Lake, LaPorte, and St. Joseph counties, located closest to the Dunes except for Porter County, strongly supported the idea of the state park. Moreover, Porter and Lake counties' Sen-

ator Will Brown agreed to sponsor the legislation. Prior to its introduction park opponents had realized that they could not muster
enough votes to prevent the location of a state park in Porter County.
Consequently, they mounted a campaign to trim the measure to their
specifications. The Valparaiso Chamber of Commerce participated
in two meetings in Gary on the proposed language. They telegraphed Senator Brown: "Understand you will introduce bill for a
two-mile park fronting Lake Michigan. We see no objection to a two-
mile park, providing it does not interfere with the three natural harbors."[52] With the NDPA still fighting for a nine-mile frontage, Brown's
bill provided for three miles of park but did not specify the exact
location, leaving the determination of boundaries to future negotiations. The legislation also included a seven-year property tax of two
mills per $100 to pay for the land. After the legislature convened,
Sheehan went to Indianapolis to join other clubwomen in working
for passage of the Dunes bills. Much to their consternation, they
learned that the Democratic caucus had decided to punish any
member who favored legislation providing for a tax increase, since
Hoosier farmers faced an agricultural depression. No wonder the
House bill languished in the Ways and Means Committee! Thirty
years later Sheehan described what confronted the Dunes proponents in the legislature: "This General Assembly of 1923 was, like
most others, a complex body. Politically, it was almost evenly divided—52 Republicans and 48 Democrats—so that it would be necessary to secure bipartisan support. Many of the members were
farmers, who could see nothing good in a hill of sand. Many of them
came from southern and central Indiana and there was always present some feeling of jealousy and suspicion of all measures being
actively supported by the new and prosperous Calumet Region."[53]
As weeks passed without any progress toward passage, Sheehan's
understanding of pressure politics grew. Between the bill's auspicious introduction and hairbreadth passage, she acquired a real political education and graduated a skilled practitioner.

Fearing the bill would die in committee, Indianapolis clubwomen
made arrangements for their leader to give a stereopticon lecture for
a group of legislators and their wives. For two hours, on the evening
of January 30, Sheehan described the Dunes, their beauty, and the
support that the women of Indiana gave to the state park.[54] Two days
later the joint Ways and Means Committee held a hearing on the
bills, and Dunes lovers came from Chicago, Gary, Michigan City,
and South Bend to testify in favor of the legislation.

The days dragged on without a vote. At Lieber's prodding Sheehan went to the press to subdue a potentially damaging whispering campaign that had aimed at convincing Dunes landowners that they would not receive fair compensation. She exhorted recalcitrant legislators; she lined up influential friends of the Dunes to reach unresponsive members. Partly by instinct, partly by trial and error, she learned to deploy her woman-power through the halls of the statehouse. Despite her constant pressure, with only nine days left in the session, the House Ways and Means Committee voted for indefinite postponement.

Frantically Sheehan and her supporters begged the chairman to withhold the report for one day "to give us time to see what we could do."[55] She appealed to a fellow woman's club member, the wife of a personal friend of Tom Taggart. Early in the session Sheehan had tried to reach him but never made contact. Nonetheless, she knew of his affection for the Dunes and hoped he might help to prevent defeat of the Dunes legislation. Taggart responded to his friend's request and came to Indianapolis on February 24. "Just what do you want me to do?" he asked Sheehan. Forewarned to have a plan ready, she urged the former senator to influence the vote of the six Democrats on the Ways and Means Committee. With Taggart's help assured, she returned to the statehouse and barged into Mc-Cray's office. Confronting the startled governor, she reminded him of his commitment to the Dunes and underscored the crucial importance of the next few hours. McCray promised to help. Something potent happened. After voting twice for indefinite postponement, the committee reported the bill without recommendation, leaving its fate to the House membership.

A week later the bill came up for final passage. Sheehan telegraphed Taggart for more help. Taggart returned to Indianapolis to her "delight and gratitude." On March 1, the last day of the session, with the galleries packed by Dunes advocates, the crucial vote occurred. Passage required fifty-one votes; the measure carried with fifty-two. Within thirty minutes the Senate safely and anticlimactically passed the bill, thirty-nine to eleven.

In a letter to Catherine Mitchell, Sheehan recounted how close to disaster the bill came. "The people here all gave up the struggle; seemed I was the only one who stuck. Had I known how discouraged the others were I guess I would have given up too. I only began to sense it about the time I began to dare to hope for success and that was the eleventh hour. . . . So we were very lucky. Providence surely saw us through an almost impossible situation."[56] Although she attributed "much of the credit . . . to Taggart without whose support the bill undoubtedly would have failed," the victory resulted from far more complex factors.[57] Without the political clout of both McCray and Taggart, the necessary bipartisan support would never have materialized. Lieber's behind-the-scenes role counted immeasurably. Yet without Sheehan and the army of Dunes advocates, the dream of preserving the Dunes might never have become reality.

Each side claimed victory. The NDPA's recommendations on site selection prevailed over those of the Valparaiso Chamber of Commerce. Moreover, President Gleason announced his group would again try to raise $1 million to purchase an additional 2,000 acres. The Valparaiso chamber saw the result as a triumph. Instead of losing nine miles of lake frontage, the State would acquire only three while the remainder stood waiting for industrial development.

The bill's passage in 1923 proved fortuitous for the Dunes because in 1924 long-time Dunes supporter, Governor McCray, resigned his seat and was sent to jail for mail fraud.[58] It also appeared ominous that his successor, Edward Jackson, became governor in 1925. The long-time Republican politician had won office with the support of the Ku Klux Klan, and during the campaign had promised to oust Lieber and give his job to a political crony. Yet after his inauguration Jackson became a supporter of conservation. On his first visit to the Dunes on May 20, 1925, he climbed Mount Green (later renamed in his honor), Mount Holden, and Mount Tom with Bess Sheehan as guide. The beauty of the lake and the sand hills captured his enthusiasm; he personally arranged for land acquisition for the park to begin.

With Dunes land prices rising and only $105,000 a year accumulating from the property tax, Lieber appealed for private contributions to philanthropist Julius Rosenwald, Judge Gary, Colonel Robert Stewart, president of Standard Oil of Indiana, and Samuel Insull of the Northern Indiana Public Service Company. A similar drive by the Indiana Society of Chicago produced no help. Eventually Judge Gary contributed $250,000. Lieber's salesmanship resulted in another gift of $50,000 from Rosenwald and a $200,000 loan from Insull, as well as a donation of land. Finally, in 1927, the state owned the 2,000 acres comprising the Indiana Dunes State Park.

In retrospect, given the strength of the opposition, preservationists achieved a surprising success in gaining a Dunes state park. Victory resulted from continuing bipartisan political pressure that overcame Porter County's jealousy of its industrialized neighbor to the west and its refusal to relinquish any land that had industrial potential. The effort also surmounted the Indiana legislature's antipathy to giving benefits to the northwestern part of the state. The intrinsic value of Dunes preservation never merited much consideration. Exhausted after years of struggle, the preservationists seemed satisfied with the small size of the state park and for the next twenty-two years made no further attempt to save any other portion of the Dunes.

NOTES

1. Horace Albright to authors, July 21, 1977.
2. Cottman, *Indiana Dunes State Park*, p. 1.
3. Bess Sheehan to Catherine Mitchell, Mar. 23, 1923, Dunes Park Manuscript Collection (S2112), Indiana Division, Indiana State Library, Indianapolis.
4. Louis Adamic, *From Many Lands* (New York: Harper and Row, 1940), p. 326.
5. Emma Lieber, *Richard Lieber* (Indianapolis: privately printed, 1904), p. 24.
6. Ibid, pp. 43–52.
7. For a more detailed account of Lieber's civic activities, see Robert Allen Frederick, "Colonel Richard Lieber, Conservationist and Park Builder: The Indiana Years" (Ph.D. diss., Indiana University, 1960); Lieber, *Richard Lieber*, pp. 64–68.
8. Indianapolis *News*, Sept. 7, 1912, as quoted in Frederick, "Colonel Richard Lieber," pp. 102, 103.
9. Frederick, "Colonel Richard Lieber," p. 104.
10. Ibid., p. 2.
11. Lieber, *Richard Lieber*, p. 53.
12. Indianapolis *News*, Dec. 14, 1908, as quoted in Frederick, "Colonel Richard Lieber," p. 106.
13. Lieber, *Richard Lieber*, p. 68.
14. *Proceedings of the Indiana Academy of Science for 1974*, 84 (1975):401.
15. Ralph Wilcox, *The Price of Forestry Neglect in Indiana, 1897*, publication no. 61 (Indianapolis: Indiana Department of Conservation, 1928), p. 4, as quoted in Frederick, "Colonel Richard Lieber," p. 138; Phillips, *Indiana in Transition*, pp. 212–15.
16. *Indiana Year Book for 1920*, p. 725, as quoted in Phillips, *Indiana in Transition*, p. 192.
17. Phillips, *Indiana in Transition*, pp. 192–97.
18. *Proceedings of the Indiana Academy of Science*, p. 400.
19. Phillips, *Indiana in Transition*, pp. 181–84.
20. *Proceedings of the Indiana Academy of Science*, p. 401.
21. Phillips, *Indiana in Transition*, pp. 383, 353.
22. Ibid., p. 220.
23. Ibid., p. 211.

24. Ibid., p. 118.

25. "Taggart Boosts Park Funds," Warsaw *Daily Union*, May 10, 1916, p. 6.

26. Howard Michaud, "State Parks," in *Natural Features of Indiana*, ed. Alton Lindsay (Bloomington: Indiana Academy of Science, 1966), p. 561.

27. Charles Roll, *Indiana: One Hundred and Fifty Years of American Development*, 2 (New York: Lewis Publishing Co., 1931), p. 413; Wilbur Peat, *Portraits and Painters of the Governors of Indiana* (Indianapolis: Indiana Historical Society, 1978), p. 70.

28. Editorial, Indianapolis *Star*, Mar. 17, 1917.

29. Frederick, "Colonel Richard Lieber," p. 181.

30. Ibid.

31. Ibid., p. 182.

32. Runte, *National Parks*, p. 1. Runte discusses this thesis in detail in his provocative book.

33. State Park Memorial Committee, Report, Jan. 1916, quoted in Frederick, "Colonel Richard Lieber," pp. 119–20.

34. Richard Lieber, *America's Natural Wealth* (New York: Harper & Brothers, 1942), pp. 163, 165–66, 168–69, 171.

35. Mildred Marshall Scouller, "Mrs. Frank Sheehan," in *Women Who Man Our Clubs* (Chicago: John C. Winston, 1934), p. 177; authors' interview with John Bowers, Edgewood, Ind., 1977.

36. Bess Sheehan, "Gary Pioneer Recalls Struggle for State Park," Gary *Post Tribune*, May 12, 1963.

37. Scouller, *Women Who Man Our Clubs*, p. 177.

38. Ibid.

39. Roll, *Indiana Development*, 2:18; Sheehan, "Gary Pioneer."

40. Cannon, Loring, and Robb, eds., *Lake and Calumet History*, p. 680.

41. John O. Bowers, "History of State Park," manuscript, Local History Scrapbooks, Gary Public Library.

42. General Federation of Woman's Clubs, Announcement, "Save the Dunes," State Parks—Dunes File, Indiana State Library.

43. Quoted in Frederick, "Colonel Richard Lieber," p. 110.

44. Minutes of the meeting, Sept. 5, 1919, Board of Directors of the NDPA, Local History Scrapbooks, Gary Public Library.

45. Sheehan to Mather, Local History Scrapbooks.

46. Cottman, *Indiana Dunes State Park*, p. 36.

47. Quoted in Frederick, "Colonel Richard Lieber," p. 257.

48. Ibid., p. 261.

49. Lieber to Mather, Feb. 3, 1921, Record Group 79, Records of the National Park Service, National Archives, Washington.

50. Frederick, "Colonel Richard Lieber," p. 236.

51. Mather to Mr. Keller, Mar. 21, 1922, Records of the National Park Service.

52. Valparaiso Chamber of Commerce, Board of Directors, Report, Jan. 17, 1923, Valparaiso Chamber of Commerce File.

53. Sheehan, "Gary Pioneer."

54. Ibid.

55. Ibid.

56. Sheehan to Mitchell, Mar. 23, 1923, Dunes Park Manuscript Collection (S2112).

57. Sheehan, "Gary Pioneer."

58. Peat, *Portraits and Painters*, p. 72.

CHAPTER 5 Industrial Conquest

Fifty years elapsed between the construction of U.S. Steel's Gary Works in the Lake County Dunes and Bethlehem Steel's Burns Harbor plant in the central Porter County Dunes. Although only twelve miles apart, the half-century interval between the erection of the two facilities critically affected their receptions. While the nation's number one steelmaker drew almost universal praise, its arch rival faced national opposition. The growth in the national conservation ethic over the span of five decades made the difference.

Both steel corporations built in the Dunes for the same reason—to capture a larger share of the growing and important midwestern market. Geography, economics, and the requirements of steel manufacturing intertwined to make a steel plant along Lake Michigan's southern shore desirable in 1905 and essential in 1955. Remarkably, in spite of the rapid urbanization of undeveloped land close to large metropolitan centers that had occurred elsewhere in the country, Bethlehem acquired land closely resembling U.S. Steel's. The same dune barrens, the same untouched shoreline, and the same absence of power lines, roadways, and other signs of settlement, which had attracted U.S. Steel at the turn of the century, captivated Bethlehem at mid-century. Both received a warm welcome from Indiana's political leaders, who consistently favored any and all additions to the state's economy. Historical differences between the two giant corporations and the evolution of the steel industry accounted for the time lag between the development of the two steel mills. Shifting American values contributed to the approbation that greeted U.S. Steel and the controversy that enmeshed Bethlehem.

Whether in the pre–World War I era or in the post–Korean War days, the physical attributes of the Dunes location met the basic requirements of steel production: ample land, plentiful water, and convenient access to water transportation. An integrated steel mill needs vast acreage on which to house the many operations necessary to turn raw materials into finished products. When organized efficiently, the complicated production system used in large-scale steelmaking involves "individual units, both spacious and specially designed to fit the specific process. . . . The larger the site, the smoother the development of these operations."[1] Both U.S. Steel's and Bethlehem's Dunes sites met this criterion handsomely. In addition, and fortunately for both corporations, they were able to purchase a substantial portion of their tracts from a single, though different, owner, making acquisition far simpler than the assemblage of many small parcels.

In the steel industry a plant's waterside location ranks in importance with the size of the site. Both U.S. Steel's and Bethlehem's Lake Michigan frontage resulted in three vital benefits. First, it allowed lake transit of raw materials from sources controlled or owned by the compaies. "The bulkiness of raw materials used in steelmaking, the great quantities of these used daily and the location of their sources near or on the borders of the Great Lakes [made] the transportation of ore, coal and flux [limestone] by lake carriers not only cheap but efficient."[2] Second, it permitted free and easy intake of Lake Michigan's clean, soft water without initial treatment costs. Steelmaking demands "an enormous supply of water for steam, for cooling, and for gas washing purposes."[3] Third, it made both steel producers automatic riparian owners. Due to Indiana's "Made-Land" law, they could legally fill in their Lake Michigan borders for a nominal fee. "This confers an enormous advantage, because a company can add very considerably to its total acreage by such filling. It is less expensive to fill in waterfront than it would be to buy more land. Lakefront land is where it is needed most and where it can be best utilized."[4]

Whereas U.S. Steel had to secure the relocation of the Baltimore and Ohio and Lake Shore railroads to service the Gary Works, the already extant rail and road transportation pattern suited Bethlehem quite admirably. The New York Central tracks offered direct access to the East. The South Shore line, via its parent, the Chesapeake and Ohio Railroad, provided linkage to the Appalachian coal fields. Truckers could use the Dunes highway to connect with the Indiana Tollroad and the soon-to-be completed Interstate 94.

Both corporations enjoyed other advantages accruing to their location: the availability of skilled steelworkers in the Chicago metropolitan region and the complete cooperation of state and county government officials eager to add a giant taxpayer to the property rolls. In Bethlehem's case the fifty years of steelmaking in the Calumet region made the availability of workers even greater and the degree of Indiana and Porter County government cooperation even stronger. Moreover, Bethlehem stood to gain from the prospects for a public port adjacent to its land, while U.S. Steel had paid for the construction of its private port from company coffers. In addition, Bethlehem had the advantage of an increased shipping range that the St. Lawrence Seaway, then under construction, would bring to its site. The seaway, designed to provide, at long last, the connecting link between the Great Lakes and the Atlantic Ocean, would allow cargos from around the world to reach any point in the Great Lakes as well as permit less expensive shipment of midwestern products to European ports.

Although both corporations found their sites perfectly suited to steel production, neither would have made the huge investment in an integrated plant except for the same compelling reason. Both required increased capacity to serve more effectively the always growing Midwest demand for their products. For U.S. Steel, building the Gary Works meant a logical expansion of its national dominance; for Bethlehem, developing Burns Harbor constituted a sharp break with its previous eastern orientation. Gary met the early twentieth-century demand for "heavy" steel; Burns Harbor responded to the mid-century call for "light" steel.

The formation of U.S. Steel in 1901 resulted in "the greatest of all trusts at the time."[5] Among its holdings, a number already served the Midwest, most notably the Illinois Steel Corporation's facilities in the Chicago environs. Small plant sites, poor river transportation, and rising land costs due to urban growth caused the announcement in the 1905 U.S. Steel *Annual Report* that "although the capacity of the producing furnaces and mills located at Chicago and vicinity has been materially increased from time to time, it has not kept pace with the increased and rapidly increasing consumption tributary to this location, and therefore a large percentage of this tonnage is now supplied from Eastern Mills. In consequence of these conditions it has been decided to construct and put into operation a new plant to be located on the south shore of Lake Michigan, in Calumet Township, Lake County, and a large acreage of land has been purchased for that purpose."[6] The nation's economic outlook propelled that decision. A growing economy flourished. Farming prospered. Steadily increasing demand for steel reflected the nation's rising gross national product (GNP). In the Midwest the importance of agriculture produced a high volume of orders for steel plows and fencing wire. The region's role as the hub of train transportation led to major requirements for steel railroad tracks and cars. Massive midwestern industrial development created needs for steel in heavy machinery fabrication.

The Midwest steel market continued to grow for the next two decades. In 1924 it received a further impetus when the Federal Trade Commission abolished the Pittsburgh Plus system, a price-basing formula under which all steel companies located outside Pittsburgh charged their customers the Pittsburgh-quoted price plus the cost of transportation from Pittsburgh. "Pittsburgh Plus was more than a convenient method of pricing; it was for years 'the keystone of organization, location and alignment of the American steel industry.'"[7] With the discontinuation of this pricing system a gradual but relentless shift occurred in the center of iron and steel production from the older eastern producing areas to the regions bordering on the Great Lakes.[8] Together with the end of Pittsburgh Plus, population increases and industrial growth gave steel manufacturers every incentive in the 1920s to invest in Midwest plants.

For the next fifty years the Midwest continued to use more steel than it produced. Its steel demand ranked 0.5 to 1 percent over the national average.[9] Its share of the country's steel consumption grew to almost 50 percent, and the forecast seemed ever brighter. Analysts claimed that the Midwest market could grow half again as fast as the national rate in the next ten years. Its market extended from the Rockies on the west, north to the Canadian border, south to the Gulf of Mexico, and east through the middle of Ohio.[10] Along with this strong demand for steel, the Midwest market also reflected shifts in product mix. These changes in the types of steel produced responded to significant alterations in the American economy. In the first part of the twentieth century production of capital goods dominated the nation's growth. Both U.S. Steel and Bethlehem built their empires on the basis of heavy steel production. After the Great Depression, manufacture of such consumer goods as automobiles and household appliances began to rise in the economy. By 1940 the automobile industry became the principal user of steel.[11] This trend continued into the 1970s, when car manufacturers accounted for 22 percent of steel output while railroads declined to 2.9 percent.[12] Consumer-oriented orders for steel required the output of lighter steel. In addition, in the mid-1950s steel, for the first time in its history, began to face strong competition from other materials such as cement, plastics, copper, and aluminum. Both U.S. Steel and Bethlehem experienced the effect of this displacement most heavily, since both devoted much of their output to structural steel. On top of this growing intrusion into the traditional steel market, and in spite of a rising GNP, steel production began to drop in the mid-1950s. Part of this loss was a result of a sharp rise in foreign imports, which in 1955 amounted to 1,100,000 tons and by 1960 had risen to 3,250,000 tons.[13]

Faced with this complex and threatening competitive situation, Bethlehem in December 1962 finally made its momentous announcement of plans to build a billion-dollar, fully integrated steel works at Burns Harbor. Fifty-seven years after U.S. Steel, Bethlehem's decision was the product of long and weighty considerations. In no sense a hasty solution, it seemed to the corporation's policymakers perhaps the only remaining alternative available to maintain their number two position in the industry. Some critics, in fact, charged that Bethlehem had "blundered" in waiting so long to establish "a plant in the Midwest area, the world's biggest market for flat-rolled light steel."[14] Defenders countered that canny Bethlehem had waited until exactly the right moment. Once the corporation had acquired the most desirable site at the best possible price, had completed architectural and engineering plans for the most efficiently designed plant, and had assured publicly financed construction of a port to serve its fleet of lake carriers, Bethlehem decided to build. Vice-President James Slater summed up the corporation's philosophy: "We move as fast as we need to and no faster. Unlike many who can't wait, we don't have to add to capital unless we are sure it will pay out."[15]

However, more than its fiscal conservatism, Bethlehem's singular genesis and subsequent corporate development decided the timing of its Midwest construction. The corporation began in 1904 when its founder, Charles Schwab, left the presidency of U.S. Steel after losing a struggle with Judge Elbert Gary for control of the nation's premiere steel company. According to one commentator, "Gary's pious mouthings irritated Schwab." More important, Schwab, "the greatest salesman that ever lived," could not and would not play second in command to Gary. Schwab had masterminded the sale of the Carnegie steel facilities to the J. P. Morgan banking interests and, in turn, "persuaded Morgan to finance the organization of U.S. Steel."[16]

Having lost the battle to guide development of the corporate giant whose formation he had initiated, Schwab turned his considerable talents to nurturing a competitor. Starting small with a $7 million investment in a little firm known as the Bethlehem Iron Company, Schwab's fledgling grew big with the acquisition of additional steel mills, shipping facilities, coal mines, and ore fields. In its early years the corporation became known as the American Krupp because of its dominance of steel production for munitions. By 1916 it boasted the most favorable profit and loss statement of any steel company in the world. After World War I the enterprising Schwab turned to commercial expansion. In less than forty years Bethlehem grew from 1.5 percent of U.S. Steel's capacity to second position in international steel manufacture. "Most of its growth came from earnings lavishly plowed back in the business."[17]

Along with the corporation's post–World War I emphasis on commercial steel production, Bethlehem developed a second definitive corporate strategy. It focused on building an integrated and balanced steel company with "a clear cut objective: to manufacture steel in the east."[18] The corporation's 1925 statement summed up this stance explicitly: "In acquiring and developing its properties, the objective of the management has consistently been the establishment of commercial steel plants advantageously located to supply the steel requirements of the Eastern part of the United States, the country's largest steel market and from which their products can be distributed by water along the Atlantic and Pacific coasts, to the industrial centers on the Great Lakes and to foreign countries."[19] To secure eastern predominance, Bethlehem "acquired through merger all the important steel plants east of the Pittsburgh District [where U.S. Steel had its concentration of steel-making mills] and expanded them greatly."[20]

In spite of its preoccupation with controlling the eastern steel market, as early as 1922 Bethlehem began its inexorable movement to meet the growing Midwest steel demand. In that year it acquired the Lackawana Steel Company near Buffalo, New York, in order to gain "access to the Great Lakes market for rails, plate and structurals."[21] The corporation also investigated acquisition of Porter County Duneland, which would later become the community of Beverly Shores.[22] This Midwest site had some advantages that Burns Harbor would not duplicate thirty years hence. The tract included four miles of Lake Michigan shoreline. A single owner held the entire parcel of virgin duneland, bordered by the South Shore tracks and close to the New York Central line.

Bethlehem decided against purchase of this land because it expected to use the less costly merger procedure for further penetration of the Midwest market. In 1930 the corporation attempted to consolidate with the Youngstown Sheet and Tube Company. This steel producer had operated a large basic steelmaking facility in Lake County, Indiana, since 1923. A minority stockholders' suit blocked the amalgamation.[23]

For the next two decades Bethlehem continued to narrow the gap between its position and that of U.S. Steel. Bethlehem's steel capacity increased from 2.1 percent in 1904 to 8.3 percent in 1948, while U.S. Steel dropped from 45.8 percent to 33.1 percent.[24] By the mid-

1950s a rosy economic outlook pervaded the nation. New Dow Jones highs signaled a booming private sector. With Dwight Eisenhower in the White House, suburbia blossomed. Two-car families proliferated. Public and corporate confidence reached new levels.[25] Against this background of prosperous times and the especially strong and growing Midwest demand for steel, Bethlehem's management once more courted a merger with Youngstown. Such a combination would have resulted in a corporation even bigger than U.S. Steel, with combined assets of $2,710,000,000. Bethlehem proposed to expand Youngstown's Indiana Harbor plant at a cost of $358 million and then use the increased output of raw steel in new nearby finishing mills. However, the federal government filed an antitrust suit to block the merger on the grounds that the action would "lessen competition in the steel industry." The court agreed with the government's contention, and Bethlehem and Youngstown decided not to appeal.[26]

Eugene Grace, veteran chairman of Bethlehem's board of directors, "had a premonition that the Youngstown merger wouldn't clear the courts."[27] After the court ruling, he knew that Bethlehem's twenty-five years of on-again, off-again merger negotiations to acquire a Midwest production facility had reached an impasse. He also knew that Bethlehem's reliance on its aging urban Pennsylvania plants or investment in their modernization did not make economic sense. Forecasters predicted a bull market for steel now that the Korean War had ended. Well known for its financial prudence, Bethlehem had accumulated the cash necessary for a major investment. Construction of a greenfield plant (one constructed entirely on undeveloped acreage) became the only answer.

While the Bethlehem-Youngstown merger still remained a possibility, the corporation embarked on a land acquisition program in the Indiana Dunes, hoping to use the acreage for a finishing mill but reserving the option to site an integrated plant there, if necessary. For that purpose, it formed a subsidiary, the Lake Shore Development Corporation, "as a land buying agency."[28] Precluded by subdivision and settlement from returning to the land it had considered thirty years earlier, Bethlehem focused on the only remaining undeveloped shoreline property in Porter County. That a few conservationists agitated for this same land to become part of a national park did not in any way deter the company.

Over the centuries man's hand had only lightly touched the central Porter County Dunes. Between the communities of Ogden Dunes to the west and Dune Acres to the east, and extending midway between route 12 and route 20 to the south and to Lake Michigan on the north, 3,600 acres remained virtually undisturbed until well into the mid-1950s. Conservationists prized the tract for its vast open space, spectacular blowouts, towering dunes, and 3.8 miles of shoreline. Nature lovers, for more than half a century, had hiked from the Dune Park, Shadyside, Meadowbrook, and Baileytown railroad stations through the land. They climbed its many trails, which meandered up and down bare and forested dune ridges. They wandered alongside twisting creeks and around interdunal lakes to reach glorious beaches. Remarkable plant life flourished there. "At one time Floyd Swink of Illinois's Morton Arboretum compiled a list of a dozen species which grew on the Bethlehem property and nowhere else."[29]

Lake Shore Development set about buying these dunelands. Bethlehem, thereby, became the industrial savior that Porter County agitators had sought for decades. First, Bethlehem's subsidiary acquired the entire 1,200-acre holdings of the Consumers Dunes Corporation.

Behind this seemingly innocent initial real estate transaction lay a history of Dunes land speculation reaching back to 1905 and the time of Gary's formation. In that year, as U.S. Steel acquired its Lake County land, a Chicago firm, Consumers Company, assumed possession of 2,300 acres previously owned by the Knickerbocker Ice Company in the central Porter County Dunes.[30] In an early example of land banking, Consumers held onto its property awaiting future industrial development. The first intrusion occurred in 1923, when Burns Ditch cut through the western section of the acreage. Weirton Steel Company became the first industrial purchaser when, in 1929, it acquired 750 acres on both sides of the ditch. Weirton, later to merge into the National Steel Corporation, foresaw using the property for a future Midwest plant. (National organized the Midwest Steel division, now known as Midwest Steel, which became the owner of Weirton's Dunes property.) The stock market crash, the Great Depression, and World War II delayed plans to build on the site. Nor did any of the company's efforts to promote construction of a federally financed port near its land materialize. When peace returned, neither "labor, construction money nor equipment were available," and National, "a very, very financially conservative company was not about to borrow for such a purpose."[31]

Another industrial land purchase in the central Porter County Dunes occurred in 1929. Northern Indiana Public Service Company (NIPSCO), the region's public utility, acquired 300 acres in the eastern part of the tract. Both Weirton and NIPSCO obtained lake frontage, but neither turned a single spade on their holdings during the ensuing thirty years.

In fact, all the land either owned or previously owned by the Consumers Company remained fallow until 1958. However, in 1954 Consumers merged with the Union Chemical Company and spun off its remaining 1,100 acres of Indiana land holdings as the assets of a new Indiana enterprise, the Consumers Dunes Corporation. To sell land in Indiana, state law required Indiana incorporation. Consumers Dunes' stated purpose involved "speculating in dune land." Controlled by the Dallas-based Murchison interests, Consumers Dunes quickly bought another 100 acres of adjacent duneland and thus held a significant parcel. Less than two years later, Lake Shore Development purchased the entire tract for Bethlehem at a cost of $3,326,500. The sale netted Consumers Dunes' stockholders an $85 profit per share. Its purpose accomplished, Consumers Dunes Company was liquidated.[32]

Both Consumers Dunes and Lake Shore Development had notable political affiliations. Consumers Dunes' resident agent, the C.T. Corporation System, "was located in the office of [Indiana's Governor George] Craig's old Indianapolis law firm of White, Raub, Craig and Forrey. Craig had quit the firm when he became governor." The largest Indiana stockholder of Consumers Dunes, Thomas W. Moses, served as president of the Indianapolis Water Company in which the Murchison interests held major stock. Moses also sat on the board of the American Fletcher Bank of Indianapolis. Board Chairman Frank McKinney formerly chaired the Democratic National Committee. He would help the Murchisons in their forthcoming successful drive to gain control of the Allegheny Corporation, "a holding company whose assets include the New York Central Railroad."[33] Lake Shore Development appointed a Porter County representative, James Chester, whom many considered the behind-the-scenes boss of both the county Democratic and Republican parties.

JAMES CHESTER

For many in Porter County, the Horatio Alger message remained gospel. They pointed to the career of Jim Chester as proof of their belief that hard work ensured success. Orphaned at two, a teenage polio victim, a poor, struggling college student at Valparaiso University, he had risen to own the largest, most influential law firm in the county. Chester successfully ran Charlie Halleck's reelection campaign in his one and only visible political undertaking, hobnobbed with Washington politicians, and, as the crowning climax of his long and illustrious career, became Bethlehem's Porter County man.

No one questioned Chester's legal prowess. Starting as county prosecutor after graduation from Valparaiso Law School, Chester could hardly support his new bride, Mae. Once in private practice, however, he began to attract clients and income, eventually becoming Porter County's top lawyer and the president of Farmers Trust Bank.

A perhaps apocryphal, though widely told, story relates that a million-dollar deposit suddenly appeared in Chester's bank account. The attached instructions directed him to purchase land in the central Porter County Dunes using dummy buyers and assigning lots to dummy trusts in the accepted tradition of Indiana real estate practice. His widow lends credence to the tale. "For a long time, we had no knowledge of the true buyer—though of course we had our suspicions."[34] To avoid escalating land prices, Chester undertook the entire acquisition in great secrecy. Lake Shore Development bought "360 separate properties ranging in size from 1,200 acres to a lot 40 × 100 feet."[35] Chester directed the whole show with an expertise derived from decades of Porter County real estate dealings. He relished the long hours, the intricate maneuverings, and the victories that the task entailed.

A quiet, assured man, his intelligence and long years of Porter County legal experience made him the logical choice as Bethlehem's agent. Moreover, his ability to succeed as a Catholic in an overwhelmingly Lutheran environment, his talent in winning control of county Democrats, though a staunch Republican, and his personality, which caused even the most critical onlooker to ignore his limping left leg, ensured that Chester would remain Bethlehem's local outside counsel. Once his land-buying activities terminated, he continued to serve the corporation in many legal matters relating to the Burns Harbor plant. His more important function involved organizing local support for Bethlehem within the county and, when necessary, arranging for Porter County representatives to plead Bethlehem's case in Washington.

Intensely persuasive, unquestionably honest, and ferociously loyal, Chester made a major contribution to Bethlehem's ultimate success in the Dunes. His role bore no resemblance to the ordinary lawyer-client relationship. Part of the Valparaiso world since childhood, he shared the business and political communities' profound "desire for the benefits of industrial growth."[36] As Bethlehem's attorney, Chester reaped rewards beyond the merely financial. He eagerly sought to realize the dream for which generations of his fellow townsmen had labored. He also brought rich dividends to his bank.

With his mastery of legal tactics, his command of legal argument, and his peerless courtroom performance, Chester effortlessly fulfilled the role of Bethlehem's land buyer from 1956 to 1965. He became, as well, the corporation's most artful local tactician during the crucial period between 1958 and 1962, while Bethlehem awaited the arrangement of zoning and other matters necessary for the construction of its Burns Harbor plant. Chester also played his usual behind-the-scenes role in aiding and abetting Bethlehem's cat-and-mouse game with port proponents. They needed Bethlehem's assurance that it would build an integrated facility in order to obtain federal financing of the port, while "at the same time Bethlehem [would] not promise to build such a mill until guaranteed that a port would be built to serve it." [37]

Chester found politics as fascinating as the law. His childhood memory of a relative who served in the Ohio legislature convinced him, first, never to seek elective office and, second, that participation in party politics would aid his legal career. Republican contacts—and what else mattered in Valparaiso then—brought him the county prosecutor's post. After that tenure he never again sought an appointed position. Instead, by supporting his party with time and contributions, he became Porter County's most influential Republican. Astutely realizing that a party frozen out of any power can become lean and hungry enough to mount a successful campaign, he insisted that the Democrats receive enough patronage to keep them pacified. Because of this clever strategy, he earned the Democrats' gratitude and allegiance. He also insisted that all candidates possess at least minimum qualifications for office, thereby keeping the Republicans from any nasty scandals.

Chester began his career when wooden sidewalks still graced Valparaiso's downtown. He lived to see Bethlehem build its huge Burns Harbor plant. Starting out as a small-town lawyer, he became a corporate factotum. His counsel helped an industrial giant achieve its goal in Porter County. [38]

While Bethlehem's land purchases continued, the corporation refused to reveal its intentions for the Porter County site. Board Chairman Grace would only laconically comment, "Well, it's not a bird sanctuary." [39] Nor did the corporation publicly commit itself to any construction plans until 1962. However, in the midst of completing its land acquisition, Bethlehem made an agreement, which simultaneously signaled its decision to build in the central Porter County Dunes and aided the promotion of a state-owned port. In 1957 the corporation gave the State of Indiana's Board of Public Harbors and Terminals a purchase option for approximately 260 acres of its property at a price of $2,062 per acre.[40] The agreement contained the stipulation that the land would revert to Bethlehem's ownership unless state port construction began by 1968. During the preconstruction period Bethlehem made few, if any, public announcements. Similar secrecy cloaked the state-company port agreement. Bethlehem's strategy kept the company's plan in the background. The corporation preferred quiet cultivation of government officials to operating in the glare of public attention. The location of the optioned land at the western boundary of Bethlehem's property clearly indicated the future port site. The same year, Midwest Steel's option for sixty-eight acres on its eastern boundary, at a price of $144,097, fixed the port site, a mile east of Burns Ditch.[41] During the next five years Bethlehem quietly proceeded with the task of preparing architectural plans and engineering studies for the first phase of construction at its Burns Harbor plant.

Meanwhile, the corporation outsmarted and outmaneuvered the conservationists, who coveted its Porter Countand. Most county officials and residents applauded the corporation's land purchases. They did everything possible to hasten the day when Bethlehem's jobs and taxes would improve the county's economy. Nevertheless, Bethlehem faced considerable opposition. Locally, the Save the Dunes Council led antidevelopment forces. With the involvement of Senator Paul Douglas in 1958, the corporation also had potent problems at the national level. Each of the Douglas bills for a federal enclave in the Dunes from 1958 to 1963 included the Bethlehem property as "the principal area worth preserving."[42] The corporation used surrogate spokesmen in its Washington battles, rarely making an official statement. Congressman Halleck, successive governors of Indiana, and Porter County leaders argued Bethlehem's case in the halls of Congress. Even Albert J. Berdis, president of Midwest Steel, represented Bethlehem. At one of the many hearings on the Douglas bills, he said, "The National and Bethlehem tracts are the only remaining sites available for plants to serve the Chicago market area, and if we and Bethlehem may not use the properties we have selected, we cannot compete in this market."[43]

All of Douglas's bills, proposed with maximum fanfare, languished in committee. Back in Porter County, Bethlehem moved ahead with its construction program. In 1959 it negotiated a land swap with NIPSCO to permit the utility to build a coal-fired power station. NIPSCO's site abutted Bethlehem's. The $30-million generating plant would supply power to the Burns Harbor mill. NIPSCO and Bethlehem also agreed to share a vital Lake Michigan water intake pipe. Still Bethlehem refused to reveal publicly its construction timetable, only admitting "Bethlehem most certainly is interested in developing its Porter County property as promptly as it is feasible to do so."[44]

For Bethlehem, feasibility meant assurance that a publicly financed port would become a reality. Though port opponents could point to U.S. Steel's private construction of its harbor facilities, as well as those financed by other Lake County industries, it seems undoubtedly true that even in the earlier era "corporations would have left the development of harbor facilities to the government had the latter been willing to take over the task. The tardiness of the government in assuming responsibility and the impatience of the corporations led to the provision of these facilities by private enterprise."[45] Bethlehem had both the patience and the corporate acumen to await state construction of the Burns Waterway. While U.S. Steel settled for federal maintenance of its harbor beginning in 1920, Bethlehem's thrifty managers wanted the cost of construction borne by the public.

Bethlehem's desire to avoid investing its corporate capital in port facilities dovetailed perfectly with Indiana's aspiration for a state-owned port. Beginning in 1932, successive state administrations, both Democratic and Republican, promoted the project. Seven governors touted harbor facilities in Porter County as an conomic bonanza for state, county, and local governments. They backed the port to stimulate further industrialization of northwest Indiana. They foresaw the proposal providing thousands of construction jobs and envisioned Indiana's farmers and industries using the port to send their products more cheaply to world markets.

Though Indiana badly wanted a deep water port on the Great Lakes, like Bethlehem it did not want to pay the construction costs. Instead, official Hoosierdom agitated for the federal government to finance Indiana's access to the world's greatest inland waterway. However, federal financing depended on congressional assent, which, in turn, needed Army Engineers' approval. They required evidence of a major industrial commitment to use the port. Thus, Indiana's thirty-year quest for a port always floundered for lack of an industrial sponsor. Indiana, therefore, courted Bethlehem with all the ardor of a lovesick suitor chasing a shy maiden. The state gladly supported the corporation's ownership of Dunes land, knowing full well that its harbor depended on Bethlehem's decision to build steel facilities there. Indiana propagandized for the steel mill and the harbor, promising "7000 three-year jobs for the building trades; 15,000 direct jobs in the steel mills; 25,000 jobs in service, allied industries, transportation and miscellaneous occupations; $2 billion in home and industry construction; and federal condemnation costs of $50 million."[46] Before Bethlehem's construction plans reached the drawing boards, the state asserted, "Modern steel mills do not emit excessive smoke, dirt, grease, objectionable odors and noise." Indiana insisted its "economic future depends upon development of this vital waterfront area."[47]

In the midst of the state's courtship of Bethlehem, the port received its first important boost from Bethlehem's neighbor, Midwest Steel. After thirty years of vacillation, Midwest, the port's original industrial proponent, announced plans to build a $100-million finishing plant on its Porter County land. "Along with the NIPSCO plant begun the same year, this development simultaneously disposed of a major tract of unspoiled Dunes and rendered the prospect for the port much stronger. Although its finishing plant did not require a harbor, Midwest reserved space for a harbor-side blast furnace operation, should the port materialize."[48]

In March 1961 steel shipments from Midwest's new plant began. Recognizing that a fait accompli had occurred, Douglas from then on excluded Midwest's land from his bills. The steel company continued to proclaim its intention to "within ten years expand into a fully integrated mill."[49] In spite of periodic flurries of excitement caused by rumors of a pending announcement, Midwest has yet to add another facility to its original steel finishing plant. According to General Manager George Lively, the 750-acre plant site has proved too small for a modern integrated steel facility.[50]

While construction of its finishing mill progressed, Midwest continued to press for the public port. The two steelmakers, in another secret pact, promised to underwrite the cost of the breakwaters and docks that would serve their plants.[51] In 1960 Midwest and Bethlehem jointly agreed to pay $4.5 million to the State of Indiana for part of the port's installations. The action came as a result of entreaties by state officials, who needed tangible commitments from the steel corporations to justify federal financing of the port.

By 1961 Midwest and Bethlehem had nullified zoning restrictions through which preservationists had tried to thwart construction plans. This attempt, although ultimately a failure, encouraged antidevelopment forces to believe, for a time, that legal rather than political tactics could stop destruction of the Dunes.

Porter County still held to the Jeffersonian belief that the government which governs best governs least. Until the 1960s the county had neither a master plan nor a zoning ordinance to regulate unincorporated areas. The central Porter County Dunes fell within this category. Further, Indiana law at that time permitted municipalities to annex and zone any contiguous, unincorporated land within two miles of their borders, providing no county zoning existed. Ogden Dunes tried to capitalize on this situation. An incorporated community of 500 acres, its zoning authority encompassed 8,000 acres, including "all of the Midwest land, the proposed harbor site and 1100 acres of the Bethlehem property" to the east and the Inland Steel tract to the west and south.[52]

Ed Osann led the town's challenge. A patent attorney, a Save the Dunes Council member, and the chairman of the Ogden Dunes Planning and Zoning Comittee, he used the law advantageously. The town adopted an annexation plan to protect itself from the undesirable effects of the two proposed steel mills and port. It zoned all of the central Porter County Dunes and the Inland property for single-family housing. The ordinance "specifically prohibited steelmaking operations" on any of the annexed land.[53] The ninety-four-page town law banned "the smelting and reduction of metallic ores, including but not limited to blast furnace, open hearth, electric furnace, Bessamer converter and non-ferrous smelter." It also listed "hammer mills, rolling mills, and drop forges" among its prohibited uses.[54]

Ogden Dunes's bold stroke provoked expected corporate outrage. Six suits in the Porter County Superior Court sought to enjoin the ordinance "on the grounds [it] was restrictive legislation and was arbitrary, unreasonable and not uniform."[55] While the court hearings dragged on from 1958 through 1960, Porter County hastened to act. To close the loophole that lack of a county zoning ordinance had opened, the commissioners hired an Indianapolis firm, Metropolitan Planners Inc., which devised a zoning ordinance to cover all unincorporated land throughout the county. Land contiguous to Lake Michigan naturally received a heavy industry designation.[56] Ogden Dunes's annexation plan became moot with the final passage of the Porter County zoning ordinance.

Because of the town's temerity in bucking industrial expansion, it received a further and more damaging reward. In the midst of the county's belated planning effort, Midwest, with Bethlehem's encouragement, took an additional step to protect the industrial turf. In 1959 it assisted in forming the new city of Portage. This new municipality's carefully drawn boundaries included all of Midwest's property and most of Bethlehem's.[57] Moreover, Portage's corporate limits abutted Ogden Dunes on its eastern, western, and southern boundaries. The Portage zoning ordinance copied the county's heavy industry zoning classification for the central Porter County Dunes.

In the next biennial session of the Indiana legislature, Hoosier solons overwhelmingly voted to legalize the establishment of Portage, thereby giving the city ordinance precedence over county zoning. This series of local, county, and state actions effectively protected industrial development and demonstrated the harmony of interests that allied all levels of government in Indiana with Midwest and Bethlehem's cause.

Bethlehem, however, still owned considerable land in unincorporated Porter County. Emulating Midwest, it aided the establishment of the city of Burns Harbor, whose boundaries lay between Dune Acres to the east and Portage to the west. It "agreed to assist the city by funding the operation of their local government until the first tax collections were made."[58] Following the already established pattern, Burns Harbor, too, zoned the Bethlehem land for heavy industry. This zoning protection assured on the local level at least that Bethlehem's construction plans could proceed without hindrance.[59] Furthermore, Bethlehem enjoyed a substantial tax advantage. In 1970 its $250 million plant received a $37 million assessment.[60]

Throughout 1962 Bethlehem continued to "grapple with a circular dilemma. According to the Corps of Engineers, the feasibility of the port depended on its heavy use by a major Bethlehem steel mill; at the same time Bethlehem could [or would] not promise to build such a mill until guaranteed that a port would be built to serve it."[61] Bethlehem's public pronouncements proclaimed its intention to build a private port, if necessary.[62] Such statements had their intended effect, goading state officials into an even further frenzy of action. If Bethlehem built its own docking facilities, any hope of obtaining federal support for a public port would disappear and, with it, jobs and other anticipated economic benefits. In spite of its many protestations to the contrary, Bethlehem wanted a publicly financed port. Otherwise, the corporation had no compelling reason to wait four long years before beginning construction. With the St. Lawrence Seaway already open, the economy prospering, and its funding assured, Bethlehem could have started building its plant months, if not years, earlier. Only the levelling of the Dunes on the corporation's property, which it had optioned for the port, assured that a national park would not acquire the land and that a public port would materialize.

A MOMENTOUS EVENT

For an hour-and-a-half on Friday morning, April 19, 1962, a two-story high conveyor belt relentlessly carried sand from a 120-foot pile northward to the Lake Michigan shoreline. There, a barge belonging to the Merry-Missouri Valley contracting consortium waited to receive each load. Members of the Indiana Port Commission watched the operation with genuine satisfaction. They had eagerly awaited this day. They knew that they were witnessing a momentous event. Once the first barge filled up, it moved out of a specially built canal and headed northwesterly across the lake toward Evanston. There its load would become part of a landfill under construction for Northwestern University's campus expansion.

In the afternoon a second barge moved into place to await its cargo. The commission members could only marvel at the efficiency of the project. Standing on land they had recently purchased from the Bethlehem Steel Corporation for their proposed public port, they knew, by summer's end, 2.5 million yards of sand would leave the site.

Only in moments of reflection did the long struggle cross their minds. Then the trio remembered the agonizing delays, bureaucratic red tape, and countless times when the project seemed doomed to fail. Without the adamant position of Bethlehem Steel, the scheme could not have come to fruition. Bethlehem had staunchly allied itself with them and withstood a barrage of unfavorable publicity. Together they had shrugged off entreaties from Senator Douglas, critical editorials, and columns of bad press. The commissioners hoped today's events would accomplish their two fondest ambitions: persuade Congress to approve an appropriation for a state-owned port and effectively destroy Douglas's latest attempt to include both the port site and Bethlehem's property in a Dunes National Park. Time would prove them right on both scores.

The weather had prevented Clint Green from joining them for the occasion. Yesterday's storms had kept him in Indianapolis. The men missed sharing the excitement with their tireless secretary-treasurer. They all appreciated the many hours he had spent laying the groundwork for today's results. Green had done the negotiating with Bethlehem to make sure the sand came out of the port site.

Chairman Jim Fleming wished Halleck could have come from Washington. Together he and fellow Commissioners Robert Schram and Al Yeager agreed that the port never had a better friend than Charlie. Well, they consoled themselves, at least Charlie knew about the deal long before the public did. Chester had seen to that.

As the commissioners continued to follow the conveyor churning away, they thought back to that explosive day over a year before when Bethlehem had revealed the sale of the sand. Huddled to-

gether under overcast skies, the three traded recollections of Douglas's angry protests when he heard the news. He called it "a brutal
and anti-social act," Yeager remembered.[63] "Imagine comparing some
sand mining to attacking and mutilating a beautiful woman so that
she may not belong to anyone else," Schram contributed.[64] They all
agreed that builders had sand mined there since the 1880s.

The wind began to pick up. The commissioners, unable to tear
themselves away from the scene while the work continued, soon
felt the sand stinging their eyes and dusting their clothes. They
looked about the site. In contrast to the activity at the water's edge,
virgin duneland stretched everywhere else they gazed. The men, try
as hard as they could, missed even a glimpse of the Midwest plant
to the west. High dunes blocked their view. In their minds the commission members could envision the soon-to-be-accomplished
transformation of this wasteland. The sand dredging would create
a big hole in the Dunes for their port. Then they expected Bethlehem to get on with leveling its property. The three foresaw with
pleasure the men and machines that soon would descend on this
God-forsaken wilderness.

A Vidette Messenger photographer broke their reverie. "How about
posing nearer the conveyor belt?" he asked. Glad to oblige, the
commissioners moved closer to the noisy machinery. Then they noticed the second barge seemed ready to leave. A midafternoon sun
lighted the sky as the group turned to depart for their homes in
Peru, Michigan City, and Fort Wayne. Now they could put behind
them the months of meetings with the Portage Plan Commission
and Board of Zoning Appeals to get a special exception for the sand
mining. Obtaining the permit surely had taken a lot of time and
allowed opportunities for those noisy Save-the-Duners to protest.

As the commissioners reached their cars, Schram recalled the
Army Engineers' hearing in Valpo. What a time that had turned
into. Just to get approval for a pier they had had to sit through days
of objections from conservationists. Colonel J. A. Smedlie had tried
to limit the testimony to the question of navigational obstruction,
but those Dunes lovers had wandered all over the lot, attacking the
Engineers, the state, Bethlehem, Midwest, and Northwestern.

Now they had to say good-by. Each of the commissioners hated
to go. They reminisced further. How could they ever forget how
Douglas had almost defeated them? He tempted Northwestern with
free sand from his friends on the Metropolitan Sanitary Commission. Only Chester's prowess in drawing the contract as tightly as
only he could do had saved them. Northwestern could not break

the agreement no matter how much pressure professors, students, and alumni had put on the school.

The commission members had half-expected to see some of their opponents come climbing over the Dunes during the day. Those pesky folks had badgered them constantly, finding new ways to delay the project at almost every turn. Fleming felt his anger return over one particular maneuver. The Army Engineers had had to schedule another public hearing because of all the letters against a plan to dredge out the shoreline for a 12-foot-deep, 100-foot-wide basin.

The chairman took comfort in the result. The Army Engineers had approved the outer harbor in spite of all the rhetoric about dunes-wrecking. As a newspaper publisher, he professionally but begrudgingly admired the skillful use of the press that the nature crowd had displayed. The flak from the Chicago papers and the Louisville Courier-Journal *might have bothered less committed public officials. Fleming knew most of Indiana stood solidly behind the commission.*

As the sun disappeared behind the clouds again, the conveyor stopped running. The first important day of work had ended. The commissioners decided not to wait around any longer. Assured that no more obstacles could interfere with the operation and that trains of sand-filled barges would continue to leave daily, they could head home. The latest threat by Save the Dunes Council attorney, Leonard Rutstein, to obtain an injunction against the sand mining had failed. Whatever new criticisms or objections might come along in the future, they believed nothing could stop the project now. At long last they agreed with Council President Dorothy Buell. She had predicted their bulldozing of the Dunes would destroy the natural scenery. The commissioners had seen it with their own eyes, and nothing could have pleased them more.

Nine months following Bethlehem's announcement of the sand sale, the corporation made an even more important public declaration. On December 3, 1962, Bethlehem broke years of silence regarding its building plans. It revealed a $250-million plan for finishing mills. "Construction will begin as soon as possible to provide finishing facilities for plates, hot and cold rolled sheets and tinplates which will be processed from semi-finished steel supplied by our existing plants in the East," said Bethlehem Board Chairman Arthur B. Homer. He stated that the Porter County plant would initially include a 160-inch sheared plate mill, a cold rolled-sheet mill, a tin mill, and an 80-inch hot rolled-sheet mill with a capacity of 1.9 million tons annually.[65] Thus the corporation finally committed itself to the mills that its planners had projected seven years earlier as complementary to the doomed Youngstown merger. Two important events triggered the date of the announcement. First, NIPSCO completed its nearby station ensuring power for the Burns Harbor Works. Second, and much more significant, newly elected Indiana Senator Birch Bayh threw his support to the port and the industrialization of the central Porter County Dunes. Bethlehem required certainty that he would not become a spokesman for the conservation interests before going public with its intentions. "Announcement of the project was delayed until the firm received assurances from Senator-elect Birch E. Bayh Jr. D-Ind. that he would support the proposals for the port. Bayh was reached at Orlando, Florida Sunday morning and flown in an Indiana National Guard C-47 to his Terre Haute home that night. He met Governor [Matthew] Welsh Monday afternoon, and the announcement came a short time later."[66] Bayh appeared at a statehouse press conference with Welsh after Bethlehem's news went over the wire service. "Welsh explained that Bethlehem officials wanted to hear from Bayh personally his support of the harbor project before announcing plans for their mill. Bayh gave Homer his personal assurance that he is back of the port plans and industrialization of the area."[67]

Welsh summed up the feelings of triumphant Indiana officialdom by predicting that the Bethlehem announcement meant "that any opposition to the port based on use of that particular area for a park will evaporate." Douglas blasted back, "Bethlehem is proposing to destroy beautiful Indiana sand dunes in order to build a steel plant. They do not have to do this. They could have located it elsewhere. But the dunes once destroyed can never be replaced. By destroying the open space around cities they create a new crop of neurotics and psychotics. This is apparently what Bethlehem is trying to do." Board Chairman Homer's revelation also added a tantalizing picture of things to come: "As conditions warrant, this facility will be developed into a fully integrated steelmaking plant incorporating the latest technological advances and using the most modern tools and processes available for producing a wide range of steel products."[68] Homer's reference to "as conditions warrant" alluded to the continuing, though diminishing, threat to expropriate Bethlehem's land that the Douglas bills promised.

Casting aside such a possibility, the corporation immediately began preparing the plant site. Road building started quickly. In four months, the New York *Times* reported, "the company has stripped

1000 acres of vegetation. Now grading equipment is on hand to begin leveling the 100,000,000 year old dunes for a new steel mill."[69]

Bethlehem's plans provided for the erection, by 1965, of a plate mill 3,000 feet long and 175 feet wide, covering a total floor area of 800,000 square feet; a complex of buildings with 1 million square feet of floor space for the production of cold rolled sheets and tinplate; and a hot rolled-sheet mill 2,900 feet long and 250 wide.[70] The design of the buildings projected production on a huge scale: plate up to ten inches thick, 900 inches long, and weighing up to 40,000 pounds; thirty miles of pipe monthly, "large enough for a truck to drive through"; coils weighing up to 1,000 pounds per inch of width and six-foot wide bands of steel.[71] The largest single undertaking in the company's history promised to employ 2,500 workers.

By July 1963 giant earthmovers swarmed over the tract. "Leveling the sand hills and filling the swamps and marshes [involved] transferring 20-25,000 cubic yards of sand a day."[72] Drag buckets pulled vast quantities of peat from drained sections of the site for later use in landscaping. Almost 1,000 construction workers labored to bring the property up to a grade 14 feet above the lake level. The building of a contractor's village and laying of more than 10,000 feet of railroad spur pointed to the growing tempo of construction for the new steel plant.

Bethlehem's finishing facilities met the corporation's target date for starting production. With the passage of port legislation Bethlehem proceeded with plant expansion. The long-awaited, long-promised integrated plant became a reality in 1969, when the first coke oven began operation. A second coke oven came on line in 1972. Together they have a daily capacity of 10 million tons. The plant now includes a strand casting unit and a sintering unit. The work force climbed to 5,000.

Bethlehem's presence changed Porter County in many ways. Some will argue for the better, others for the worse. Its tremendous economic impact raised income levels, increased urbanization, and boomed new communities. As a result of the Burns Harbor plant, political alignments changed. Once totally conservative Republican, Porter County developed pockets of Democrats. Where concentrations of unionized steelworkers now live—in Portage, Porter, South Haven, and Burns Harbor—Republican control slipped. The creation by the Republican-controlled state legislature of a new congressional first district in 1981 demonstrated the increasing Democratic complexion of northern Porter County. The Republicans chose to lump the Dunes communities with solidly Democratic Lake County to dilute Democratic strength in Porter County. Though the state and county governments remain solidly united with the corporation, municipalities have shown increasing evidence of independent stances.

Foreign steel competition, which had begun to affect American producers by the time Bethlehem started to build the Burns Harbor plant, has cut the market far more than most steel producers, including Bethlehem, ever dreamed. "Imported steel amount[ed] to 14 percent of the domestic market in 1960–1974."[73] The American share of raw steel production has plummeted from 47 percent in 1950 to 20 percent in 1978.[74] Hit not only by the lower prices of primarily Japanese steel but also by the national decline in demand for steel caused by the economic slump of the early 1980s and reduced car production, Bethlehem experienced bad times. Layoffs and plant slowdowns occurred at Burns Harbor, raising questions about the viability of the corporate decision to locate there. Its defenders argued that the nation's hard times will soon pass, and Burns Harbor would resume its round-the-clock production. The jewel in Bethlehem's collection of steelmaking facilities, Burns Harbor seems destined to continue for many decades as the corporation's most efficient, most technologically advanced producer. Yet despite Burns Harbor's superiority to older American steelmaking facilities, it does not match Japanese steel productivity. For example, Bethlehem's management waited until 1975 to acquire a continuous slab caster for Burns Harbor. Combining a number of steelmaking processes, this machinery "saves large amounts of energy and manpower and produces a higher-quality product compared with the old-fashioned ingot casting system."[75] One commentator has described the continuous caster as "a piece of equipment that is as important to the efficiency of a plant as a touch-tone is to the speed of a telephone call."[76] Critics of the American steel industry's unwillingness to invest in capital improvements claim the plant should never have gone into production without such equipment. In 1981 Bethlehem announced plans to double its continuous casting capacity at Burns Harbor.

An observer has called Bethlehem's decision to sell its sand for the Northwestern landfill "a crucial and Machiavellian contribution" to the resolution of the conflict over industrial development versus preservation in the central Porter County Dunes.[77] From the corporation's perspective, such a characterization seems patently false. Bethlehem operated consistently and with great skill to further its own interest. Its corporate plans, policies, strategies, and tactics reflected the dominant values of American society: profitability remained the sole purpose of business and industry and ownership of property brought the inalienable right to use one's land for one's private purposes. The company perceived no reason to include social concerns in its corporate decision-making and did not expect to deal with opponents who expressed alternative values. Bethlehem had a clear purpose and the resources to accomplish that purpose. In spite of a nationwide campaign, opponents could not develop sufficient political strength to deflect the corporation from its chosen course.

By beginning construction of its plant while Congress still ponderously weighed legislation affecting its property, Bethlehem effectively broke the stalemate. For several years conservation and industrial development interests had prevented each other from achieving either the port or the park. Bethlehem's action both allowed resolution of the controversy and brilliantly protected the corporation.

Bethlehem's construction in the Dunes demonstrates the absolute power of private property owners in the mid-1960s. No mechanism then existed to mediate among competing land use interests. Because of its giant economic resources, Bethlehem's desires outweighed the concerns of neighboring property owners in the minds of local, county, and state officials. The national interest in conserving natural resources had no voice. Only subsequent to Bethlehem's erection of its Burns Harbor plant would the Congress enact legislation that might have affected the placement of steel works in the Porter County Dunes. That legislation came too late.

NOTES

1. Bate, "Chicago Iron and Steel," p. 16. See also Kenneth Warren, *The American Steel Industry* (London: Oxford University Press, 1973), p. 143.

2. Bate, "Chicago Iron and Steel," p. 14.

3. John B. Appleton, *The Iron and Steel Industry of the Calumet Region: A Study in Economic Geography*, Studies in the Social Sciences, vol. 13, no. 2 (Urbana: University of Illinois, 1927), p. 91.

4. Ibid., p. 89.

5. Bate, "Chicago Iron and Steel," p. 14.

6. Quoted in Warren, *American Steel*, p. 142.

7. A. O. Hackett, *Iron Trade Review* (Jan. 1925), as quoted in J. Bernard Walker, *The Story of Steel* (New York: Harper & Brothers, 1926), p. 182.

8. Bate, "Chicago Iron and Steel," p. 5.

9. "Too Much Steel in the Midwest," *Iron Age*, Oct. 3, 1963, p. 34.

10. "The Battle for the Midwest Steel Market," *Steel*, Apr. 4, 1966, p. 34.

11. Bate, "Chicago Iron and Steel," p. 102.

12. U.S. Department of Commerce, *Steel Demand, Capital Costs and Imports.* Report prepared by William Hogan (Washington: Government Printing Office, 1975), p. 13, hereafter cited as Hogan, *Steel Demand.*

13. Charles Silverman, "Steel: It's A Brand New Industry," *Fortune*, Dec. 1960, pp. 127, 125.

14. Gilbert Burck, "The Private Strategy of Bethlehem Steel," ibid., Aug. 1962, p. 105.

15. Ibid., p. 112.

16. Stewart Hall Holbrook, *Iron Brew: A Century of American Ore and Steel* (New York: Macmillan, 1939), p. 278; Arundel Cotter, *The Story of Bethlehem Steel* (New York: Moody Magazine and Book Company, 1916), p. 54.

17. Cotter, *Bethlehem Steel*, p. 43; "Bethlehem Steel," *Fortune*, Apr. 1941, pp. 62, 61.

18. "Bethlehem Steel," *Fortune*, Apr. 1941, p. 61.

19. Bethlehem Steel Corporation, *The Properties and Plants of the Bethlehem Steel Corporation* (Bethlehem, Pa., 1925), p. 3.

20. Gertrude Schroeder, *The Growth of the Major Steel Companies* (Baltimore: Johns Hopkins University Press, 1953), p. 199.

21. Warren, *American Steel*, p. 154.

22. *Iron Age*, Aug. 20, 1925, p. 47.

13523. Bethlehem Steel Corporation, *Recollections* (Bethlehem, Pa., 1979), inside front cover; Schroeder, *Major Steel Companies*, pp. 98–99. The shareholders led by Cleveland financier Cyrus Eaton preferred Youngstown to the Republic Steel Corporation but failed in the attempt.

24. Schroeder, *Major Steel Companies*, p. 197.

25. Herbert Parmet, *The Democrats* (New York: Oxford University Press, 1976), pp. 116–19.

26. "Bethlehem Plans Came to Light in 1956," Gary *Post Tribune*, Dec. 4, 1962, p. B–1; "Steel Merger Goes to Trial," *Steel*, Jan. 20, 1958, p. 37; "The Big Merger Is Off," ibid., Feb. 3, 1959, p. 52.

27. Stewart S. Court, "The Building of Burns Harbor," *Chicago Commerce*, Feb. 1966, pp. 18–19.

28. William Peeples, "The Indiana Dunes and Pressure Politics," *Atlantic Monthly*, Feb. 1963, p. 86.

29. Peggy Moran, "The Dunes and Dunes People," *Calumet Review*, 3 (1969): 20–21.

30. Richard Pough to Dorothy Buell, July 7, 1955, Save the Dunes Council Files. See also George A. Brennan, *The Wonders of the Dunes* (Indianapolis: Bobbs-Merrill, 1923), p. 133.

31. Authors' interview with George Lively, Portage, Ind., 1978.

32. Peeples, "Dunes Pressure Politics," p. 86.

33. Gordon Englehart, "The Battle of the Dunes," Louisville *Courier-Journal*, July 23, 1961; a reprint is in the Save the Dunes Council Files.

34. Authors' interview with Mae Chester, Valparaiso, 1980.

35. Court, "Building Burns Harbor."

36. Rutherford H. Platt, *The Open Space Decision Process: Spatial Allocation of Costs and Benefits*, Department of Geography, Research Paper 142 (Chicago: University of Chicago, 1972), p. 161.

37. Ibid., p. 157.

38. Authors' interview with lawyer James Lyons, Valparaiso, 1980, and Chester interview. Other Porter County lawyers who knew Chester supplied additional information.

39. "Bethlehem Plans," Gary *Post Tribune*.

40. Englehart, "Dunes Battle," Louisville *Courier-Journal*.

41. Platt, *Decision Process*, p. 156.

42. Ibid., p. 170.

43. "Bethlehem Plans," Gary *Post Tribune*.

44. Ibid.

45. Bate, "Chicago Iron and Steel," p. 14.

46. Indiana Department of Commerce and Industry, undated brochure, Save the Dunes Council Files.

47. Ibid.

48. Platt, *Decision Process*, p. 156.

49. Englehart, "Dunes Battle," Louisville *Courier-Journal*.

50. Lively Interview.

51. Englehart, "Dunes Battle," Louisville *Courier-Journal*.

52. Platt, *Decision Process*, p. 160.

53. Ibid.

54. "Bethlehem Plans," Gary *Post Tribune*.

55. Ibid.

56. Ibid.

57. Ibid.

58. Edward H. Frank, district manager of public relations, Bethlehem Steel Corporation, to authors, May 10, 1977.

59. U.S. Congress, Senate, Senator Paul E. Douglas in extension of remarks to include "Battle of the Dunes, tiny community battles to keep industry out," fourth of a series by Richard Lewis, Chicago *Sun-Times*, Aug. 20, 1958, as found in 85th Cong., 2d. sess., Aug. 22, 1958, *Congressional Record*, 104:19029.

60. Platt, *Decision Process*, p. 160.

61. Ibid., p. 157.

62. See, for example, "Expect to Have to Construct Own Port—Bethlehem," Gary *Post Tribune*, Feb. 20, 1963, p. 1.

63. News Release, Senator Paul H. Douglas, "On the Threatened Destruction of the Indiana Dunes," Mar. 31, 1962, Save the Dunes Council Files.

64. Ibid.

65. Christina Kirk, "Bethlehem Steel—Mid-West Invader," New York *Herald Tribune*, Dec. 4, 1962, pp. 37, 45.

66. "Bethlehem Mill Plans Strengthen Indiana's Case for Port in This Area," Chesterton *Tribune*, Dec. 4, 1962, p. 1.

67. "Mill Plan Boosts Harbor," Gary *Post Tribune*, Dec. 4, 1962, p. 1.

68. Ibid.

69. Donald Janson, "1,000 Dune Acres Cleared for Mill," New York *Times*, Apr. 14, 1963, p. 94.

70. "Bethlehem Lists Details of New Mill Buildings," Gary *Post Tribune,* Feb. 22, 1963, p. 24.

71. "Women Learn about Steel Plant," ibid., Nov. 6, 1963.

72. Ibid.

73. Hogan, *Steel Demand,* p. 3.

74. Newsletter of Senator Richard Lugar, "Special Report on the State of the Steel Industry," Fall 1980, chart, pp. 2–3.

75. Douglas Sease and Urban Lehner, "Trailing the Japanese, U.S. Steelmakers Seek to Use Their Methods," *Wall Street Journal,* Apr. 2, 1981, pp. 1, 20.

76. "Steel Industry's Year of Crisis," New York *Times,* June 20, 1982, p. 15.

77. Platt, *Decision Process,* p. 157.

6 Battle Cry: Save the Dunes

With the realization of the Indiana Dunes State Park in 1927, the Dunes preservation movement disappeared without a vestige for twenty-two years. Conservationists, who had spent themselves on the state legislative effort, seemed satisfied with their achievement and drifted off to other projects and concerns. Neither the hardships of the Great Depression nor preoccupation with the sacrifices of World War II stimulated conservationist ideals in northwest Indiana; no external threat forced renewed efforts to save the Dunes. Indeed, port proponents, who had barely articulated their interest when the crash came in 1929, seemed to go underground for the duration of the depression. Their proposals did not become common currency until World War II had come and gone. By that time two decades had elapsed since anyone in Indiana had attended to Dunes preservation.

Ironically, however, the depression of the 1930s stimulated a greater national commitment to conservation and to the care and mainte-nance of the nation's parks than had ever occurred in more prosper-ous times. Interest in conservation grew in tandem with the nation's greatest need for economic growth and development in two decades. Two factors contributed to the rise in conservation-mindedness: Franklin D. Roosevelt's concern and the necessity to find work for the unemployed. Early in his first administration, FDR proposed the Civilian Conservation Corps (CCC) as a means of providing work for thousands of unemployed young men between the ages of eigh-teen and twenty-five. By sending these youths to care for the na-tion's parks and forests Roosevelt underscored the need for "conservation of human and natural resources on a national scale."[1] Congress used emergency appropriations liberally to fund conser-vation work. New legislation "established the National Park Service [NPS] as the federal agency primarily responsible for nationwide park, historic and recreation programs." By 1935 the NPS, together with other federal agencies, operated 2,916 CCC camps servicing both national and state parks and forests. In addition to its pick-and-shovel functions, the program contributed enormously to the evolution of national thought and philosophy about parks and recreation.[2] Under the auspices of the CCC the NPS undertook a series of studies, both immediate and long range, which surveyed park and recreation programs on a nationwide basis. The reports covered everything from park structures to laws governing camping and to tree preservation as well as fees and charges for public recreation; the results influenced park planning and financing for many years.

During the intense conservation activity of the 1930s the NPS for the first time studied the nation's shorelines as part of its overall planning. Although by then the predepression land boom, which had leveled dunes for homesites in Florida and along the eastern shores, had temporarily subsided, it had caused sufficient destruction to warrant concern about future shoreline preservation. In 1934 and 1935 the NPS began studies of the seashores of the Atlantic Coast and the Gulf of Mexico. Six months later the agency included the Pacific Coast as well. The findings enabled the NPS to identify fifteen areas worthy of inclusion in the national park system as well as thirty areas of lesser importance for attachment to state recreational systems. The studies resulted in the establishment of Cape Hatteras National Seashore, the nation's first, in 1937.

World War II and the cold war that followed kept national park activity at a minimum. Shoreline preservation was stalled because of the cost-cutting policies of the Dwight Eisenhower administration and by the president's disinclination to consider the setting of national conservation goals as a legitimate role for the government. Twenty years elapsed before Congress authorized the next national seashore, Cape Cod, in 1961. Between the establishment of Cape Hatteras and that of Cape Cod, the NPS initiated a new seashore program by means of donations from the Mellon Foundation. These studies reviewed both oceans and the Gulf of Mexico and this time included the shores of the Great Lakes. The shoreline program opened up a new phase of conservation for the United States. It began a policy of preserving and protecting bodies of water, including rivers, lakes, and streams; with the acquisition of Cape Cod it established the precedent of purchasing park land with congressional funds—a concept suggested by Stephen Mather for the Indiana Dunes forty years ahead of its time.

Despite the generous emergency funding of the 1930s, however, basic appropriations for the NPS did not pay for its increased responsibilities. Moreover, the exigencies of World War II had caused curtailment of monies for park administration, a reduction that remained in effect after the war ended. When Americans tested their postwar mobility by driving to the national parks, they found them in shocking condition. The parks failed to maintain essential sanitary facilities; they lacked adequate water, sewer, and electrical systems and juggled a short supply of security personnel. Often they looked like rural slums. Ten years after the war the national parks still suffered from inadequate maintenance, underdevelopment, lack of protection, and paucity of funds. Between 1950 and 1955 park visitation rose from 33.2 million to 56.5 million, while appropriations increased from $30.1 million to only $32.9 million.[3] Many natural, scientific, and historic sites as well as many seashores recommended for inclusion into the park system by the studies of the 1930s had been damaged or destroyed and were irrevocably lost to the nation. The commitment to conservation together with the financial muscle to do the job, so evident during the 1930s, disappeared under a national mania to catch up economically. Postdepression, postwar America wanted a return to the plenty that had been denied for fifteen years. "The citizenry waited with whetted appetites and overflowing wallets, for the economic cornucopia of peace."[4] However, not everyone welcomed the return of economic primacy if it meant suppression of other values.

In 1949 the long dormant threat to industrialize Indiana's Porter County Dunes finally resurfaced. Port proponents who had used the war years to reconstruct the groundwork for a new assault confidently attempted, once again, to secure the approval of the federal district engineer for their never-forgotten obsession. The Army Engineers' prewar recommendation, which had finally reached the Congress in 1944, justified current optimism by stating: "The Burns Waterway site is the only one on the Indiana shore of Lake Michigan at which sufficient space is available for the type of general industrial and commercial harbor desired by local interests."[5] This assertion reversed Army Engineer Captain S. N. Kerrick's 1935 directive requiring a survey of the entire shoreline to determine the best harbor site. It thus legitimized port proponents' claims and became central to all opposing arguments in the lengthy struggle that eventually commanded the entire nation's attention.

Unlike its precursors, the public hearing before Col. W. P. Trower, district engineer, held in Gary on July 19, 1949, produced a favorable report. It stated: "There appears to be a need for a public harbor and terminal in the Chicago area of the magnitude proposed by the state of Indiana; there is a reasonable prospect of developing a project which would be economically justified by its benefits; and a survey to determine the best plan of improvement and its justification is warranted."[6] Then, to the chagrin of port proponents, the Korean War halted civilian projects of the Army Engineers. Congress appropriated no funds for the survey until 1954 and then a mere $4,000, instead of the $37,000–$50,000 estimated as necessary for the job.[7]

The Gary hearing, unlike those before it, had other consequences; it attracted sizable, albeit unexpected, opposition to the port. Inarticulate, rudimentary, unorganized, and composed of an eclectic mix of Lake County steel interests, Ogden Dunes property owners, the East Chicago Chamber of Commerce, and a sprinkling of true conservationists, this assortment, "the mottliest group you ever saw— the boy scouts, Audubon Society, American Legion, Little Men's Marchers and Shouters," constituted the eventual nucleus of a new Dunes preservation movement—the first since Bess Sheehan's exhausting triumph twenty years earlier.[8] Stimulated by the renewed threat of industrialization and the testimony of the 1949 hearing, a shaky antiport assemblage formed. A small amount of money contributed by East Chicago's steel companies, Inland and Youngstown, supported the Indiana Dunes Preservation Council, an organization solely dedicated to warding off industrialization in the Dunes.[9] Its campaign pleaded for preservation and recreational use of the land, but the real interest of its members lay in preventing construction of the port. Unfortunately, the group lacked firm, positive, long-range goals; within a few years the uneasy coalition fell apart. Although it limped on, in name, into the mid-1950s, it accomplished little after an initial flurry.

The few genuine conservationists, who affiliated with the short-lived Indiana Dunes Preservation Council, those whose beliefs went beyond an ad hoc label, lamented its inevitable demise. Dr. Myron Reuben Strong, long associated with scientific and recreational activities in the Dunes, personified their frustration. His personal interest in the region dated from 1903. Then, as a young scientist working with Henry Chandler Cowles, he had become involved with protecting the ecology of the Chicago environs, an interest he sustained throughout his many years of participation in conservation causes. He joined the Chicago Conservation Council and became its president. By 1949 he could have emulated the spirited activism of a Jens Jensen or a Stephen Mather by gaining popular and political backing for Dunes preservation. Sadly, however, Strong lacked their flamboyance and magnetism, nor did the times encourage their civic style. Unknown outside of local conservation circles, Strong possessed neither the personal contacts nor the political acumen to coalesce enough strength to fight the proposed harbor—the single most significant threat to the remaining Dunes. At the age of seventy-seven he encountered formidable resistance to Dunes protection, opposition that might easily have discouraged the younger Jensen and Mather had they run up against it. Regrettably, Strong's best effort could not fill the acute need for vigorous, forceful leadership. Alarmed and impotent, Strong watched the Indiana Dunes Preservation Council deteriorate, neither preventing the port nor preserving the Dunes. He determined that he must do something to halt further erosion of the Dunes preservation organization. On February 24, 1952, therefore, eighty-year-old Strong wrote to Mrs. Dorothy Buell of Ogden Dunes, Indiana, "I wish to discuss with you the problem of leadership for our effort to save the dunes between Ogden Dunes and Dune Acres . . . we lack aggressive leadership. We need a more active campaign than we have had so far . . . it is my judgment that we need someone who will do what Mrs. Sheehan did in the promotion of the Indiana Dunes State Park, and I think you may be the person to do this." [10]

DOROTHY BUELL

Neither naturalist, scientist, preservationist, nor engineer, sixty-five-year-old Dorothy Buell seemed an unlikely candidate for national eminence in conservation. Within a decade of her initiation, however, she qualified for Who's Who in the Midwest, *she blossomed as one of the top feminine newsmakers in Indiana, and she acquired an impressive string of national conservation awards. How did an aging Republican clubwoman, a traditional person living a conventional life become the symbol of a cause that pitted Dunes preservation against the political-industrial values of the nation?*

Nothing in Buell's early life would have predicted such an outcome. One of seven children, Dorothy, nee Richardson, grew up in Neenah-Menasha, Wisconsin, in the late 1880s. Despite limited finances and a large family, the Richardsons' ambitions included higher education for their three daughters. Dorothy spent two years at Milwaukee-Downer College and then transferred to Lawrence College, where she received a Bachelor of Oratory degree from the School of Expression in 1911. For the next forty years she used her training and talents in the expected, traditional fashion. After her marriage she conducted dramatic readings and book reviews, with equanimity, wherever husband Hal's job took her. In Gary, Indiana, Tulsa, Oklahoma, or Flossmoor, Illinois, Buell enchanted audiences of clubwomen with her witty monologues and sage reviews. Her popular book clubs multiplied; her little theater flour-

ished. By the end of the 1940s their only child, Robert, had grown and gone, and Dorothy and Hal remained in Ogden Dunes to lead a seemingly complete, predictable, and uncontroversial existence.

The incident that changed her life did not appear significant at the time. In 1949, on the way home from a trip to the White Sands National Monument in New Mexico, Dorothy and Hal stopped for dinner at the Gary Hotel. They noticed a poster in the lobby announcing "meeting at 8:00 to help save the Indiana Dunes." [11] *Although they had no prior interest in conservation, on impulse they attended that evening's meeting of the Indiana Dunes Preservation Council. Her interest stimulated, Dorothy Buell became a frequent participant in the following months. Mostly she sat quietly and observed the way the men ran things. If she had any quarrel with their methods, she refrained from criticism. After all, she knew many of them as friends, neighbors, Hal's business associates, and fellow Republicans. At these meetings she met Myron Reuben Strong, the elderly conservationist who, only a few years later, selected her to wear the mantle of Dunes saver. His influence and friendship would motivate her, guide her, and support her in times of secret discouragement.*

Accordingly, at an age when most people slow down or retire, Dorothy Buell found a cause, a lifework, an obsession, a vocation, a beginning. She emerged as a leader for whom politics constituted anathema and public attention remained a cross to bear. She based her faith in the eventual outcome on the moral rightness of saving the Dunes; that faith continued, absolute and unshakeable, for the rest of her life. Not surprisingly, therefore, when Dorothy Buell initiated the Save the Dunes Council in June 1952, she believed fervently that the world would decide the case for the Dunes on its merits and that the merits spoke for themselves.

A diminutive, chubby woman like her predecessor, Bess Sheehan, Buell radiated a dignified presence that allowed her domination of any company. She dressed formally for public occasions, complete with hat and gloves. When she wished, she could silence a room full of ideological enemies with a meaningful incline of her white, waved head. Steeped in old-fashioned reserve, she dared not address Strong as "Reuben" until their comradeship had endured for the better part of ten years. Her mentor from Illinois remained "Mr. Douglas" throughout their long association. Colleagues recall that Buell had the tenacity of a bulldog. Once she got hold of something she never let it go. When she wanted to do something, she did it; nobody stood in her way. Many people neither liked nor understood her—especially the unsuspecting victims of her biting wit. A bulldog indeed! Friend and enemy alike marveled at her energy, persistence, and stubbornness. Dorothy parlayed her doggedness, her high energy level, and her ingenuous, messianic belief in the rightness of her cause into an organization whose members would rather die than refuse her. That she lacked genuine organizational ability irritated some; that she floundered uncertainly from time to time bothered others; but, to most who knew her, she embodied a symbolic inspiration providing hope and promise to a sometimes desperate cause.

With unflappable dignity and a kind of quiet charisma, Dorothy functioned best when performing in public. She left attacks on the opposition to others. "When Mrs. Buell got up to speak, you could hear a pin drop. Never on the offensive, she stuck with the basic issue of saving the Dunes, and she garnered incredible respect. No one would dare to criticize her, the high road all the way. Even Halleck didn't dare to criticize her. It would have been suicide."[12]

Charisma, however, rarely submits to dissection; nor did Buell's. The observable elements have appeared in print and linger in the memories of those who knew her. "She had a special way with people," " . . . seemed ageless, charming looking, spirited, firm, natural." "She could really do this job." "She was fun, gay, and very able." "She thought big; her success would not have surprised her; she knew it would happen." "She had an intriguing, unique personality," " . . . was a dedicated, wonderful person," " . . . a real human being who could let her hair down yet always handle everything." "She worked tirelessly; her day started at 5:30 in the morning and continued long after everyone else had gone to bed."[13] None of these qualities separately or in any combination suffices to explain Dorothy's symbolic relationship to the cause she loved. Authoritative, dignified, erect, and unfalteringly "right," she personified Saving the Dunes for a quarter century.

In 1953 Dorothy stumbled, inadvertently, into a major success for the year-old Save the Dunes Council. Naturalist Lois Howes discovered that the owners of the bog where she believed Cowles had conducted his field work owed the county back taxes. The bog exemplified all that made the Dunes unique and worth preserving and afforded a visitor the progression from lake to beach to oak savanna to beech climax forest and beyond, to interdunal ponds and wetlands that demonstrated Cowles's theories of plant succession. Each habitat exhibited its specialized array of plant and animal life, providing scientific significance as well as exceptional beauty. Howes convinced Dorothy Buell, who could hardly distinguish a bog from a meadow at the time, that the Save the Dunes

Council should purchase it. With nothing close to the $1,400 asking price in the treasury and only a few short days before the tax sale, Dorothy obtained $700 from Sheehan—all that remained of the National Dunes Park Association funds—and another $700 from a wealthy Michigan City benefactor. Hal, who had toted his checkbook to Valparaiso just in case, coughed up another $300, allowing the ladies to outbid the opposition and emerge as landowners. Thus, in less than a year, without much preplanning, the fledgling Save the Dunes Council had purchased its first duneland. In retrospect, the organization probably took no other single action as significant. For a variety of legal reasons the Save the Dunes Council kept the bog for twenty years, by which time staggering debts prevented its donation for preservation purposes. Instead, the organization sold it to the Indiana Dunes National Lakeshore—a controversial act, highly criticized by the opposition—which allowed full payment of past debts and funds for future operation.

By the middle of the 1960s, Dorothy Buell was leaving much of the work to others. Few noticed, however, for her presence and spirit sufficed. Exhausted from the years of effort and beyond her seventy-fifth birthday, she finally recognized her body's limits. In 1970 she and Hal gave in to their son's increasingly firm requests that they move to California. Both suffered poor health. The effects of age and illness had begun to show, and, though slow to admit it, they could no longer look after each other as they had always done. Reluctantly, Dorothy Buell left her beloved Dunes. Although she returned a few times to visit and to receive new honors, she had gone for good. "Nobody in California wants to hear about the Dunes," she invariably complained, "and that's all I've got to talk about."[14] Indeed she had gone for good; she died in 1976 at the age of eighty-nine, having lived several lifetimes successfully.

Dorothy Buell spent from February to June 1952 considering Strong's proposal that she lead the Dunes-saving effort. After consulting at length with Sheehan, Buell took the plunge. She fashioned the early Save the Dunes Council according to Sheehan's model, agreeing totally with Sheehan's view of the issue. "Let others fight the harbor project, but here, have one clear purpose—to add this five miles to the Indiana Dunes State Park."[15]

Twenty-five enthusiastic women responded to announcements made at the Dune Acres League and the Ogden Dunes Woman's Club and in the Gary *Post Tribune.* By the end of the June 20th meeting they had agreed to save the Dunes and to do so by buying up the land and donating it to the state park. These women, together with Buell, perceived the council to be a new species of woman's club. Happily severed from the floundering men's effort, they patterned their organization in the comfortable and familiar mold so successfully established by Sheehan thirty years before. The infant council operated according to few simple goals—spread the gospel; get as many people as possible behind us; collect money; buy the land.

Within the confines of the tasks Buell set, the Save the Dunes Council flourished in the early years. She begged and commanded attention, support, and money from any quarter, persisting with evangelical zeal. Strong provided continual approbation and praise: "I am delighted with the grand start you have made in our campaign and I am also gratified by having our judgment confirmed in asking you to undertake this important work."[16]

Despite the good start, Buell sometimes became intensely disheartened when confronted with an uncaring public. "I am very much discouraged," she complained to Strong in October 1953. "Ogden Dunes is very indifferent . . . they feel a park next door will bring the negroes into Ogden Dunes 'roaming around on the beaches!'"[17] As he had expressed approval for her achievements, Strong found sympathy for her dejection: "I know just how you feel when you speak of being discouraged. I have been that way many times, and I have been that way sometimes about the dunes project. However, I am not a defeatist and I still think we are warranted in trying to put something over. You have been just wonderful in doing as much as you have and the Mineral Springs Bog purchase alone justifies what you have done. [Local designations for the Cowles Bog included Mineral Springs Bog and Tamarack Bog.] I did not expect activity during the summer, yet you did a *lot*. In fact you were wonderful."[18]

As a drum-beater and word-spreader, Buell had no equal. In 1954 the council formed an advisory board, which included scientists Edwin Way Teale and Strong; Dunes artist Frank V. Dudley; writers Harriet Cowles and Donald Culross Peattie; nationally known conservationist Richard Pough; philanthropists Mrs. Charles Walgreen and Mrs. Norton W. Barker; and Sheehan. By 1956 the organization had acquired 1,000 members, had set itself a goal of raising $1 million, and had begun collecting signatures on a Save the Dunes petition, which would reach an unbelievable 500,000 names by 1958. The council had spread beyond its established network of support from woman's clubs and had begun to solicit and receive the backing of national conservation groups. It had conducted a tour of the

Dunes for the NPS—the first since the Mather days—and had elicited Director Conrad Wirth's cautious encouragement. Through the advisory board's prestige, recognition by conservationists outside of Indiana, and a broad-based coalition of supporters, the Dunes issue gained legitimacy and publicity. Despite these substantial achievements, however, the Save the Dunes Council did not take a more action-oriented role. Its tax-exempt status prohibited political activity, and its president adamantly opposed enlarging the group's focus. The council remained strictly educational and, as a result, increasingly impotent. From its inception Buell pursued her program of education and exhortation, while Strong worried about the lack of an organization to fight the harbor. Repeatedly he appealed to Buell to remedy the situation: "I hope you and your co-workers will explore the problem of organizing the men of nothern Indiana in this work. . . . And now about the Indiana Dunes Preservation Council! I do not like the inaction of the officers of that organization. . . . Mrs. Strong and I debated yesterday, the question of how much this group is needed, whether the men in it could be drawn into your Save the Dunes Council. How about it?" However, Buell remained stubbornly resistant, agreeing only that if either group made any headway they might "eventually merge." "We [the council] should continue for another year at least in our present setup."[19]

Unable to persuade Buell to enlarge the scope of the Save the Dunes Council, and unable to find new leadership for the Indiana Dunes Preservation Council, Strong grew more and more frustrated and concerned. Eventually, the events of the mid-1950s forced the Save the Dunes Council to change. In 1954 Governor George Craig had proposed that the State Board of Public Harbors and Terminals borrow $3.5 million from the state's revolving fund to purchase 1,500 acres for harbor development. Although the 1955 General Assembly failed to appropriate the funds, it did authorize a state feasibility study, which, not surprisingly, produced a favorable report on the Burns Harbor project. Meanwhile, the Consumers Dunes Corporation had formed in 1954, giving rise to rumors that Midwest Steel would build and Bethlehem would buy. By 1956 Bethlehem had acquired 4,000 acres of the choicest Dunes and the Lakeshore Development Company had purchased 5,200 acres—2,300 from Consumers Dunes—all headed for Bethlehem. To crown the disasters, in 1957 the Indiana legislature appropriated $2 million to purchase the harbor site pending approval from the Army Engineers.

These distressing events caused Buell to consider abandonment of the Dunes project. She saw little hope of meeting her objectives and felt overwhelmed by the magnitude of the opposing forces. Then, in the spring of 1957, acting on a bit of casual advice, an utterly exhausted and discouraged Buell appealed to Emily Taft Douglas, wife of Illinois Senator Paul Douglas. Buell entreated her to influence Douglas to support saving the Indiana Dunes. Buell's successful quest initiated a long, productive, and remarkable collaboration with Douglas and forever changed the substance and direction of the Save the Dunes Council.

PAUL DOUGLAS

People rarely felt neutral about Paul Douglas. Supporters, attracted by his charisma, his uncompromising convictions, and his lofty idealism praised him as an eloquent but lonely defender of right and principle. Detractors scoffed at his unwillingness or inability to accommodate to the political back-scratching required for power on Capitol Hill, at the same time regarding his emotional liberalism as a ploy for political gain. His Senate staff served him with devotion and, after his death, remembered him with a combination of reverence and awe. Even his choicest enemies acknowledged the power of his dogged persistence.

From his youth Douglas needed the independence and missionary spirit of his New England forebears. In Paul's early childhood his mother had died of tuberculosis. His father, a traveling salesman with a "taste for the low life," had often come home in a drunken temper, a practice which had eventually made family life impossible for his second wife and his two sons.[20] She fled with the boys and raised them as her own, inspiring Paul's lifelong love and admiration for her as well as his perpetual antipathy for the absent father. His stepmother personified selflessness, purity, goodness, and right—ideals that motivated Douglas in all his future endeavors.

Douglas spent his formative years in Onowa, Maine, living and working at the hotel owned by his stepmother's family. Primitive, surrounded by mountains, pine woods, and lakes, this isolated resort provided a hard but deeply satisfying pioneer-style life in most seasons. In the summer, however, the hotel clientele brought temporary "civilization" and new ideas, often in the form of muckraking literature, to a mind ready to ignite. Paul greatly loved these surroundings. Eventually, in later years, he found in the Indiana Dunes the only acceptable substitute for Onowa's serenity and renewing qualities.

College life introduced Douglas abruptly into financial independence, due to business setbacks suffered by his family. As he learned to become self-supporting, the study of economics became his "consuming passion" and he tasted, for the first time, the heady excitement of social reform.[21] After college, far from the protective cocoon of Maine's Bowdin, Douglas began graduate studies in economics at Columbia University. He absorbed the inspiring atmosphere of pre–World War I New York as he learned from his Germanically oriented university professors. New York led to the Midwest, where Professor Douglas brought his first wife and found his first teaching job. The marriage did not last, but the Midwest became and remained the resting place for Douglas's intellectual, spiritual, and public preoccupations. By 1930 Douglas had spent a decade in the Midwest and had fallen in love with the scholarly atmosphere of the University of Chicago, where he would teach for twenty-eight years, and with the raw, brawling, endlessly exciting city he learned to call home. He taught, he wrote, he lectured; his academic reputation grew, as did his outrage at social injustice and political corruption.

In 1932 Douglas married Emily Taft. Her father, sculptor Lorado Taft, had championed Indiana Dunes preservation with Jensen and Mather prior to World War I. Emily continued her family's tradition of love for the Lake Michigan wilderness. With royalties from Douglas's books, the couple built a spartan, rustic beach cottage atop a high dune in Dune Acres, Indiana. In the summers and on fine weekends in other seasons they commuted from Hyde Park, the home of the University of Chicago, on the South Shore Railroad. Owning no car, they taxied from the Dune Acres station and carried their simple provisions up the forty-three steps that Douglas himself had constructed. A coterie of Dunes-loving university colleagues and their families owned cottages nearby and provided what little social life Emily and Paul required. For the most part they swam, walked on the beaches and in the woods, wrote, and gratefully escaped from the pressures and obligations of university life. The Douglas family cherished the Dunes as a true retreat, a rare gift of privacy and simplicity, and a lifelong source of physical and spiritual renewal. Well aware of the preservation battles that had taken place earlier, however, they watched and listened for threats of further industrialization. Rumors of steel expansion, which had begun with Midwest Steel's purchase in 1929, ebbed and flowed during their years in the Dunes. Douglas often worried that "it seemed impossible to stop this movement, but one moonlit evening I made a secret pledge that if I could help to do so I would. Twenty years later the way opened and I followed it."[22]

Following in the footsteps of Charles Merriam and other Univer-

sity of Chicago professors, Douglas ran for public office. Their concern about local conditions caused them to descend from their ivory towers into politics. Slated by Chicago's Kelly-Nash machine as a "clean" candidate at a time of particularly widespread corruption, Douglas served as an independent, reform alderman on the city council. Tall, white-haired, aristocratic-looking, an economist of national reputation and importance, Douglas fit the part of outsider perfectly. He substituted idealism, honesty, and long hours for what he lacked in practical knowledge of politics. While a member of the City Council, he met Jacob M. Arvey, whose influence and friendship would greatly affect his later political career. Douglas's aldermanic stint established his priorities and his political style. He grew accustomed to the role of loner and maverick, outvoted by his fellow aldermen, hounded by the Chicago Tribune, laughed at by the grafters, and lauded only by the defenseless, the recipients and beneficiaries of his energies and interest.

Then World War II interrupted Douglas's political aspirations. At the age of fifty, a husband, a father of five children, a respected economics professor and theorist, a man with further political ambition, Douglas confounded his family and followers by enlisting in the U.S. Marines as a private. Despite the outpourings of national pride brought on by the war, patriotism alone could not explain his motives. Seemingly, he did not accept the notion that his mind, his training, and even his political abilities might have had greater value for his country than his aging body and a desire to prove his worth to some unnamed authority. He reveled in the hardships of Marine life; he gloried in his wounds. "A deep wave of exaltation swept through me that at my age I had shed blood in defense of my country."[23] Douglas rose through the ranks despite himself and returned from the war a decorated lieutenant colonel whose useless left arm remained as a testament to his determination and bravery.

In 1948 Illinois's Democratic boss, Jake Arvey, engineered Douglas's nomination to the U.S. Senate. Harry Truman's astonishing victory coincided with those of Douglas's and several other emotional, idealistic, impatient liberals, all of whom remained Senate outsiders throughout the Truman and Eisenhower years. As Congress's most prestigious and academically renowned liberal, Douglas repeatedly failed to achieve his legislative goals: reform of the Senate, revision of tax policy, civil rights, and consumer protection, in part because his ideas preceded a climate for national acceptance and in part because he would not or could not play the Senate game. His refusal stemmed from a powerful conviction that he must deal with issues on their merits, not from a failure to understand the power structure of the Senate. In fact, he had applied the techniques of academic research to a study of the Congress and well understood senatorial alignments and pressure points. Moreover, his daily reading of an array of national newspapers and the Congressional Record raised his level of information and understanding of the issues far above the Senate norms. He did not wheel and deal, preferring debate and study as the right way of politics; his high, implacable standards precluded any action inconsistent with what he thought just.

Midway through his second Senate term Douglas joined forces with Buell and the Save the Dunes Council's effort to preserve his beloved Indiana Dunes. Theirs became a combined effort of rare mutual dignity, respect, and compatibility. Douglas and Buell shared a single-minded belief in the absolute value of their cause as well as the conviction, outwardly at least, that right would triumph. Separated by only a few years in age, they also shared the courteousness of an earlier time. If Buell gratefully deferred to Douglas's leadership, he gallantly consulted her about each action he took. They worked together, harmoniously, always cognizant of the significance of the other's role, always with complete regard for each other and with total commitment to their common goal.

For the second time in forty years a Chicago-based mentor headed the effort to preserve the Indiana Dunes. Although he justified his involvement because of the Dunes's regional and national constituency, Douglas nonetheless first satisfied himself that he could not persuade Indiana's senators, William E. Jenner and Homer Capehart, to sponsor preservation legislation. Initially positive toward Douglas's feeler, "Capehart cautiously postponed an answer until he had consulted the 'boys in Indianapolis.' When Douglas pressed him for a reply, Capehart responded, 'I can't do it, they have other plans.'"[24] On May 26, 1958, Douglas introduced the first of a long series of bills designed to protect and preserve the still unspoiled Porter County Dunes. His first legislative proposal called for the establishment of a national monument, consisting of nearly 4,000 acres and including three-and-one-half miles of shoreline. Like his subsequent bills it included, deliberately, land targeted by the state for its long-desired port and land recently purchased by Bethlehem Steel. Douglas believed these sites to be among the finest in the Dunes; he hoped to acquire them first and to deflect Indiana's opposition by his rhetoric. "It may seem strange that I should come here from Illinois to plead with all my heart for the protection of a small part of the sovereign state of Indiana, and yet I honestly feel that no apology is necessary because the issues at stake are of national significance."[25]

The Indiana press, politicians, and industrial spokesmen joined forces and, with one voice, attacked Douglas. Together they accused him of unwarranted interference in Indiana's affairs, of representing those Chicago interests that sought to prevent Indiana's industrial development, of carpetbagging, of acting as the "third Senator from Indiana," and of wanting a playground outside his own state for blacks and other unwanted Illinois minorities.[26] These frequently embellished accusations haunted Douglas throughout the Dunes controversy. Although his first bill never received a hearing from the Senate committee responsible for national parks, Douglas did not feel defeated. Methodically he began to prepare for the next attempt by lining up regional and national support and by gently orchestrating the tactics of the Save the Dunes Council.

As the activities and successes of the port proponents escalated during the late 1950s, Douglas together with the newer and younger members of the Save the Dunes Council (which now also included men) convinced a reluctant Buell that saving the Dunes required an active effort to prevent a port at Burns Ditch. By 1959 even she recognized that the harbor issue would soon reach a climax. In January a New York court had rejected Bethlehem's proposed merger with Youngstown, thus vastly increasing the likelihood of a Porter County plant. The Indiana General Assembly had passed a resolution memorializing Congress not to buy land in the proposed port site. (In the legislation empowering counties to form port authorities, the General Assembly denied this right to counties having three or more second-class cities, thus removing Lake County from contention.) Midwest Steel had begun construction of a finishing mill, Northern Indiana Public Service Company had constructed a power plant on land included in the Douglas bill, and the St. Lawrence Seaway had opened.

Even though the men who had sat on the Save the Dunes Council board for a few years had now begun to dominate the proceedings, they seemed as reluctant as Buell in deciding to fight the port. Such activity ran counter to the self-image of the organization. Its members, unschooled in the dirty business of political warfare, denied the necessity for confrontation. Two newcomers, Leonard Rutstein, a Chicago lawyer hired by the council, and Thomas Dustin, an environmentally aware public relations adviser from Fort Wayne, finally convinced Buell and the rest of the board that they could not win the battle on its merits. According to Dustin, "It took a professional PR man sitting in on a meeting of the council to turn the trick. The public is not yet ready to back dunes over steel mills. They will opt for pay checks, not picnics. You need an issue that everyone can understand."[27]

Douglas took an active role from the introduction of his national monument bill in 1958 until he left the Senate. Kenneth Gray, Douglas's only legislative assistant, estimated that he spent one-third of his time during the early 1960s working on Dunes legislation—a monumental amount to allocate to any one piece of legislation.[28] Although Douglas looked on the Dunes as his most compelling and personally appealing project, he might have felt hard pressed to call it his most important. As he pushed ahead with his series of bills, he pursued two main avenues toward their successful realization. He concentrated, first, on creating a dependable coalition of allies— Hyde Park liberals and intellectuals who had a long-standing affection for the Dunes as well as Chicago Democrats, politicians, labor leaders, and espousers of public-spirited causes on whom he could count to rally behind him. Second, by inspired use of the media and by dogged, persistent, repetitive, personal appeals to any and all who would listen, he began to build a national constituency for the Indiana Dunes. He featured the publicity movie filmed by the Save the Dunes Council at a series of luncheons designed to introduce the Dunes to the uninitiated. He did not restrain passionate rhetoric in his speeches to the Congress. Shamelessly, he clutched a portfolio of Dunes photographs under his withered left arm, buttonholing colleagues as he marched from his office to the Capitol, exhorting, pleading, demanding, and begging attention from those who had the power to help. All the while, Douglas found time to encourage and advise his council friends in almost daily letters. He told them what approach to take, what data to collect, and how to soothe their friends and rankle their enemies. These messages never voiced discouragement. Under his patient tutoring the Save the Dunes Council began to emerge as a potent political instrument, advocating tactics that the women gathered on Buell's porch only a few years before had not imagined.

The election of Vance Hartke, an Indiana Democrat, to the U.S. Senate in 1958 signalled a shift from the southern power brokers in the Senate to domination by northern liberal Democrats. Neither Hartke's election nor that of Democrat Matthew Welsh as governor in 1960 had any positive effect on Dunes preservation. It took the election of John F. Kennedy to begin the first real movement toward a national park. More than any other political event, save the return of Douglas to a third Senate term, Kennedy's ascension decisively affected the outcome of the Dunes struggle. With a new Democratic administration, easier passage of Douglas's bills seemed possible. Kennedy, who had fought for the establishment of a national seashore on Cape Cod, appeared more favorably disposed toward conservation issues than did his predecessor. Moreover, the New Frontier brought Arizona's Stewart Udall to lead the Department of the Interior. An avowed conservationist, Udall had pledged to upgrade the NPS and seemed likely to support Douglas's cause. In addition, the 1960 election produced new legislators, more liberal, more in harmony with Douglas's concerns, and more likely to come through with votes when they counted.

Guided by Douglas, the Save the Dunes Council devised three basic strategies to fight the port. Specifics did not evolve as the result of a long-range tactical blueprint. Instead, they appeared piecemeal, as events, circumstances, and inspiration dictated. The first strategy sought to focus national attention on the disputed 10,000 acres of duneland and to keep it there by increasingly sophisticated use of the media and public relations techniques. The second strategy took the council down previously uncharted paths through the courts, foreshadowing subsequent and eventually successful legal disposition of environmental and public interest issues. The third strategy created in-house technical and engineering expertise capable of refuting official data, whether from the Army Engineers, the state, the Port Commission, or one of the many private studies commissioned by port proponents. Douglas functioned in Washington, attempting time and time again to achieve national preservation, while the council focused on events in Indiana, attempting to buy some all-too-scarce and precious time.

On July 23, 1961, Douglas succeeded in bringing some of the people who mattered in Washington to see the Dunes for themselves. Douglas and Udall joined Senate Interior Committee members Alan Bible and Frank Moss and NPS Director Wirth for a highly publicized tour. Local dignitaries, including Mayors George Chacharis of Gary, Walter M. Jerose of East Chicago, Edward C. Dowling of Hammond, Mary Berchic of Whiting, and Richard J. Daley of Chicago, together with Representative Ray J. Madden of Indiana's first district, also participated in the ballyhooed event that drew a crowd of more than a thousand.[29] The Save the Dunes Council had organized both the tour and the spectators who came, despite the rain, to hear the dignitaries praise and support preserving the Dunes as a national park.

Second District Congressman Charles Halleck considered the council's failure to include him among the notables a "personal affront."[30] According to Halleck, Democratic Governor Welsh and Democratic Senator Hartke felt similarly nettled at not receiving invitations. Though demonstrators opposed to preservation turned out with signs reading "Let Illinois Have Its Senator Back" and "Should an Illinois Senator Run Indiana?", the volume of "Save the Dunes" placards made them virtually unnoticeable.[31] The tour attracted wide local press coverage and became one of the first events to direct national attention to the Dunes controversy. This result greatly satisfied Dustin, who had long sought a way to get the Dunes issue in front of a national audience and keep it there. While the tour opened the way to wider recognition, it could not rival the effectiveness of the Reuterskiold drama that unfolded in 1962.

THE BEST SINGLE STORY WE HAVE EVER HAD

Late in 1962 Dr. Virginia Reuterskiold and her physician husband, Knute, rejected an offer of more than $100,000 ($250,000 in 1980 dollars) for their ten acres and seventy-year-old house in the Dunes. As staunch supporters of the Save the Dunes Council, the elderly Reuterskiolds had attempted to prevent Bethlehem from building a new steel mill by refusing to sell their land to the company. Their modest holding had commanded this immodest sum because it sat strategically in the midst of Bethlehem's 4,000-acre tract and represented a major thorn in the steel company's side. Upon hearing the news, Dustin recognized that the Reuterskiold saga exhibited all of the elements necessary to capture the national imagination. He had searched without success for such a vehicle since becoming public relations director for the Save the Dunes Council and now could not believe his good fortune. Dustin spent a moment of sheer pleasure fantasizing the copy to be made from the specter of the mild, nature-loving Reuterskiolds single-handedly restraining the force of tons of steel. Then he set to work, prepared to "get every mile out of it that is possible."[32]

Dustin started his blitz with immediate releases to UPI and AP, both in Indianapolis and Chicago, followed by special delivery copies to the wire services in Washington. He called Don Underwood of Life *magazine, who suggested contacting Paul Welch of the Chicago* Life *bureau. Underwood assured Dustin that "*Life *would definitely be interested in a Reuterskiold story." He composed a press release and communicated the substance to Interior Secretary Udall. Dustin wrote to attorney and council board member Ed Osann,* urging him to call Ed Gorlick of the Chicago Daily News who "would give it a real sendoff." He instructed Osann to contact also Gorden Englehart of the Louisville Courier-Journal and Don Janson of the New York Times. He recommended that NBC's commentator, Len O'Connor, get the material, that same evening if necessary, to allow him "a special break . . . as far as timing goes."[33]

Dustin worked with manic intensity, knowing that "time was of the essence." He viewed the item as "the best single story we have ever had."[34] It guaranteed publicity and, for Dustin, bad publicity did not exist. It catapulted the issue into the news; it forced people to notice the conflict; it projected the Indiana Dunes as a national concern.

Dustin's press release presented all the components of the Dunes drama in simple, direct, black-and-white terms. It did not indulge in subtlety; no reader could have failed to identify either the heroes or the villains. In the release, purportedly from the lips of Buell, the Reuterskiolds' decision emerged as "a dedicated and heroic act of an unselfish family which places long-term public benefit and scientific value above personal fortune and profit."[35] Dustin utilized a "high source in the Interior Department" to say, "This development is a significant indication of the dedicated support the save the dunes effort is attracting."[36] His document stressed the achievements of the Save the Dunes Council and the failures of its industrial opponents. It pitted the small, humble individual against a greedy, mechanized giant, the efforts of scientists and educators against the avarice of the Indiana Port Commission and Bethlehem Steel, the good of the nature-lovers against the evil of the Duneswreckers.

Both Dustin's hunch and his hyperbole paid off. The national press did take up the Reuterskiold story, and, as Dustin had predicted, the Dunes controversy remained alive to a national audience in the years that followed. With the exception of Indiana newspapers, which almost uniformly approved the port effort and avoided mention of saving the Dunes—so much so that Dustin and others posited a deliberate southern Indiana press blackout—newspapers far from Indiana followed the conflict and reported it in Dustin's fashion. By reducing a complex issue to its simplest terms, Dustin and the national press allowed the public easy grasp of the dimensions of the problem and increasing identification with the merits of the Save the Dunes Council's solution.

As early as 1959 the council had formed a legal committee consisting of board members, attorneys, and Buell. It functioned as an ad hoc decision-making body often operating in secrecy with a kind of paranoid intensity. After failing to find an Indiana attorney to represent them, the committee hired a young Chicago lawyer named Len Rutstein. With constant consultation between the committee and Douglas, Rutstein prepared a long series of cases that he later described as "a catalog of legal disasters in which the Save the Dunes Council sued and lost, not in a single instance achieving a victory on the merits."[37] Several problems plagued Rutstein in all his Dunes cases. First, he believed that no issue even peripherally connected with the proposed port would get a fair hearing in Indiana. He attempted, therefore, to remove his cases from the Indiana courts to the federal courts, where he assumed the presence of unbiased judges. At that time, however, Rutstein could not find any easy means of gaining access to the federal courts. No law yet existed (and would not until the National Environmental Policy Act [NEPA] of 1969) that allowed him to sue in the federal courts on environmental grounds. Moreover, he often failed to find any adequate grounds upon which the federal courts would accept jurisdiction. Unfortunately, Rutstein and the Save the Dunes Council broke legal ground too early. By the late 1960s, class-action suits on a wide variety of public interest issues had become common in the federal courts because new legislation provided ample justification to sustain a federal jurisdiction.

The court action that best illustrates the crucial nature of obtaining a federal jurisdiction began when the Reuterskiolds negotiated with Bethlehem and Rutstein represented them in their refusal to sell. By 1963 they believed that Bethlehem would go ahead and build the mill around their small parcel. Having a better use for the money, they at last capitulated and agreed to sell. Save the Dunes Council Board member Herbert Read had conjured up the better use for the Reuterskiolds' newly acquired cash.

Read had identified a small piece of land—about an acre depending on the lake level—without which, he firmly believed, the state could not build the port. Borrowing Bethlehem's payment from the Reuterskiolds, the council bought this strategic parcel of land in the port site. While the purchase never prevented construction of the port as Read and the others had envisioned, it did cause substantial delays for the state. Unable to construct its harbor without this land, the State of Indiana proceeded to condemn it. Under Indiana law the state had the right to take the property first and then let the owner litigate the value. To do this, Indiana only needed to establish its right to condemn. Rutstein built his case on a statutory procedure allowing a challenge to this right. He conducted it with utmost care, because he believed that the condemnation issue contained a constitutional violation—grounds, at last, for access to the federal courts. Rutstein explained:

> Our basic argument was that there was no public interest being served. All the figures established by the Army Corps [of Engineers] indicated that the port would be solely for the benefit of two steel mills and therefore it was a private, not a public thing. We had a series of about thirty legal objections to the state's authority to condemn.
> There was a substantial hassle over the filing of objections. We decided to first file the objections so that our challenge of the state's authority to condemn would be "of record." The state would thereby be prevented from taking possession of the property until the trial on that issue had taken place. Then, *immediately* after filing the objections, we would seek to remove the case to federal court on the grounds that to condemn for private use exceeded the authority of the state making its attempt a violation of the 14th Amendment and therefore, a constitutional issue. It was critical that the filing be done in that sequence.[38]

Rutstein considered that protection of his right to challenge the constitutionality of Indiana's proceedings took priority as his most urgent consideration. With the crucial sequence in mind, he hand-carried the necessary documents to the court clerk and had the exact times of the filing stamped on them. Using the time machine in the office, he stamped in his objections to the proceeding and two minutes later stamped in a motion to remove. "The first question at the beginning of the trial was whether we were entitled to try the right of the State to condemn, or whether that issue had already been determined and thus all we were entitled to was a trial for damages. The judge ruled that we hadn't filed our objection and therefore the only thing before the court was the question of the damages. He ordered the condemnation forthwith and proceeded to a trial on the amount of money we were entitled to receive for the land."[39]

Rutstein protested that he had indeed filed objections, that he had filed them in the correct order, and that he possessed copies of the hand-stamped documents to prove his contention. The judge recalled otherwise and, despite overwhelming evidence to the contrary, refused to take it into account. He stuck to his story that Rutstein had presented the motions in reverse order. The judge's position prevailed. He ruled that he did not have to try the issue of the state's right to condemn, that he had already granted the state authority to proceed, and that only the amount Indiana owed the Save the Dunes Council constituted grounds for a trial.

Thus, even when constitutional grounds existed, the council never could have gained access to the federal court. Immediately after the trial for damages, Rutstein took concurrent appeals to the Seventh Circuit Court of Appeals and to the Supreme Court of Indiana. He attached copies of the documents in the sequence filed and "let them sit in both courts for a period of time." Before the resolution of the appeals, however, legislation establishing the Indiana Dunes National Lakeshore passed the Congress. The council settled with the Port Commission, receiving "a nice chunk of money" from the state, paid off Virginia Reuterskiold, and put the remainder in the coffers to carry on the fight.[40]

Read, however, never agreed with Rutstein's contention that the port site purchase had served its purpose. He never changed his view that the tactic could have and should have prevented the port's construction. He blamed Rutstein for its failure. In his letter of June 6, 1966, Read expressed his dissatisfaction to the Save the Dunes Council board. Its tone ranged between earned petulance and righteous outrage.

> The land was purchased for the purpose of furthering the Indiana Dunes National Lakeshore in decent and respectable form. The specific objective was to prevent construction of a harbor until such time that the Lakeshore was a reality, including some portion of Bethlehem's properties. . . . As the strategy was originally conceived, such objectives would have been possible . . . the purchase of the land was a bold step toward the offensive . . . for the first week after our land purchase we had the possibility of total victory in our grasp . . . caution and inactivity prevailed and one by one the opportunities for the necessary offensive action were lost. Even worse was the unwillingness of our legal counsel to devote the time for research, preparation and securing of needed documents.[41]

Unswerving belief in total victory had fired Read's inventiveness and unceasing activity for more than six years. He could not accept the reality of partial victory—a port and a park—but none of his colleagues begrudged him his weary outburst.

Less than three months later, after eight years of unpaid work for the council, Rutstein submitted his bill—the grand total due as of September 1, 1966: $25,513.53. Funds to pay him came from the sale of Cowles Bog to the Indiana Dunes National Lakeshore.

The Save the Dunes Council's decision to fight the port, head-on, required development of in-house engineering expertise. When asked how he came to be a technical expert in the intricacies of harbor construction, Read responded: "Probably because I didn't know I couldn't do it. My training as an architect was adequate, all I needed was knowledge of the formalized steps the Corps [of Army Engineers] took. Once knowing that, I found myself taking the same steps by deduction."[42] Read's deductions, however, led to conclusions far different from those of the Army Engineers. They provided the foundation for the port-fighting strategy followed by the council's Engineering Committee: architect Read and engineer George Anderson.

Political events in Indiana in 1960 had made a new strategy imperative. By the time Governor Welsh took office, he had already dashed the council's optimistic hope for support in Indianapolis. The first Democrat since Paul McNutt to occupy the governor's mansion, Welsh lost no time in sounding more Republican than his opposition when it came to supporting the port. During his campaign he had promised to defer a decision on the port's location until he had completed a study of the entire shoreline. That promise consisted of campaign rhetoric and not much else; Welsh never honored it. Instead, he pressed hard for action on the port. First he created the Indiana Port Commission, which replaced the Indiana Board of Harbors and Terminals and which had as its stated goal the construction of Burns Ditch Harbor. In addition to lobbying for federal funds and engaging in the by now familiar pursuit of trying to persuade Midwest and Bethlehem to make firm commitments to build, the commission went one step further than the agency that preceded it. It exercised the new authority to issue revenue bonds for land purchase, thus freeing appropriations from the whims of the legislature.

Prodded by the Save the Dunes Council, which for the first time had a full-time lobbyist in Indianapolis, and by increasingly unfavorable press coverage, Welsh and the Port Commission held a hearing in May 1961, allegedly to determine the best site for a harbor. Anderson called the hearing a sham at best and at worst "a fraud and an insult to the public."[43] Just six months later, in November 1961, Midwest Steel's president disclosed that fifteen months prior to the hearing the State of Indiana had entered into a binding contract with that company fixing the location of the harbor.

The council's first tactical priority, therefore, became promoting an alternate site for the harbor and its second was providing the engineering and economic back-up data to refute all claims to the Burns Ditch location. Although harbor surveys of various sorts had cost hundreds of thousands of dollars over the years, Read and Anderson proposed to beat the experts at their own game for nothing. The Army Engineers' favorable report of 1960 had attributed 97.3 percent of the benefit to the traffic of the two proposed steel mills. The council hammered away at the unjustified expenditure of federal funds when so great a part of the direct benefit would go almost exclusively to the two mills. The council's strident exposure of the state's attempt to build a private harbor with public funds accomplished a number of things. First, it interrupted what port proponents anticipated as an orderly progression of the proposal from the district engineer's office to the Secretary of the Army, to the congressional Public Works Committees, and finally to the Congress for approval. Instead, the proposal got routed back to the Army Engineers for further study. Second, the shrill campaign forced the Army Engineers to hold a new hearing on the matter in 1961. Third, it caused Interior Secretary Udall to speak at the hearing. Despite meticulous refutation of port proponents' data by Read and Anderson, and despite Udall's intervention, the Army Engineers' revised report, issued in 1962, while changing the figures somewhat, did not change the conclusion. It again affirmed the economic feasibility of the proposed harbor.

Read and Anderson found the 1962 report riddled with errors and accordingly requested a new hearing and ninety days to prepare rebuttal. Although they made the request to the congressional Rivers and Harbors Committee's Board of Engineers, that seven-man board consisted entirely of Army Engineers who promptly denied both requests.

Douglas, angered by the 1962 report, vowed to fight the port proponents "before the Budget Bureau, in the House and in the Senate with every bit of strength we've got."[44] Anderson and Read had their work cut out for them, because the fight that Douglas planned to wage depended on an economic analysis more detailed than anything they had yet produced. Completed in August 1962, their study contained twenty-six pages, including twenty-eight tables dealing with the costs and benefits of the proposed harbor. Though the Army Engineers only produced three pages and two tables, their conclusions prevailed.

As a result of the Army Engineers' static position, the Save the Dunes Council decided to press for a review of the economic feasibility of an old proposal: a harbor straddling the border between Illinois and Indiana. This tactic had the obvious advantage of a built-in constituency ready to join forces with the council in opposition to the Burns Harbor project. Originally proposed in 1918, the Illiana or Tri-Cities Harbor never materialized because Indiana politicians eschewed any activity that involved cooperation with Illinois, even if potentially beneficial. Useful in the 1960s as another buyer of time, the Tri-Cities proposal additionally provided the council with some convenient rhetoric: park supporters did not oppose a port for Indiana, they strongly supported jobs and industry, but neither industry nor the port needed to exist in the Dunes that they wanted to preserve when these groups could find better sites. At the same time that the council denounced the Army Engineers for finding Burns Harbor economically feasible, its members promoted Tri-Cities. According to the University of Chicago's Harold Mayer, one of its chief advocates, this plan had always lacked a favorable benefit-cost ratio. With the exception of Lake County public officials, no one in the Indiana political establishment took notice of the Tri-Cities Harbor proposal.

Just as the council's legal battles had never once succeeded on merit, the tactics of its Engineering Committee probably never changed a single conclusion of the Army Engineers. Both strategies did cause substantial delay in the outcome of the Dunes conflict. During the months and years of slowdown, national attention remained riveted on the Indiana controversy. Gradually at first, and then with increasing frequency, Dunes preservation became synonymous with changing land use values nationally. With the advent of the New Frontier, preservation gained a new respectability as well as a more promising climate for executive support and legislative action.

Meanwhile, the Save the Dunes Council had come of age. During its first ten years the organization grew into an effective precursor of the powerful single-interest lobbying groups that, to the dismay of Congress, multiplied in the 1970s. Its petition and fund drives of the early 1950s introduced the Dunes environmental dilemma to a public outside of Indiana. The Council's early "tea party" demeanor slowly dissipated with the increasing male domination of the group's policy-making function. Men's leadership caused essential changes in direction and allowed the organization to become politically focused and more action-oriented. Douglas's devotion and efforts in Washington meant the council did not have to organize political activity there. Instead members concentrated political work exclusively in Indiana.

After Douglas's departure from the Senate, the Save the Dunes Council learned, from necessity, how to manipulate the Washington scene. Their mentor gone, Save the Duners eventually performed his many roles with admirable success. In 1966 the Internal Revenue Service revoked the tax-exempt status of the Save the Dunes Council because of blatant lobbying for Dunes legislation. Sylvia Troy, the council's second president, believes, in retrospect, that the group's real political stance dates from this act. No longer required to abstain from such activity, the council began to take an aggressively active political role. Its leadership raised substantial contributions and campaigned for sympathetic candidates in local, state, and national elections. Had Buell lived to see the Save the Dunes Council's participation in the elections of 1976 and 1980, she would not have recognized the tough, mature organization she had spawned. Perhaps she would not have liked it either.

NOTES

1. Conrad L. Wirth, *Parks, Politics and the People* (Norman: University of Oklahoma Press, 1980), p. 73.

2. Ibid., pp. 126, 127, 150.

3. Ibid., p. 234.

4. Joseph C. Goulden, *The Best Years, 1945–1949* (New York: Atheneum, 1976), p. 8.

5. Lawrence M. Preston, *The Port of Indiana Burns Waterway Harbor*, Bureau of Business Research, Graduate School of Business (Bloomington: Indiana University, n.d.), p. 14.

6. Ibid., p. 17.

7. Ibid., p. 18.

8. Authors' interview with George Applegate, executive secretary, East Chicago Chamber of Commerce when the Indiana Dunes Preservation Council began, East Chicago, Ind., 1977.

9. Ibid.

10. M. Reuben Strong to Dorothy Buell, Feb. 24, 1952, Chicago Conservation Council Files, Chicago Academy of Sciences Collection.

11. "Heroine of Indiana Dunes," *Chicago Sun-Times*, Dec. 1, 1966, p. 52.

12. Authors' interview with Tom Dustin, Huntington, Ind., 1979.

13. Composite portrait drawn from interviews with original Save the Dunes Council members, Laura Gent, Lois Howes, and John and Hazel Bowers, and also later members, Sylvia Troy, Tom Dustin, and Leonard Rutstein.

14. Authors' interview with Laura Gent, Ogden Dunes, Ind., 1976.

15. Buell to Strong, July 14, 1952, Chicago Conservation Council Files.

16. Strong to Buell, Aug. 9, 1952, Chicago Conservation Council Files.

17. Buell to Strong, Oct. 7, 1953, Chicago Conservation Council Files.

18. Strong to Buell, Oct. 12, 1953, Chicago Conservation Council Files.

19. Strong to Buell, June 22, 1953, Buell to Strong, July 2, 1953, Chicago Conservation Council Files.

20. Paul Douglas, *In the Fullness of Time* (New York: Harcourt Brace, Jovanovich, 1972), p. 5.

21. Ibid., p. 24.

22. Ibid., p. 77.

23. Ibid., p. 123.

24. Ibid., p. 537.

25. U.S. Congress, Senate, Senator Paul H. Douglas speaking for the "Preservation of the Indiana Dunes as a National Monument," 85th Cong., 2d sess., May 26, 1958, *Congressional Record*, 104:8468–70.

26. Douglas, *Fullness of Time*, p. 537.

27. Dustin interview.

28. Authors' interview with Kenneth Gray, Washington, 1977.

29. "Udall: 'Need Area for Park,'" Hammond *Times*, July 24, 1961.

30. Ibid.

31. Ibid.

32. Thomas Dustin to Edward Osann, Oct. 29, 1962, Save the Dunes Council Files.

33. All quotes in this paragraph are taken from the letter cited in n. 32.

34. Ibid.

35. Press Release, Save the Dunes Council, Nov. 1, 1962, Save the Dunes Council Files.

36. Ibid.

37. Authors' interview with Leonard Rutstein, Chicago, 1976.

38. Ibid.

39. Ibid.

40. Ibid.

41. Herbert Read to Save the Dunes Council Board, June 6, 1966, Save the Dunes Council Files.

42. Authors' interview with Herbert Read, Beverly Shores, Ind., 1978.

43. Chicago Conservation Council, minutes of meeting of Jan. 16, 1964, Save the Dunes Council Files.

44. Gary *Post Tribune*, quoted in Preston, *Port of Indiana*, p. 37.

7 A Shaky Peace

The late 1950s and early 1960s saw Indiana politics lose the doctrinaire, conservative image of its Republican leadership. In 1958, the same year the John Birch Society was formed in Indianapolis, Hoosiers elected Vance Hartke to the U.S. Senate. Indiana voters followed up this first Democratic senatorial victory in twenty years by electing Democrat Matthew E. Welsh as governor in 1960. He and the only Democratic state senate in twenty-two years entered office together. Not yet satisfied with the changes, Indiana's electorate replaced conservative Republican Senator Homer Capehart with Democrat Birch Bayh in 1962. Voters produced another Democratic governor, Roger Brannigan, in 1964 and in the same year elected the first Democratically controlled General Assembly in twenty-eight years. (Long overdue legislative reapportionment contributed to this latter victory.) In 1967 Gary, Indiana, elected Richard Hatcher mayor, joining Cleveland as the first of major American cities to have black men in the top municipal post.

Although by any measure an active two-party state, Indiana had always appeared to lean in the Republican direction. On the state level, although Hoosiers had elected nine Republican governors and eight Democrats since 1900, they had consistently put the Republicans in charge of one or both houses of the legislature between 1939 and 1963. In national elections, between the end of World War I and the late 1950s, many more Hoosier Republicans than Democrats filled the House and Senate seats in Washington. Of these "[most] have been almost always conservative and frequently provincial and isolationist."[1] Moreover, in the seventeen presidential elections between 1900 and 1964, Indiana voted Democratic only four times: for Woodrow Wilson in 1912, for Franklin Roosevelt in 1932 and 1936, and for Lyndon Johnson in 1964. By 1964 only second district Representative Charlie Halleck survived the Democratic rout, and even he could number his days.

The political turnaround of the 1960s took place both because of significant changes in Indiana as a state and the condition of its major political parties. All the elements for a long-lasting, if not permanent, shift to a Democratic Indiana seemed in place. Despite virtually automatic Republican victories through the mid-1950s, supported by bipartisan-in-name-only groups like the State Chamber of Commerce and the Indiana Farm Bureau, the times and demography had ripened for change. Industrialization, with its shift of population from the cornfields to the cities, continued and accelerated. Of the ninety-two Indiana counties, the fourteen most urban contained 60 percent of the population by 1960. The five leading urban counties contained 40 percent of the state's citizens, with 25 percent residing in the largest two. Less than 10 percent of the people still farmed. Moreover, of the new mass of urban workers, more than half a million belonged to labor unions; they repudiated Indiana's lingering Republican conservatism. Union members found the Republicans' right-to-work law of 1957 particularly galling. Elderly voters bristled at the Republican state chairman's attack on Social Security in 1959.

Nor did Indiana fail to conform to national trends, albeit with fewer pronounced changes. The state's black population, which almost tripled between 1950 and 1965, turned to the Democratic party on the national wave of civil rights enthusiasm that helped to elect John F. Kennedy. In addition, Indiana reflected the nation's increasingly younger population, half of which had yet to reach its twenty-sixth year by 1970. Nationally, 53 percent of these young urban Americans regarded themselves as Democrats in 1965, as compared with 38 percent in 1940. While not as great a percentage of young Hoosiers identified with the Democrats, enough so labeled themselves to help alter the political complexion of the state. Indiana's Democratic party gained a large urban vote from blacks, the young, people with foreign ancestry, and religious minorities. Hoosiers of German-Lutheran descent who had voted Republican since 1920 switched back to the Democrats in 1958, 1960, and 1962, lured by German-Lutheran candidates Hartke, Welsh, and Bayh.

By 1960 Welsh's control of the statehouse assured good health and riches to Indiana's Democratic party. Through its 2 percent club—"a two percent levy on the annual salaries of approximately 8,000 state employees who were outside of civil service"—and other assessments, the party could afford to wage substantially funded, winning campaigns.[2] The Democrats engaged in such revenue-collecting practices with impunity since the Republicans, who "followed the same time-hallowed means of raising funds when they were in office," felt little inclination to criticize.[3]

By contrast, the Republican party had problems, some of longer duration than its members recognized. In the preceding decade the Republican percentage of the off-year election vote had slid from 56.2 in 1946 to 53.9 in 1950 to 51.4 in 1954 to a disastrous 44.2 in 1958.[4] Party members had paid scant attention to the political implications of a changing Indiana. They sat "immobilized, wedded to orthodox conservatism, oriented to the business and rural viewpoints, hoping like Dickens' Micawber that something would surely turn up."[5] They made little attempt to deliver attractive candidates to the voters. To make matters worse, highway scandals during the administration of Republican Governor George Craig (1952–56) shocked even those Hoosiers who usually closed their eyes to political corruption. The resulting exposés contributed, in part, to Democratic victories in 1958, 1960, and 1962. GOP losses in those years, however, really stemmed from the sharp division within the party between the Republican professionals and party ideologues. "The professionals, as a group, were not very concerned with ideology. Their main interest was in winning elections in order to control the emoluments of power. Much of the professionals' time was spent in placating and soothing the injured feelings of the party's conservatives while attempting to secure the nomination of candidates palatable to urban Indiana."[6] Party leaders blamed the ideological split on Senator William E. Jenner. Earlier "Republican moderates [had] devoted considerable energy and ingenuity in efforts to keep [Jenner] out of Indiana."[7] They banished Jenner, who badly wanted the governorship, to the Senate in 1946. Such moderates as Governor Ralph F. Gates and Halleck reacted warily to Jenner. Realizing that he might well win the statehouse, they contrived to keep him in "this crazy Communist joint"—Jenner's designation for Washington—until 1958. In that year, to his great relief, Jenner returned to "America," as he labeled his Hoosier home, to divide and weaken his party. When the Republican ideologues again took charge, voters defected to the Democrats.

A new breed of Indiana Democrat—Hartke, Welsh, Bayh, Roush, Brannigan—took over. Perhaps a shade or two to the right of Democrats in other places, varying markedly among themselves in the amount they leaned left of center, they nonetheless all looked like liberals as compared with the Capeharts, Jenners, Hallecks, and Jacksons who had complacently dominated Indiana politics for so many years. That the newcomers sometimes abandoned their erudition for a folksier, Hoosier twang when they stumped the back home byways should have surprised no one. While they could afford a liberal attitude toward issues in faraway Washington, the expression of such views, face-to-face, on home territory, often required verbal sleight-of-hand. Though voters became Democrats, they did not automatically become liberals. Right-wing Democrat Alabama Governor George Wallace cashed in on almost 30 percent of the Democratic vote in Indiana's 1964 primary and garnered 12 percent of the Hoosier vote in the 1968 general election. While the state as a whole experienced political upheaval, no such ferment occurred in the second district. There Halleck reigned as always, not recognizing that he, too, faced an uncertain future.

CHARLES A. HALLECK

After he retired from the Congress, Charlie Halleck lived with his memories in a characterless tract house that stood in a new section at the edge of Rensselaer, Indiana. Only the two long black Cadillacs in the driveway and the stone elephant on the lawn distinguished it from its neighbors. Nearby the shopping centers and fast-food franchises encroached on the somnambulant, once typical Indiana town, which the almost eighty-year-old Halleck now called home. Though lonely and bitter and not yet adjusted to the death of his wife of many years, Halleck could still muster more than a trace of the folksy Hoosier charm he had flaunted like a trademark during the height of his power. He spent his days puttering about the house or driving a gleaming black car to one of the many local functions honoring him and the glories of his notable political past. Halleck retained vigorous memories of his thirty-four years in the House, of the power he had wielded, and of the further power he had coveted.

Halleck considered himself a political moderate; the facts did not always support his perception.[8] Although he had supported Indiana's Wendell Willkie for the Republican presidential nomination in 1940 and 1944, he soon abandoned Willkie and grew steadily more conservative. By 1948 he had become Thomas Dewey's man in the House. Always a pragmatist, he had tempered his rightism with political reality. By the early 1950s he had abandoned his longtime conservatism to become a middle-of-the-roader in tune with the views of the Dwight Eisenhower administration. In outrage Senator Jenner used the issue to lead an unsuccessful dump-liberal-Halleck attack. By 1964, however, Halleck again courted the conservative wing, seconding Barry Goldwater's nomination for the presidency. "I didn't want to do it," Halleck remembered, "[but] there were Goldwater clubs set up in Porter County—those people thought I was a wild-eyed radical."[9]

Meanwhile, in 1947, the House had elected Halleck majority leader at the start of his seventh term. By 1948 he hoped and expected to become the vice-presidential candidate. Convinced that Dewey's advisor, Herbert Brownell, had offered him the second spot, Halleck never lost his sense of betrayal at its failure to materialize. Dewey, however, denied any knowledge of such a commitment. Halleck badly wanted the vice-presidency and bitterly decried Eisenhower's selection of Richard Nixon. Having failed to get the nomination, he would gladly have settled for Speaker of the House. However, when Joe Martin became Speaker for the second time, Halleck could only fume and wait for revenge. For four years he stood poised to oust Martin from his twenty-year post as floor leader but failed twice because twice Eisenhower refused to support him. By 1959, however, Halleck finally had the votes to bolster his ambition. At that time a coalition of fourteen disgruntled Republican members, including Michigan's Gerald R. Ford, blamed November's election disaster on Martin's lack of leadership. The fourteen, who rarely agreed on anything, felt in perfect accord about getting rid of Martin and replacing him with Halleck. This time Eisenhower promised to stay out of the fight and by a close vote, 74–70, the rebels maneuvered Halleck into the top spot.

His leadership style—personal and highly partisan—did revive the demoralized Republicans. He courted selected members in small, informal sessions called the clinic by those on the inside. Martin and the outs referred to the clinic as Charlie's drinking room, a not entirely inaccurate designation.

Though less powerful than he would have preferred, Halleck nonetheless was a formidable enemy to Paul Douglas and the Save the Dunes Council. In addition to his philosophic differences with Douglas about the best use for the disputed duneland, Halleck had developed an intense, personal, and long-lasting animosity toward the Illinois Senator. Eleven years after the Indiana Dunes National Lakeshore became a reality, the mere mention of Douglas's name continued to infuriate Halleck. His antipathy carried over to the Save the Dunes Council as well.

> I won't challenge the motives of some of the people involved in the park effort—some were undoubtedly very sincere about it, but some were making big money out of it, the Save the Dunes Council, no doubt. And there were others, certainly from Illinois, who didn't want Indiana to be in any sort of competitive

position. In fact, they wanted a playground for the great mass
of people in Chicago, especially that part of Illinois closest to
the Dunes [Chicago's South Side, predominantly poor and
black]. All through this controversy, and it finally got to be a
real vicious sort of struggle, I've wondered why the hell Doug-
las didn't take some of the North Shore.

I remember going over on the Senate side to testify for the
port and against the park and there were a bunch of women
from that area with placards on who sat right up front and
sneered at me. I can deal any one of them all the aces and
spades and still beat them any time. It was a damn, disrepu-
table, rude operation—the more they did, the madder I got.

Yet Halleck grudgingly admired Douglas's persistence:

Douglas was indefatigable in pressing. I remember one time he
pulled up his sleeve and said, "Take my blood, take my blood."
I might well have accommodated him . . . hell, he was kind of
a phony in my opinion.[10]

Kennedy's victory in 1960 and the election of Democratic Sena-
tors Hartke and Bayh to replace conservative Republicans Jenner
and Capehart set the stage for the establishment of a national park
in Halleck's district over his most vigorous objections. Halleck didn't
care that the new Indiana Democrats in Washington wanted the
port as much as he. To his mind, they, like Douglas, had no busi-
ness interfering in his territory. He adhered to a primary, unwritten
rule of the Congress—you don't put parks in the districts of mem-
bers who don't want them. And Halleck didn't want this one! "Most
of the land consists of buckerbrush you wouldn't be caught dead
on."[11]

By the end of 1962 some of the younger Republicans in the House
began to question the quality of Halleck's leadership; they had little
use for his methods. They perceived his cronyism as contributing
to a negative Republican image; they objected to his tendency to
oppose for opposition's sake. With a display of infighting skill that
Halleck, especially, could have admired, they contrived to get rid
of him. These critics had discovered a useful statistic. A majority
of the Republican members soon to convene for the 88th Congress
would arrive with six years or less of seniority. Among this group
the makings of an insurrection surely existed. The rebels recog-
nized that they lacked the votes to attack either Halleck himself or
Republican whip Les Arends immediately. Instead, they began with
Charles Hoeven, chairman of the House Republican Conference.
By a vote of 86 to 78, they replaced Hoeven with Gerald Ford. Pub-
licly they maintained the fiction that they had designed the move

to strengthen Halleck's position. *Two years later, in a coup reminiscent of Martin's unseating in 1959, Ford replaced Halleck as minority leader. The Valparaiso* Vidette Messenger *explained the demise of the second district's fair-haired boy. "Halleck . . . was in effect a casualty of the lopsided Republican defeat in November. Although no one blamed Halleck for the Democratic election sweep, House Republicans wanted a new face. In Ford, they got one generally considered handsome and youthful. Halleck is 64. Ford is 51. Their voting records show little difference. But Halleck is one of the 'old pros' of the GOP and one of the most widely known men in the party and that fact was his undoing."* [12] *The Save the Dunes Council liked to believe that it had contributed substantially to Halleck's defeat. In December 1964 Tom Dustin had proposed the following strategy to Dorothy Buell:*

> I suggest an immediate and concerted effort to topple Halleck from his post as Minority Leader of the House of Representatives. There is obviously some thought being given to this by 20th Century Republican Congressmen. Anything the Second District can do to discredit Halleck should be undertaken immediately. I would certainly contact . . . members . . . and urge them to write to Gerald Ford. [He] is said to be among the "young Turks" who would like to knock the old sot over; and criticism of Halleck, directed to Ford, from Second District people will certainly help. [13]

By 1964 Halleck had lived with the port project from its inception. As the congressman from the district, as an accomplished power broker and a man of high position, he should have seen it realized long before. Although he could demand and receive a hearing, his success lay only in holding the opposition at bay and keeping the issue alive. He had wanted the port. He had never wanted the park. Unswervingly, lauded by his constituents, he held to the view that Porter County had enough park and could not afford the loss of tax base that more park would entail. Moreover, he believed the port would lead to a Democratic Porter County. By 1965 one of his supporters at least had chided him for his stubbornness:

> Many of us feel the clobbering we received in the 1964 election and the Great Society with all its reverberations and implications give impetus to the park proposal. Also the fact that you . . . were chastised for your honorable stand for Goldwater leads many of us to believe our feelings, as expressed through you, will carry less weight now than in the previous Congress. . . . The 11,000 acre plan for the park as passed by the Senate is as you know ridiculous! But I'm afraid that unless we come up

*with a reasonable counter plan it will get passed in the House
over the heads of all of us. . . .*

*I guess I feel so strongly at this time because the last election
taught me one thing if nothing else and that is: that Barry lost
. . . primarily because he had no definite plan for conservatism.
He was "agin" almost everything proposed . . . but he offered
no positive plan to guide us back or forward or sideways to a
reasonable road of conservatism. So, instead of getting what
you and I believe would have been best, we got our "Big Daddy"
and his "Great Society."*[14]

No evidence exists to suggest that Halleck ever took this advice.
Years later Halleck could produce a philosophical, matter-of-fact
explanation of why he could not prevent the park:

*When we had the two Republican senators, the thing was pretty
much under control. But when Capehart and Jenner lost or quit
or got beat, that situation was reversed. I was down there pretty
lone-handed for awhile, I'd pretty much lost the powerful position by the time [park legislation] came along. You understand, that the Republicans controlled the Congress [only] four
years out of the last 40-some. Now, in the 80th in '47 and '48,
I was the Majority Leader—in that situation, they couldn't
get that damn park thing through. We took pretty much of a
licking.*[15]

But some contemporary political observers believe that Halleck
surely must have gotten something in return for letting the park go
through. As one of the "great horse traders of our time," he could
not have failed to exploit the quid pro quo opportunities of that
situation.[16]

On October 14, 1966, the House of Representatives, on a roll call
vote, approved the Indiana Dunes National Lakeshore—Halleck's
abhorred park—over Halleck's howling objections. The media, nationwide, declared the measure a triumph for the people of the
country and a particularly cruel defeat for Halleck. His ouster as
minority leader left him with but one trump card to play. He joined
the Public Works Committee as its most junior member in order to
make sure that Indiana got reimbursed for the state funds spent on
the port. No doubt the reimbursement would have gone forward
without him.

The political changes that took place in Indiana and throughout
the country accounted for the outcome of the Dunes conflict, but
only in part. The controversy's resolution also depended on changes

in land ownership and proposed use during the four crucial years between 1958 and 1962. Acceptance of the reality of these changes by Douglas and the Save the Dunes Council permitted a climate for the complex negotiations that both sides called compromise.

In 1958, the year Douglas introduced his first Dunes bill (S3898), a little less than half of Porter County's total shoreline remained undeveloped and in private ownership. The principal site, called the Central Dunes, lay between the towns of Ogden Dunes and Dune Acres. It consisted of four-and-three-quarters contiguous miles of beach and high dunes considered by conservationists as the most desirable parcel in the entire Dunes region for preservation. Midwest Steel, Bethlehem Steel, and Northern Indiana Public Service Company (NIPSCO) divided its ownership. In addition to this tract, Inland Steel owned 830 acres west of Ogden Dunes. Purchased in 1919, Inland's land still remained undeveloped. Douglas's first bill called for only 3,600 acres, but these encompassed the entire Central Dunes and five uninterrupted miles of shore. It called for nothing else. His last bill, in 1966, called for 8,000 acres of noncontiguous land parcels; it entirely excluded the Central Dunes. "The process by which the Central Dunes were gradually removed from park consideration to be replaced with areas more acceptable to industrial-port interests was the very essence of the Indiana Dunes controversy."[17] Substitutions occurred as construction began at the Midwest and NIPSCO sites and continued as industries rendered more and more of the land unfit to preserve. Although successive bills provided more total acreage, they called for successively less desirable parks. Douglas's 1961 bill (S1797) proposed a 9,000-acre park, patchy perhaps, but still containing 2,054 acres of Central Dunes.[18]

Then, in April 1961, Bethlehem contracted with Northwestern University for the sale of sand from the Central Dunes. Though two years elapsed before the bulldozers rolled, two years of agony and supplication for Douglas and the Save the Dunes Council, indeed for preservationists everywhere, the agreement had sealed the fate of the Central Dunes and changed the configuration of any future park. With "the central and crucial area for the park" gone, park proponents and port proponents alike could finally speak of compromise.[19] Ironically, Senator Hartke had introduced a compromise bill in 1961 (S2317), which proposed a 6,000-acre park that eliminated the Central Dunes entirely. Conservationists, who attacked it as a sellout to industry, would triumphantly hail an almost identical park in 1966. Hartke's support for a park, however unacceptable to Save the Duners in 1961, marked a significant change in the status quo. As the first Indiana politician to express the idea that both a park and a port could exist together, Hartke had broken the stalemate. Kenneth Gray of Douglas's staff downplayed Hartke's role as "just a way of saying he did something, a paper bill."[20] Howard Shuman, Douglas's administrative assistant, retrospectively depreciated Hartke's role: "Hartke has never been a very important figure—useful in that he wasn't outwardly negative, but I don't think you ought to make heroes out of neutrals. He wasn't a major person in our calculation."[21] Major or not, Hartke had suggested a new direction, which predicted the final outcome and which his detractors eventually had to accept.

Meanwhile, park advocates and port proponents pursued identical but parallel procedures to move their incompatible proposals through the legislative machinery. Each group participated in Senate and House hearings held by the appropriate committees. Although each committee dealt with the same land, neither could deal with the whole question. According to Rutherford H. Platt, a student of land use decision-making, this dual system caused a

> schizoid federal attitude toward the Dunes . . . rival proposals for port and park were being advanced through separate bills assigned to entirely different committees. Since there necessarily were two concurrent sets of hearings largely dominated by the proponents of one or the other proposal, the representatives of the Corps of Engineers and the Department of the Interior seldom if ever confronted each other. . . . The problem was that as long as the Central Dunes were the focus of controversy, both proposals applied to the same land and therefore cancelled each other out.[22]

Then, beginning in 1962, a series of critical occurrences nudged the controversy toward its climax. On February 1, 1962, Laurance Rockefeller, chairman of the Outdoor Recreation Resources Review Commission, submitted his report to President Kennedy and the Congress. It called for the acquisition of new lands for recreation, particularly shoreline areas, a new Federal Bureau of Outdoor Recreation, and massive federal financing for planning, acquisition, and development of such recreational land.[23] Douglas hailed the report as a "compelling essay in support of the proposed Indiana Dunes National Lakeshore."[24] He delighted in having acquired a new hat, that of mass recreation, on which to hang his preservation efforts.

On February 23 Chicago District Engineer Colonel J. A. Smedlie issued the latest Army Engineers' report indicating the Burns Ditch site as the most suitable for a deep water port.[25] During the same week the Senate Public Lands Subcommittee held hearings on

Douglas's 9,000-acre park bill (S1797 amended) at which all Indiana political officials, except Representative Ray Madden of Gary, testified in favor of industrial development and expansion in the Dunes. At the same hearing Douglas produced two highly significant union endorsements. Walter Reuther, head of the United Auto Workers, and Joseph Germano, leader of District 31 of the United Steel Workers, which included 80,000 workers in the Chicago-Gary area, spoke out in favor of preserving the Dunes. Their testimony undermined port proponents' claims to labor support.[26]

In reality, however, port proponents' views on labor's position held up better than the Douglas forces liked to acknowledge.

> Neither the steel workers nor their leaders supported a park most of the time. Indiana union members had no use for the Lakeshore and Illinois steel workers didn't care one way or the other. But they could not fight Paul Douglas openly. They went along with Douglas on a lot of things because he was Paul Douglas— to them he was charismatic. [Although] Joe Germano used to grouse about Paul Douglas, that idiot professor, [he] had carried the mail many times for the steel workers. He didn't call in the chips, but [the unions] weren't going to get into a spitting contest on something that was so important to him.[27]

At the same time that Germano publicly supported Douglas on the Dunes, he lambasted as antilabor the vote of a few members of the Illinois legislature that would have prohibited U.S. Steel from filling more of Lake Michigan at its South Works site.

On March 1, 1962, President Kennedy sent his conservation message to Congress. It recommended the establishment of a Land Conservation Fund for national parks' land acquisition; the fund signified a radical departure from past practices. Kennedy's message urged favorable action on a number of park bills then before Congress, including an Indiana Dunes National Lakeshore, and proposed that Congress make funds for their purchase available through annual appropriations.[28] Douglas's jubilation over Kennedy's implied support for his bill turned to out-and-out ecstacy in response to a Bureau of the Budget (now Office of Management and Budget) letter of March 19. Addressed to Senator Clinton P. Anderson, chairman of the Senate Committee on Interior and Insular Affairs, the letter stated:

> This is in response to your request for the views of the Bureau of the Budget on S1797 . . . and S2317 [Hartke's bill]. The report which the Secretary of the Interior is submitting on these bills describes the significant features of the area proposed for addition to the National Park System and alludes to the fact that

there are conflicting views concerning the highest and best use to which some segments of the Indiana Dunes area should be put. The report endorses the purposes of S1797 . . . and expresses the belief that legislation along these lines should provide for the inclusion of the maximum acreage that is practical from the standpoint of preserving the unique and outstanding recreational and scenic values. This bureau concurs in that report. The President, in his recent message on conservation, urged favorable action on legislation to create a national lakeshore in northern Indiana. Enactment of legislation for this purpose *along the lines of S1797* would be in accord with the program of the President.[29]

Douglas took the letter to mean the Bureau of the Budget and the president favored a park rather than a port and endorsed his proposal for its land area rather than Hartke's.

On March 23 the Army Engineers' Board of Rivers and Harbors approved the proposed Burns Ditch Harbor. Port proponents expected no trouble with the next step in the process; as they presumed, state officials promptly affirmed the board's action. The following requirement, approval by the Bureau of the Budget, threatened to cause problems. Port boosters angrily disputed Douglas's claims of administration support. They contended that the wording "along the lines of S1797" ruled out specific support for Douglas. Clinton Green, secretary-treasurer of the Indiana Port Commission, administrative aide to Governor Welsh, and the port's most vocal supporter, spent the week in Washington. By the end of his stay, and after a "frank and friendly talk" between Welsh and Interior Secretary Stewart Udall, the secretary began to talk compromise.[30] "We have agreed to work actively toward a solution which would be acceptable to both the conservation and economic interests of the people of Indiana and of the nation."[31] Douglas, meanwhile, blasted the Army Engineers for failing to study alternative sites for the port. He continued to believe that the president fully supported his bill.

On April 2 Douglas wrote a long, detailed letter to Lee C. White, assistant special counsel to the president, urging delay of the Bureau of the Budget's approval for the port pending a study of alternative sites. He included the data assembled by the Save the Dunes Council's Engineering Committee, which refuted the Army Engineers' cost figures.

In July Welsh and Green paid a call on President Kennedy to make him "aware of the importance we attach to this project."[32] A few weeks later the Bureau of the Budget held the first of a series of conferences to discuss the Army Engineers' report recommending the Burns Ditch site. Green sat in for Welsh. Representatives of the Bureau of the Budget and the Army Engineers and presidential aide White joined Green and attempted to work out the particulars of a port recommendation to Congress. Green felt especially confident because on August 1, two days before the four-way meeting, he had secured all but about 100 acres of the 440 needed by the state for the port. The complicated deal had involved action by the Indiana Conservation Commission granting Bethlehem permission to fill in 331 acres of Lake Michigan in exchange for 252 acres of Bethlehem property at $179,000 below what the company had paid for the land.[33] The advantageous price plus a few other concessions put Green in a strong bargaining position.

By August 15, however, Representative Sidney Yates (D., Ill) loosened $50,000 from the House Appropriations Committee for the study of a deep water port in Lake County, Indiana. The move brought yelps of protest from Halleck and from J. Edward Roush, Indiana's fourth district Democratic congressman and the House sponsor of Hartke's compromise bill. While Madden speculated that the study might take several years, port proponents worried that the tactic would delay the approval by the Bureau of the Budget for the Burns Ditch site. By the middle of September, however, they confidently anticipated the long-awaited approval. After weeks of intensive scrutiny by the administration, "more top-level consideration than any other project of its kind," the Associated Press leaked the information that the Bureau of the Budget would approve the harbor.[34]

ROSE GARDEN PROMISE

Early in the first week of October 1962, the phone rang in Douglas's office. When Ken Gray answered, he heard the familiar voice of Joe Mohbat, an AP-UPI reporter, who checked in frequently looking for news. This time, however, Mohbat had some to pass on. "Well," he said, "I see you're getting the old blankety blank on the Dunes again." Gray had no idea what he meant, and Mohbat continued, "As a reporter, I have a talent that's very useful. I can read upside down. I won't tell you who I was talking to at the Bureau of the Budget, but on his desk I saw the authorization, signed by the President, for the harbor to be included in the Public Works bill. I found out that it's being sent by messenger right now to the committee. This afternoon the committee is going to put it in the bill— it'll be in and you'll never get it out."[35]

Gray didn't wait to hear any more. As implausible as the story seemed, it had the ring of truth about it. He rushed into Douglas's office and repeated Mohbat's grim tale. Douglas grabbed his coat and with one foot out the door told his secretary to call Evelyn Lincoln, President Kennedy's personal secretary. "Tell her I know the President doesn't have me on his schedule, but I'm coming down and I must see him."[36]

While Gray sat in the cabinet room and waited, Kennedy and Douglas walked together in the Rose Garden. Their leisurely pace belied the urgency Douglas felt. He began quietly to talk of Cape Cod, of its beauty and its value, of its personal meaning to the president. He talked of the nation's good fortune in having such places preserved and of Kennedy's role in the achievement. Then he spoke of the Indiana Dunes, comparing both its uniqueness and his private identification with the land to Kennedy's feelings about Cape Cod. Douglas reminded Kennedy of his conservation message, which recommended Dunes preservation, and of the relevance of the Rockefeller report.[37] Douglas urged that if Kennedy could not reject the port outright, he must not let it go forward without adequate study.[38] He promised that the Save the Dunes Council could prove that the Army Engineers had inflated cost-benefit projections if only it were given the time.[39] He sympathized with the political problems Kennedy would face if he reversed himself: a Democratic governor, two Democratic senators, a Democratic congressman, almost all of Indiana's Democratic elected officials solidly behind a Burns Ditch port. In addition, Douglas appreciated that Kennedy courted Halleck's cooperation. Again and again Douglas underscored his belief that the issue superceded politics, that Kennedy must help preserve the Indiana Dunes.

Either Douglas's eloquence or his sense of desperation got through to the young president. As quickly as the port had appeared on the list of the administration's recommended projects, so did it disappear; the Bureau of the Budget did not manage to get around to considering the Burns Ditch harbor again until September of the following year.[40]

On October 3, 1962, when the Bureau of the Budget rejected Indiana's proposed Burns Ditch port, astounded port proponents reacted angrily. Green, who had spent almost two months lobbying in Washington, led the bipartisan attack against Douglas. Calling Douglas "short sighted and uncompromising," Green went on to declare, "True conservationists have been lead [sic] down a blind alley by Mr. Douglas in order to satisfy the vanity and private interests of a crotchety old man."[41] Halleck howled even louder: "I serve notice that I'm not going to continue to take this lying down. Either they'll send up that report or we may forget about the ground rules. We're going to have our harbor one way or the other."[42] Halleck did his best to include the port in the omnibus public works bill. He went so far as to delay adjournment of the Congress because of the port. Nevertheless, he did not succeed. Douglas had prevented the appropriation of federal money for the Burns Ditch harbor, at least for 1962.

By the end of that year, although they may not yet have realized it, park proponents had lost the Central Dunes and with them any chance for the park they originally envisioned. Slowly, pushed by the unfolding reality of the opposing forces, they retreated from their original dream. Despite the presence of Bethlehem, Douglas still believed that he and his allies could beat the port. They pursued the tri-cities harbor proposal throughout 1963. They offered other alternatives, such as the proposition that Bethlehem move its plant one-half mile south and use the Burns Ditch channel to establish inland water transfer terminals, thus leaving the lakefront free for preservation. They litigated on many fronts. They countered each new tactic of port supporters.

From October 1962, when the Bureau of the Budget rejected the port, to September 1963, when the agency finally accepted it, Douglas and the Save the Dunes Council concentrated on blocking the port. Through the efforts of Herb Read and George Anderson, Douglas challenged the Army Engineers' figures and conclusions, an unheard of notion at that time. He believed that "the evidence we presented to the Bureau of the Budget showed conclusively that local commitments could not be met, that traffic in coal, grain and general cargo would be insufficient to support the port and generally that this harbor is not economically justified. Moreover, we pointed out again and again that the primary justification for the harbor was the alleged use to be made of it by the two steel companies."[43] By the end of 1963, Douglas had resigned himself to the inevitable. "It is indeed disheartening to think that the most beautiful and the most scientifically valuable portion of the Dunes is to be left to the bulldozer and the steel mills, but I believe that we must not fail to take advantage of the chance . . . to establish a national dunes park that will preserve much of the remaining unspoiled dunes area."[44]

Meanwhile, at the end of 1962 Governor Welsh, too, faced unpleasant realities. Unlike the preservationists, Welsh, Green, and their confreres never considered the idea of no port at the Burns Ditch site. They concerned themselves rather with trying to get a public port before Bethlehem and Midwest built their own. They had until 1968 to accomplish the job. At that time, if port construction had not yet begun, Bethlehem could reclaim the land it had sold to Indiana so cheaply. Concluding that federal money would take too long to get, Welsh proceeded to try to win a state appropriation. He proposed a $34.5 million State Economic Development Fund, earmarking $25.5 million for harbor construction at Burns Ditch. To raise the money, Welsh planned to double the state cigarette tax. With a kind of perverse political logic, a coalition of Republicans and Lake County Democrats voted down the plan. The Republicans who had directed the port promotion effort since 1929 argued that since the federal government routinely funded similar projects, they saw no reason for Indiana to pay. Douglas used the occasion to imply that rejection of the appropriation indicated that the legislature no longer supported the port.[45] Bethlehem attorney James W. Chester sent a copy of Douglas's remarks to Halleck's office. Chester railed at Douglas: "Of course, Senator Douglas has some real wrong conclusions, the main one being that the refusal of the Indiana Legislature to pass the recent port legislation indicated a rejection of the port. Everyone in Indiana knows that the legislature was overwhelmingly in favor of the port but many thought that the same should be financed by Federal authority. I'm sure Mr. Douglas knows this also but is deliberately misstating and confusing the record."[46] Chester spared no scorn for the Save the Dunes Council either: "I cannot help but feel that it is most unusual that an organization such as the Save the Dunes Council, with paid public relations representatives, attorneys, etc. is enjoying tax free status. If there was ever an outfit organized for one purpose and used for another, it is this one."[47]

The politics of the situation grew so peculiar that in 1964, the Valparaiso *Vidette Messenger*, that most Republican of Republican newspapers, commented in a column called "The Hoosier Day": "Election of an overwhelmingly Democratic State Legislature promises to give Indiana the Burns Ditch deep water port on Lake Michigan. . . . Governor Matthew E. Welsh who has put all the resources of his administration behind the efforts to get the deep water port will ask the upcoming January legislature to advance 25 million dollars. It being a dominate [sic] Democratic legislature, the governor is apt to get what he seeks to start the port now."[48]

While Douglas and the Save the Dunes Council attempted to prevent the port, while Welsh and the Indiana Port Commission tried to find the money to get construction underway, the Kennedy administration pondered the politics of the situation as it tried to solve the problem. On the one hand, solid (with the exception of Lake County's Madden) Indiana Democratic support for the port made out-and-out rejection impossible. On the other hand, powerful Democratic forces such as Reuther, Germano, Richard J. Daley, and assorted liberal allies supported Douglas's bid for a national park. Moreover, the park accorded with Kennedy's stated conservation objectives. Most important, however, the Dunes issue dovetailed with one of the president's primary priorities. "Kennedy was building a new Democratic coalition—he had done very well with pieces of it, the unions, the blacks, but he did not have the liberals. He did not have the intellectuals; he did not have the kids. They all came around on an issue like [the Dunes.]"[49] As a conservative machine politician, Kennedy needed to establish his credentials as an environmentalist and as a liberal with the wing of the Democratic party that had supported Adlai Stevenson. Douglas spoke for both those positions. By supporting Douglas on the Dunes, Kennedy stood to gain the kind of credibility Douglas represented and to solidify the Democratic coalition that he intended to build.

So the Bureau of the Budget, with help from the Department of the Army, the departments of the Interior and Health, Education, and Welfare, and perhaps others, studied, analyzed, and reviewed until they could find nothing else to investigate. Accordingly, on September 24, 1963, the Bureau of the Budget announced its Solomon-like decision. In a letter to Secretary of the Army Cyrus Vance, the bureau's Deputy Director Elmer Staats unfolded his agency's compromise. Relying entirely on the Army Engineers' revised report of August 1963, the bureau recommended the authorization of the Burns Waterway Harbor. The approval stipulated a number of stringent conditions regarding tonnage requirements for coal shipment, local provisions for public terminals, and water and air pollution controls. The Bureau of the Budget also recommended an 11,700-acre Dunes park, stating, "It is the President's wish to see a deep-draft harbor for Indiana made a reality while at the same time preserving as much as possible of the priceless heritage of Indiana Dunes for future generations. Early acquisition of remaining dunes and natural areas is essential if they are to be preserved for public use and enjoyment. Accordingly, it would be highly desirable that the Congress give early consideration to both harbor and park proposals in order that appropriate plans for a balanced development of this important area may be made."[50] The balanced development took three more years to accomplish.

Why did the Congress take so long to authorize both the port and the park? The administration had discharged its obligation by producing a compromise, but clearly neither side accepted it completely. Each faction continued to try to maximize its advantages. Further, Douglas no longer felt it improper to engage in trade-offs, accommodations, and compromises. For the Dunes, he had learned to play the game.[51] Though the alliances had shifted somewhat—since Senators Bayh and Hartke and Representative Roush now felt at political liberty to join the park proponents—the struggle persisted. No doubt Kennedy's untimely death a month after announcement of the compromise slowed down park and port bills as it did other pending legislation. In addition, the advent of Johnson's administration surely must have put Douglas on guard. Even though Johnson pledged to carry forward the Kennedy agenda, Douglas probably suspected the worst. Adversaries since they entered the Senate together in 1948, the two had never trusted each other. Johnson seemed to take special delight in sabotaging Douglas's fondest causes, and so Douglas expected no help from the new president. Port proponents, on the other hand, perceived Johnson as a man who would be easier to deal with. In a letter to Halleck in September 1964, Chester spelled out his new hopes: "While you and I may have some very definite reservations about some of the activities in the White House when White was working under Kennedy, I cannot help but feel that there is a good chance that your friendship with President Johnson will now reflect itself through Lee White. Under the Daley-Douglas-Kennedy influence, he didn't have much of a chance to express himself or cooperate with us."[52]

Late in 1963 Senators Bayh and Hartke introduced a new harbor bill, containing a provision for federal reimbursement to Indiana for any monies spent on port construction prior to federal appropriations. Port boosters embraced the new concept enthusiastically. A commitment to reimbursement meant that construction could begin immediately, and the Indiana legislature would likely overcome its reluctance to include the funds for the harbor in the state budget. With strong urging from Halleck, Governor Brannigan asked for $25 million for the port in the 1965 state budget. The overwhelmingly Democratic legislature, despite a few caveats, approved the appropriation.

Meanwhile, Douglas, not trusting that the park would become a reality without further precautions, succeeded in attaching a proviso to the Public Works Omnibus Bill of 1965 that stated: "No federal funds shall be spent on the port until such time as the Indiana Dunes have been preserved and protected as a national lakeshore by an act of Congress."[53]

The Senate passed the port bill with the proviso by mid-July. The House, responding to Halleck's fury, found the proviso unpalatable and eliminated the offending item, thereby sending the port problem to conference committee. There the conferees changed the language of the proviso to read: "Any funds appropriated for the construction of this project shall not be utilized until such time as the Indiana Dunes National Lakeshore has been voted upon by both Houses of Congress in the same Congress."[54] On October 27, 1965, Congress passed the Public Works Omnibus Bill, including the Burns Harbor project. A year later, on October 14, 1966, Congress authorized a 6,539-acre Indiana Dunes National Lakeshore, a preserve containing no land in common with the original design and having 5,161 acres less than that recommended by the Kennedy compromise.

PAUL DOUGLAS

On December 2, 1966, Paul Douglas telegraphed Dorothy Buell:

Greetings and congratulations to one of the most unselfish groups of men and women whom it has ever been my pleasure to know. It has been an inspiration to have had the chance to work with you and it has given us all keen and durable pleasure at having saved some of the magnificent dunes for this and for future generations. I think I should warn that the enemies of the dunes have not given up the battle and will probably seek to throw obsticle [sic] after obsticle by trying to cut appropriations and by other means. We have won the important battle but have not yet won the war and we need to consolidate our gains to keep together and to push on. While I am now leaving public life forever, I want to work with you as a citizen and I hope I may be permitted to continue as a member of the Save the Dunes Council. Thank you dear friends, for all you have done. Let us finish the job.[55]

Perhaps the job had finished Douglas. For ten of his eighteen years in office he had devoted much of his energy, much of his staff's time, and all of his heart to saving the Dunes. Shuman compared that effort with civil rights as "the toughest thing I've ever seen around here."[56] *Douglas's tenacity and determination "got a couple of very busy people [in the Kennedy Administration] to listen. The old gladiator had Kennedy's real respect."*[57] *Eventually, Douglas accomplished his goal, and people then knew him best for saving the Dunes. Nevertheless, in November 1966, Illinois voters denied Douglas his fourth term; he seemed surprised only that he had lasted* so long. Early in his career, Douglas had viewed his role as providing the "cutting edge" for the great issues of the day. Insiders, however, soon wrote him off as a "liberal who could dominate the headlines but not the Senate." "He never became a member of the club; he functioned as the antithesis of a club member, and that made things difficult for him."[58] Even the University of Chicago avoided him when it needed help from the Senate. Despite his long identification with the school and its community, Douglas could not deliver for the university wheelers and dealers, and everybody knew it. "If an issue turned on personal influence or personal clout, Douglas didn't have it."[59] Oblivious to opinion, he had espoused and battled for such liberal causes as civil rights, truth-in-lending, and one man, one vote. By 1966, however, a combination of factors—age, his support of civil rights, the charm of his opponent, his stand on the Vietnam war—all contributed to his defeat. He had lost his coalition; he could no longer relate to the young and the intellectuals who had backed him for so long. Moreover, at the hour of the election Douglas found arrayed against him a formidable accumulation of enemies: the steel companies, the railroads, the "third-rate politicians who always went for pork," and the growing cadre of antiwar liberals who would vote their conviction.[60] In an off-year election that foreshadowed the victory of Richard Nixon two years later, Douglas lost to his former student, young, handsome Charles Percy. Even eleventh-hour detente with his old adversary, Lyndon B. Johnson, could not save the day. President Johnson had given Douglas's campaign his all. He who as majority leader had "mocked and foiled Douglas' crusading liberalism" now needed his old enemy's support for an increasingly unpopular war.[61] Johnson invited Douglas to the LBJ Ranch, the site for presidential arm-twisting. There the president informed him that he considered Douglas's election to a fourth term the most important political necessity of 1966.[62] Presidential support came too little and too late; Douglas's defeat followed by less than a month his sweetest victory. Indeed, that victory, the passage of a bill to save the Dunes, almost did not happen.

> The chairman of the House Interior Committee, Wayne Aspinal, was reluctant to take it up. But we did have a couple of members of the committee who knew Mr. Douglas personally and as a personal favor were willing to push. One was Morris Udall [brother to the Secretary of the Interior], and another was John Saylor of Pennsylvania, who worked quietly but said he couldn't take the lead. But Mr. Douglas simply [persisted]. Every week, two days a week, he would call on the members

of the House Interior Committee. He would trudge over there and he would plead with them. He did it to every Democrat and Republican on the Committee. Finally, he began to get commitments that they would go ahead. Then he began to push the administration—finally we got hearings, but Aspinal wouldn't act on the bill.

At the very end, the Republicans did something nasty and that made Aspinal mad.[63] He said, "I'm not going to let you guys do something like that—we're going to start all over again."

Douglas went to Morris Udall and other friends on the committee and shamed them into coming. Then the outside lobbyists like the ADA [Americans for Democratic Action] and labor got on the ball and began to help us. They weren't lobbyists for this sort of thing, labor and others helped because they saw Douglas losing.[64]

Douglas and his supporters felt relatively satisfied with the bill that came out of the House Interior Committee. Everyone told them that it would fail on the House floor because Halleck intended to see to its demise. The House leadership did not even want to schedule it. Meanwhile, on September 28, Interior Secretary Udall shocked the bill's protagonists by announcing at a news conference that he "[was getting] sick and tired of the failure of the State of Indiana to show any real enthusiasm for the national park." "Maybe," he suggested, "we'd be better off if we dropped the whole thing."[65] Douglas lambasted Udall, after which the secretary claimed that the press had misinterpreted his comments. Douglas again resorted to calling on a president. After half an hour of conversation with Johnson, Douglas received reaffirmation of administration support for his bill. To keep the wavering Udall in line, the Bureau of the Budget prepared a letter of support for Udall's signature. "Udall at first balked at signing it. Heatedly, Mr. Johnson ordered him to sign it anyway."[66]

While the out-of-town lobbyists saturated Capitol Hill spreading the message "Paul Douglas needs this bill to help win reelection," Johnson called Speaker of the House John McCormack with the same refrain: "Douglas wants this, can't you help him?" Vice-President Hubert Humphrey, whose friendship with Douglas went back to 1948, when they entered the Senate together, went personally to the Speaker with the same plea: "Douglas needs all our help, can't you do something for him?"

That sort of thing finally got the leadership to schedule the bill for the last week of the session. It was brought up on Monday as a committee of the whole. The Speaker himself was on the

*floor talking to people. When he came back, he said he didn't
think we had the votes. "I want to help Paul, and I'm going to
take a long shot," he said. The Speaker went down in the well
of the House and talked to Halleck. He told Halleck, "I'm puz-
zled by how this is going to go—it's really a waste of time, we
have other important bills to take up, it's the last week of the
session, I'd like to put this off."*[67]

*The idea delighted Halleck. The longer McCormack put it off, the
fewer members would attend, particularly big city members who
had close races and needed to go home to campaign. They agreed
to call the bill for a vote on the last day of the session—noon on
Friday. Halleck saw total success in the plan. Aware of the unlike-
lihood of getting a quorum on the last day of the session, Halleck
knew that by calling for a quorum he could settle the park bill then
and there. After Halleck had agreed to the new time, McCormack
stood up and asked for unanimous consent from the floor of the
House for the schedule change.*

*Minority leader Gerald Ford came rushing down the aisle say-
ing, "Charlie, what in the hell did you do?" Halleck replied
that he now had the best of all possible deals. But what Halleck had forgotten, or didn't know, was that the President had
asked the House to take up the Demonstration Cities Act (Model
Cities) and that debate had been scheduled for Friday at 2 P.M.
The President had sent telegrams to all Democrats saying, "You
be back to vote!" That meant we would have more votes than
at any other time. Speaker McCormack had tricked Halleck. It
was still close even though we had all the votes back.*

*As the members went in and out, they had to walk by the
lobbyists. I swear that all the liberal guys in town and all the
chief lobbyists, too, stood there. They would grab the members
and say, "Do it for Paul." And the members did!*[68]

*Douglas had a favorite way of putting into perspective the depth
of emotional attachment he felt toward "that little chunk of land,"
the Indiana Dunes. He used to tell it this way to those he wanted
to set straight:*

*I'm now in my 16th or 17th year in the Senate and when I first
came it was a big jump from alderman to the Senate and I
knew I was going to save the world. I was into my second term
and knew I'd be doing very well to save the Western Hemi-
sphere. Now at the end of my second term they'd got me down
to North America. Into my third term I realized I couldn't do
a damn thing about Canada and Mexico, so I was going to save
the United States, which was not a bad thing to do. Christ, it*

*wasn't very long before I gave up everything west of the Missis-
sippi and south of the Mason Dixon Line. They pushed me and
squeezed me and took away everything I wanted to save, but
Goddamn, I'm not going to give up the Indiana Dunes. That's
the only thing I can save because my days are slipping away.*[69]

*The pressing business of his losing campaign kept Douglas away
from his moment of greatest triumph and satisfaction. But with
customary modesty and grace, and with uncharacteristic political
good sense, he gave special credit to Senators Hartke and Bayh,
Representatives Roush and Madden, House Interior Committee
Chairman Aspinal, Secretary Udall, and Speaker McCormack. He
paid tribute, by name, to every congressman and senator who had
helped him; he called the roll of those newspapers which had supported him unflaggingly: Chicago's* American, *the Washington* Post,
the St. Louis Post-Dispatch, *the New York* Times, *the Milwaukee*
Journal, *and the Louisville* Courier-Journal. *He paid homage to Illinois's press and named seventeen conservation organizations as
leaders in the effort. Finally, Douglas singled out the Save the Dunes
Council, lauding its members as "completely selfless and extraor-
dinarily able," reading their names into the record for all to remember. He took no personal credit for the victory. In his closing
statement he said, "The final approval today of the Indiana Dunes
National Lakeshore marks a decisive turning point, though not the
end, I am sure, of a classic battle to preserve a significant part of
America's natural heritage."*[70] *As a prophecy, his observation had
great merit.*

The nation's press offered extravagant praise for the Dunes bill,
which passed in 1966. Headlines lauded it as a miracle, a victory for
the country, and a triumph for preservation; they acknowledged the
efforts of the elated and grateful conservationists. A conscientious
examination of the evidence, however, renders that victory far less
sweet. Without doubt, Douglas had fashioned a park in Halleck's
backyard, thereby breaking a sacrosanct convention of the Congress.
Nonetheless, the resulting park had no territory in common with
the magnificent Dunes that Douglas and the Save the Dunes Council had originally set out to preserve. The Kennedy compromise provided a resolution to the conflict after the preservationists had lost
all hope of gaining the land they wanted most to save. They achieved
a park; but in quality, in beauty, and in scientific value, it in no way
matched what they had lost. Moreover, the opposition had easily
reduced by half the 11,000 acres recommended in the compromise.

Disappointingly, the park as finally authorized consisted of noncontiguous bits and pieces that promised management problems for the National Park Service and confusion for the park's clientele. Industrial interests and port promoters, on the other hand, had conceded nothing. Rapid industrialization occurred in all the land staked out for development. While proindustry supporters like Halleck and the local construction unions had wanted to set aside land for future industrial and residential or commercial development, land-banking had not appeared as one of the options in the controversy. Proponents of industry, therefore, could hardly claim to have lost that land to the park. Nevertheless, the conservationists who had chosen to save any dunes at any price, rather than none at all, expressed satisfaction with the result.

Politically, the achievement deserved all the extravagent praise served up by the press. Douglas had managed a political juggling act with flair and finesse. He and his staff knew that, rhetoric notwithstanding, they would never pass a park bill without support from an Indiana politician. Hartke, the only possible man when the effort started in 1958, had proved useless to Douglas. A Johnson supporter from the beginning, Hartke had no political liaisons that could help Douglas, nor did he seem inclined to support Douglas's cause. Bayh's arrival in 1963 presented a different picture. The new Democratic senator had breezed into Washington tied to his state's solid bipartisan support for a port. In addition, the Kennedy administration saw Bayh as a "comer" and did not want to antagonize him. Douglas, realizing only too well that he did not have the strong active support of the administration, needed Bayh. Ken Gray recalls that he and Douglas worked on Bayh for quite a while until Bayh gradually changed his view and began to say that Indiana could have both a port and a park. They did not have an easy time. Bayh and Douglas did not always see eye to eye; in fact, they often made an ostentatious display of not speaking to each other. According to Gray, the first thing Bayh said when he got to Washington was that he wished Old Man Douglas would keep his nose out of Indiana affairs. The Douglas people kept after him because they needed an Indiana Democrat too badly to let petty considerations interfere. Gray takes personal credit for the eventual compromise. He contends that he and Robert Keefe, an aide to Bayh, worked out the details and then "forced it" on the White House, which went along with their proposals.[71]

Besides Bayh, Douglas had other balls to keep in the air. While he searched for the requisite Indiana politician, he simultaneously tried to unearth political backing sufficient to counteract Halleck's proprietary claims to the destiny of his district. He needed also to overcome the administration's deference to Indiana Democrats who supported the port. In addition, Douglas often had to prop up a not always enthusiastic interior secretary. While he managed all that, he also slowed down port approval by the Army Engineers, by the Bureau of the Budget, and by Congress until the other pieces fell into place. Douglas derived his usable political strength primarily through the leadership of those national unions whose goals he had endorsed and worked for over the years. The relationship between Douglas and the steel workers' union came to Kennedy's attention quite soon after his election. It took place at Kennedy's first appearance in Chicago as president. Joe Germano sat a few seats from Kennedy. He leaned over Douglas and Mayor Daley and said, "Mr. President, we had a lot to do with your election and I want you to do one thing— I want you to help Paul Douglas with the Indiana Dunes."[72] With union support behind him, Douglas successfully appealed to Kennedy, who called off the budget bureau's approval of the port. For a year thereafter, Douglas countered Indianapolis's pressure on the administration with elaborate rebuttals of the Army Engineers' statistics that the Engineering Committee of the Save the Dunes Council produced. He never ceased to call the nation's attention to the merits of his cause; he flailed away at the selfishness and destructiveness of port proponents; he courted the support of public sentiment. He could well afford to discuss values because he functioned immune from the wrath of the Indiana electorate.

While Douglas juggled, Bayh walked a tightrope. Unlike Hartke, Bayh had come into national office with the help and support of the in-power state Democratic machine, a powerful organization that wanted the port above all else. Although Bayh remembers supporting both park and port earlier than the evidence suggests, he indeed needed to tread carefully, making sure that he fulfilled his obligations to Indianapolis before dealing with the interloper Douglas. Bayh occupied the pivotal position with regard to negotiating a compromise. As a former member of the Indiana legislature in tune with his state's fondest hopes, as an attractive young Democratic senator who had the administration's ear, as Douglas's only hope for Indiana political support, Bayh represented an ideally situated negotiator.

White House assistant Lee White described the politics as grim. Faced with a head-on collision between Douglas and the Indiana industrial interests, White and Staats tried to find a way to accommodate everybody. White recalls the process as working, pounding, and beating until all the divergent interests came together. Fortunately, they had some time, because Douglas had bought breathing space by demolishing the Army Engineers' cost estimates. Douglas's strategy forced Vance, who rarely showed interest in the civil functions of the Army Engineers, to look at their port figures. After one glance, Vance decided that the Engineers had done a sloppy, inefficient, and inept job.[73] The Bureau of the Budget assigned a senior analyst named Robert Teeters to examine the numbers. The days and nights he spent in the office studying those figures bought time.

To Bayh it appeared as though the situation had reached a stalemate. "Both sides were mobilized more to defeat the opposition than to pursue their own goals. Neither [group] moved very rapidly toward its own end but each successfully kept the other side from moving."[74] By that time, the administration probably had as much interest in resolving the matter as either of the contenders. The port-park conflict had become a monumental headache, taking more time and attracting more attention than its political value warranted. Finally, through the urging of Douglas, Bayh began to work with White and the budget bureau toward effecting an acceptable solution.

For a brief moment the compromise seemed to satisfy all parties. By the time the park got underway, however, the preservationists felt cheated. In short order they initiated legislation to enlarge the park, claiming the remainder of the acreage mandated by the Kennedy compromise but eliminated in the final legislation. What had appeared as a resolution in 1963 merely defined the battle lines for a new assault that would continue into the 1980s.

Once Indiana had its port secured, Bayh, Roush, and, to a lesser extent, Hartke ended their balancing act and became open and fervent park supporters. Not only did they join in sponsoring the 1976 park expansion legislation, but, with some urging from the Save the Dunes Council, they led subsequent efforts to enlarge the lakeshore. To hear them tell it, preservation had always come first in their priorities.

NOTES

1. Edward H. Ziegner, "Indiana in National Politics," in *Indiana: A Self-Appraisal*, ed. Donald F. Carmony (Bloomington: Indiana University Press, 1966), p. 38.

2. John H. Fenton, *Midwest Politics* (New York: Holt, Rinehart and Winston, 1966), p. 164.

3. Ibid., p. 165.

4. Ziegner, *Indiana Politics*, p. 42.

5. Ibid., p. 44.

6. Fenton, *Midwest Politics*, pp. 169–70.

7. Ibid., p. 173.

8. Halleck interview.

9. Ibid.

10. Ibid.

11. "Halleck Tries to Use House Rule to Block Dunes Park," Chicago *Sun-Times*, Oct. 12, 1966.

12. Editorial, Valparaiso *Vidette Messenger*, Jan. 5, 1964.

13. Tom Dustin to Dorothy Buell, Dec. 4, 1964, Save the Dunes Council Files.

14. William P. Crumpacker to Charles A. Halleck, Feb. 19, 1965, Halleck Papers.

15. Halleck interview.

16. Authors' interview with Abner Mikva, Lakeside, Mich., 1981.

17. Platt, *Decision Process*, p. 151.

18. Ibid., p. 149.

19. U.S. Congress, Senate, Senator Paul H. Douglas speaking for "Indiana Dunes National Lakeshore," 88th Cong., 1st sess., Feb. 4, 1963, *Congressional Record*, 109:1589–97.

20. Gray interview.

21. Authors' interview with Howard Shuman, Washington, 1977.

22. Platt, *Decision Process*, p. 170.

23. "Outdoor Recreation Activity Will Triple by 2000, Report Says," *Wall Street Journal*, Feb. 2, 1962.

24. Press Release, Senator Paul Douglas, Feb. 2, 1962, Save the Dunes Council Files.

25. "Burns Site Best: Port Study Finds," Gary *Post Tribune*, Feb. 24, 1962.

26. "Union Backs Douglas on Dunes," Chicago *Sun-Times*, Feb. 27, 1962.

27. Mikva interview.

28. John F. Kennedy, "The White House Message on Conservation," Mar. 1, 1962, Save the Dunes Council Files.

29. Press Release, Senator Paul Douglas, Mar. 22, 1962, Save the Dunes Council Files.

30. "Port-Park Compromise Being Talked," Gary *Post Tribune*, Mar. 24, 1962.

31. Ibid.

32. "3-Way Capital Talk on Port," ibid., July 6, 1962.

33. "In Triple Play State Gets Title to Most of Land for Harbor Site," Fort Wayne *News Sentinal*, Aug. 2, 1962.

34. "JFK Decision on Port This Week," Hammond *Times*, Sept. 17, 1962.

35. Gray interview.

36. Ibid.

37. U.S. Congress, Senate, Senator Paul H. Douglas speaking on the "Indiana Dunes National Lakeshore," 88th Cong., 1st sess., Oct. 21, 1963, *Congressional Record*, 109:18843–849.

38. Ibid.

39. Gray interview.

40. Ibid.

41. "U.S. Bars Port at Burns Ditch," Hammond *Times*, Oct. 4, 1962.

42. Ibid.

43. *Congressional Record*, 109:18843–849.

44. Ibid.

45. U.S. Congress, Senate, Senator Paul H. Douglas speaking on "Hoosier Support for Indiana Dunes Growing," 88th Cong., 1st sess., May 2, 1963, *Congressional Record*, 109:7204–5.

46. James Chester to Robert G. Allett, assistant to Halleck, May 21, 1963, Halleck Papers.

47. Ibid.

48. Frank A. White, "The Hoosier Day," Valparaiso *Vidette Messenger*, Nov. 6, 1964.

49. Mikva interview.

50. *Congressional Record*, 109:18843–849.

51. Mikva interview.

52. Chester to Halleck, Sept. 23, 1964, Halleck Papers.

53. U.S. Congress, Senate. S. Rpt. 464, 89th Cong., 1st sess., Oct. 21, 1963, p. 9.

54. Halleck to Harold C. Conru, Oct. 21, 1965, Halleck Papers.

55. Telegram, Douglas to Buell, Dec. 2, 1966, Save the Dunes Council Files.

56. Shuman interview.

57. Authors' interview with Lee White, Washington, 1977.

58. Rowland Evans and Robert Novak, *Lyndon B. Johnson: The Exercise of Power* (New York: New American Library, 1966), p. 38.

59. Mikva interview.

60. Shuman interview.

61. Evans and Novak, *Lyndon B. Johnson*, p. 565.

62. Ibid.

63. The "something nasty" was former Postmaster General J. Edward Day (a lobbyist for Inland Steel at this time), urging committee members to stay away from the committee when the vote was taken. Day wanted Inland's 800 acres removed from the House bill and thought this maneuver would work. Consequently, Aspinal found half his committee absent on June 29, and Halleck's "man on the committee" (Joseph Skubitz, R., Kan.) succeeded in getting the Inland property removed. Douglas, by means of a friendly call from President Johnson, convinced Aspinal to oppose his own committee's recommendation and put the Inland property back in the bill. Charles Nicodemus, "The Dunes Bill: Story of a Miracle," Chicago *Daily News*, Oct. 17, 1966.

64. Gray interview.

65. Nicodemus, "The Dunes Bill."

66. Ibid.

67. Gray interview.

68. Ibid. For a different version of the passage of the Dunes bill, see Nicodemus, "The Dunes Bill."

69. White interview.
70. U.S. Congress, Senate, Senator Paul H. Douglas Statement, "Indiana Dunes National Lakeshore Truly a National Park and a Great Victory for the People of Illinois and Indiana," 89th Cong., 2nd sess., Oct. 18, 1966, *Congressional Record*, 112: 26291–293.
71. Gray interview.
72. Ibid.
73. White interview.
74. Authors' interview with Birch Bayh, Washington, 1977.

John Nelson

Patterns in the sand, Indiana Dunes.

Herbert Read

Mining the Central Dunes in 1962—the sand is destined for the Northwestern University landfill.

Bethlehem Steel

Bethlehem Steel's Burns Harbor plant. Ore storage is in the foreground; steelmaking facilities are in the center; sheet, plate, and tin mills are in the background.

This huge conveyor system facilitated the excavation of Bethlehem Steel's Burns Harbor plant.

James Chester, Porter County counsel for Bethlehem Steel, not only handled the company's land transactions but also masterminded its political strategy.

Congressman Floyd Fithian worked for expansion of the Indiana Dunes National Lakeshore during his three terms in office.

Thomas Dustin was the first public relations chairman for the Save the Dunes Council; his professionalism brought national attention to the Dunes struggle.

Herbert Read, a Save the Dunes Council stalwart, battled against the building of the Port of Indiana and NIPSCO's Bailly plant.

Burns Waterway Harbor, 1981, was the dream come true for port propo

The experts gather, left to right: Nature Conservancy Director Richard Pough, Save the Dunes Council President Dorothy Buell, Senator Paul Douglas, Chicago Conservation Council President Reuben Strong, and Morton Arboretum botanist Floyd Swink look over maps for the Douglas bill in 1958.

Lakeshore Dedication Day—Julie Nixon Eisenhower and Secretary of the Interior Rogers Morton stroll along the beach.

Dunes Veterans: Save the Dunes Council President Sylvia Troy and Senator Birch Bayh look over the Department of Interior Conservation Service Award that Troy received in 1976.

Proponents and opponents of a Dunes park demonstrate in 1961.

Touring the Dunes, left to right: Secretary of the Interior Stewart Udall, Senator Alan Bible, Senator Paul Douglas, and National Park Service Director Conrad Wirth on a Save the Dunes Council–sponsored tour, 1961.

Senator Paul Douglas, his wife, Emily (left), and Save the Dunes Council President Dorothy Buell, in 1973, when the senator returned for his last stay in his beloved Dunes.

The Indiana Dunes: "There are no final solutions, only shifting forms."

PART II RELUCTANT ALLY

Our nation has long depended on the marketplace as the arbiter of competing land uses. In the Indiana Dunes conservationists tried to follow the time-honored American practice for two short periods. After the demise of the Sand Dunes National Park and between 1952 and 1956, both the Indiana Dunes Preservation Association and the Save the Dunes Council attempted to purchase unimproved Dune lands. They discovered, to their chagrin, that development interests easily could outstrip their economic resources. Subsequently, both groups campaigned to substitute public funds for the private dollars they could not amass. In both cases, the preservationists ultimately prevailed due to the involvment of state and federal governments and their considerable treasuries. Satisfied with the accomplishment, the early Dunes conservationists left management of the Indiana Dunes State Park to its ardent champion, Colonel Richard Lieber, and disbanded.

A different situation faced park proponents of the 1960s. On the federal level the National Park Service (NPS), the agency charged with park land preservation, had ambivalent feelings about the Dunes. Initially the second wave of Dunes park advocates assumed they had enlisted a savior; the NPS's record in the legislative battles to establish and subsequently to expand the Indiana Dunes National Lakeshore painfully reeducated them. They learned that the agency had lost its authoritative voice on park land preservation and management and that the decision-making power had shifted to Congress and to the executive branch. They also discovered the inherent dichotomy of purpose in the agency's mandate and its often prevalent emphasis on use rather than preservation.

The Save the Dunes Council's increasing knowledge and sophistication forced abandonment of any thought of dissolution. Instead, in step with the growth of the environmental movement, the preservationists assumed the role of NPS watchdog to ensure resource protection in the management of the lakeshore. The agency's unwillingness or inability to prevent deterioration of the park's natural

qualities brought the Save the Dunes Council into increasing conflict with the region's industries.

Part II focuses on the third party in the contemporary Dunes land
use controversy: the National Park Service. Chapter 8 reviews the
agency's performance in the legislative process. Chapter 9 considers
its management record. Both chapters delineate the political constraints under which NPS operates as a bureau attempting to mediate development and preservation.

8 Another Battleground

Stephen Mather would hardly recognize the National Park Service (NPS) he started in 1916! Created to impose centralized management for a small number of widely scattered parks and monuments, the agency has grown into a far-flung, multipurpose bureaucracy. A gigantic expansion of its holdings and the accelerating influence of the executive branch and Congress on national park policy have shaped the service's evolution.

Originally the agency controlled the process for enlarging the national park system. The NPS studied the desirability of further land preservation, evaluated specific sites, and negotiated their acquisition through private or state donations. The administration of John Kennedy broke that mold. With the adoption of a new public policy for purchasing park land, decision-making about additions to national parks shifted to Congress. This significant change relegated the agency to the role of consultant. NPS's views still determined a project's fate in the 1960s. In the 1970s Congress often chose to ignore them. In the struggle to preserve the Indiana Dunes, the agency's role reflected the pressures of a changing status, conflict in mission, and increasing politicization.

In 1980 the NPS domain encompassed 323 units totaling 72 million acres.[1] The initial jurisdiction consisted of twenty-one national monuments and fifteen vast, spectacular enclaves in the West, all of which Congress had previously carved from federal land.[2] Today the NPS administers a vast potpourri of national, historical, and recreational areas all around the country, increasingly acquired through the purchase of private land.[3]

Establishment of the national park system marked a radical departure from the country's long-held policy of selling off federal land to private interests. The new approach retained some land (with special characteristics) for public use. To this day, conflict continues about its merits. The more recent practice of buying private land for national parks has added fuel to the controversy over whether or not the federal government should have responsibility for land preservation.

Neither the nation nor the NPS has ever resolved the dichotomy between the mandates of preservation and public use in the agency's charter. Preservation maintains park land in its natural state and makes it available for public enjoyment. With its original, large, and pristine holdings, NPS encouraged viewing nature's grandest sights—the Grand Canyon, Yosemite Falls, and the geysers at Yellowstone. Largely middle-class park visitors traveled long distances to appreciate the scenic beauty and undisturbed wilderness preserved in the first national parks. Much has changed in the last half century. Large-scale public attendance and demand for modern conveniences (like running water and indoor plumbing) turned portions of the older parks into playgrounds. Later acquisitions, though located nearer to population centers, lacked the isolation that initially protected the first parks. Moreover, human habitation has changed natural characteristics.

Critics within and outside of the NPS resisted such later additions. They held to the standards established for the first national parks and opposed altering the criteria for preservation. These purists strove to maintain the system as Mather had fashioned it.

STEPHEN MATHER

Acknowledged as the best director the NPS has enjoyed in its sixty-five-year history, Mather imprinted an image and ethic the agency has since sought to maintain. He devoted himself to building his National Park Service, for he and the agency became inextricably associated in the public's and the NPS's mind. He succeeded beyond even the most ardent conservationist's hopes, recruiting a professional cadre of employees, winning large budget appropriations, and carefully adding selected, choice parks. By the time illness forced him to retire in 1929, seven new national parks, which Congress transferred from federal land, belonged to the system, as well as fourteen new national monuments. In addition, Mather's charm, energy, and contacts produced successes in soliciting private donations that ultimately became Acadia National Park and Smoky Mountain National Park. Moreover, he "established the Park Service's universally acclaimed interpretive programs, standardized concession contracts, and fought off repeated forays against the parks by power, grazing, lumbering and mining interests."[4] Mather also expended considerable effort to increase public use of the parks. He built roads to make the parks accessible, sometimes paying for them with his own funds. He also persuaded the rail-roads to construct hotels in the parks near their lines.

During Mather's era the conflict between the agency's dual responsibilities—to "preserve for all times the wonders within its boundaries in a natural state" and to make them "available for the enjoyment of all people"—remained hidden.[5] Public use of the almost 6 million acres increased only gradually. Much of the land remained too far from population centers to experience any appreciable impact from visitors. However, Mather's insistence on dramatically increasing attendance created in his agency a regard for numbers that has continued.

Nevertheless, Mather set a standard for NPS directors that his successors have not matched. His personal integrity and his devotion to the highest standards for national parks caused four presidents, Democrat and Republican alike, to retain him in the post. He combined flamboyance with practical idealism, persuasiveness, and optimism. His free-wheeling style made him irresistible to everyone he met. His hand-shaking, back-slapping charm covered a steely drive. He fashioned an administration imbued with esprit de corps. He succeeded in building a public image of the NPS as an able agency, devoted to duty, and concerned above all with protecting the national heritage entrusted to its care. Because of Mather's influence, succeeding generations of conservationists viewed the NPS as clean and inviolate, while legislators and businessmen applauded its lean management and ability to attract private donations.

Although Mather drew back from the crassest attempts to commercialize the parks, such as building an aerial tramway across Grand Canyon, his business orientation often prevailed over his conservationist ethic. He always courted chambers of commerce and the private sector and responded positively to their development orientation.

Mather tried hard to isolate agency personnel and decision-making from politics. Unfortunately, he could not ensure that succeeding directors would possess his private means or his ability to shield the NPS from legislative or presidential pressures.

In retrospect the Mather era formed the agency's golden years. A strong, rich leader willing to spend his personal fortune on agency programs, sympathetic administrations, and friendly Congresses helped the NPS develop a superlative image and a proud record of accomplishments. During the 1920s America found much to favor in a park agency that preserved the national heritage and kept costs down. Under Mather's leadership "the National Park Service al-

*most doubled in size and extended into the eastern United States,
historic holdings were quadrupled and the groundwork laid for a
coordinated national historic preservation program."* [6]

The succeeding half century of NPS's history reflected an altered
world. Just as the country experienced profound changes, so did the
NPS, its growth in personnel and responsibilities paralleling the expanding role of the federal government after the 1920s. When President Franklin Roosevelt named Harold Ickes as his secretary of the
interior, he brought an action-oriented liberal to a department heretofore tilted toward conservative development interests. Ickes determined to polish up Interior's reputation, tarnished in the 1923 Teapot
Dome scandal. He failed to achieve his greatest ambition: to reorganize Interior into a Department of Conservation. However, Ickes,
a wheeling-dealing, power-hungry reformer, did persuade Roosevelt
to add considerably to the NPS's holdings and functions. Through
executive order the NPS gained exclusive jurisdiction over all federally owned parks, monuments, and memorials. Its properties increased through the addition of "12 natural areas located in nine
western states and Alaska and 57 historical areas located in 17 pre-
dominately eastern states and the District of Columbia." [7] More significant, Mather's single-purpose agency expanded to administer
diverse lands with different uses. [8] The reorganization of the national
park system in 1933 involved the transfer of jurisdiction from the
War Department (in the case of military parks and monuments established on military reservations) and the Department of Agriculture (for monuments in national forests). These additions also
increased the geographical dispersion of NPS lands. Most important,
the agency became involved in parks devoted chiefly to recreation,
even though it had never defined recreation in any of its policy statements. (Does camping in a natural area fit within the rubric of recreation? Does hiking in a recreational area differ from hiking in a
traditional park? This confusion, both in concept and terminology,
permeates National Park Service literature. Perhaps the classification of "natural" and "recreational" relates to intensity of use. However, the number of visitors to Yellowstone, a natural park, exceeds
that of the Indiana Dunes, a recreational park. The policy of zoning
all parks according to use, adopted during the Carter administration,
holds promise for more precise classifications.) After 1933 a new
national park system emerged, an assemblage of lands preserved for
scientific, historical, scenic, and recreational purposes.

The New Deal also altered the NPS's functions. The agency became not only the planner and operator of federal parks but also of state parks. Mather had promoted the growth of state parks to protect national park standards. Under his aegis the NPS remained aloof from doing more than encouraging local citizens to establish or expand state parks. The history of the establishment of the Indiana Dunes State Park exemplifies the NPS's minimal involvement. The Roosevelt era erased that limitation. With the formation of the Civilian Conservation Corps (CCC), NPS became heavily involved in expanding state open-space programs. Using federal funds to purchase submarginal agricultural lands and employing CCC workers in their development, the agency supervised the creation of forty-six recreational demonstration areas in twenty-four states. With this program Congress showed its first willingness to spend general tax revenue for parks, albeit under emergency economic conditions, when creating jobs held the highest priority.[9]

In 1935 the passage of the Historic Sites Act made the NPS the steward of the nation's scenic glories and the keeper of nationally significant historic sites, buildings, and objects as well. Once again the agency's functions broadened beyond the federal level to include planning and cooperation with local groups.

The NPS's planning responsibility received further emphasis through the Park, Parkway, and Recreational Study Act of 1936, which directed the agency to become the nation's planner for a coordinated program of local, state, and federal parks and recreational lands. In the next two decades the NPS gradually increased its recreational land holdings and assumed responsibility for national parkways and reservoir-related recreational areas. Some agency members accepted the desirability of this step-by-step involvement in recreational planning and operations; however, many in the NPS continued to oppose such responsibility. They contended that the states or other jurisdictions should administer land used primarily for outdoor recreation.

By the mid-1950s the conflict between these two factions of the NPS over the agency's future direction resulted in two major, but separate, park programs. On one hand, with the blessings of the Dwight Eisenhower administration, the NPS put its emphasis on a large-scale program of park improvements. Director Conrad Wirth and NPS officials devoted their energies to the Mission 66 program, which involved refurbishing existing park facilities sadly neglected since 1930. Congress independently established the Outdoor Recreation Resources Review Commission in response to the demand for additional outdoor recreation space and facilities brought about by the nation's increased urbanization, automobile ownership, and leisure time. Much to the NPS's chagrin, this blue-ribbon panel took over the agency's responsibility for devising a plan to correct the nation's deficiency in land for recreational use. In 1962 the commission issued its influential report *Outdoor Recreation for America*.

The report could not have come at a more auspicious time. Stewart Udall, John Kennedy's secretary of the interior, matched Ickes's conservation bent and action orientation. Emulating Ickes, Udall determined to enlarge, reorganize, and modernize the national park system. He put his emphasis on providing accessible park land. Heretofore, national parks had attracted a white middle-class clientele. The new secretary of the interior looked for ways to make open space available to a broader constituency. He especially decried the status quo thinking of the powerful traditionalist bloc in the NPS. Udall set out to change the NPS mind set toward the "beg, borrow or steal system."[10] Conditioned to believe that national park land had "either to be federally owned or given to the government by a lesser jurisdiction or a private donor," no NPS director for the first three-and-a-half decades of the agency's existence pushed for federal purchase of park lands after the ignominious defeat of Mather's Sand Dunes National Park proposal.[11] In large part this stance stemmed not only from the past history of park additions but also from decades of congressional unwillingness to fund acquisitions. NPS leaders, discouraged by the legislative branch's position, never dreamed of mounting an aggressive campaign to obtain a new funding source for the system.

Udall began his effort to reorient the NPS by diminishing its power. Following the recommendation of the Outdoor Recreation Resources Review Commission, he established a new Interior agency, the Bureau of Outdoor Recreation. He transferred responsibility for formulating and implementing a national outdoor recreation plan to this bureau, in spite of the NPS's adamant opposition.[12]

Udall also changed NPS directors, installing George Hartzog in place of Wirth, whom he considered resistant to new directions.[13] The secretary understood that the NPS's first loyalty remained with its natural areas and recognized that the growth of NPS historic and recreational holdings had suffered because the agency had stubbornly continued to apply its time-honored standards of size, uniqueness, and spectacular scenery to all potential new units. He knew that many NPS old-timers had accepted the addition of historical areas to the system solely to gain congressional support for existing parks.[14] He also realized the intense antipathy to recreational areas on the part of some agency personnel, who feared the spread of recreational programs into natural areas. Furthermore, Udall perceived that many NPS veterans opposed any rapid expansion of the park system. In their view only a program of highly selective, incremental additions could protect the agency's position as the keeper of the nation's crown jewels of scenically spectacular, pristine land. These members worried about the appropriateness of new parks that did not meet the criteria of vastness and significance.

Udall saw the NPS's mission very differently. He believed the agency should administer a variety of parks serving different purposes. Casting aside the standards of the 1920s, he reorganized the agency into three co-equal branches: natural, historic, and recreational, with separate resource management, use, and development policies for each. In so doing, he responded to the progressive faction within the NPS that supported the evolution of a dynamic park system and that advocated the addition of national parks throughout the country. It endorsed, as well, the inclusion of representative samples of the nation's diverse and varied habitats, a concept akin to the already established policy of adding national monuments representing the country's historical eras. Most of all, this faction wanted the NPS to overcome its fixation on western land and to provide parks closer to population concentrations.

As part of his reorganization, Udall also strengthened the NPS's efforts to preserve natural areas. He assigned the agency responsibility for administering a new National Landmark Program. It "encouraged the preservation of significant natural lands by . . . state or local governments, conservation organizations, and even private persons."[15] Cowles Bog in the Indiana Dunes received the designation of a national natural landmark in 1966, while it was still owned by the Save the Dunes Council.

The Kennedy administration had even more ambitious plans for the NPS. The Outdoor Recreation Resources Review Commission had recommended a new funding source for park land acquisition to overcome congressional unwillingness to spend general revenue for this purpose. In 1962 Udall persuaded the legislators to establish the Land and Water Conservation Fund.[16] Revenue for the fund comes from national park user fees and offshore oil drilling leases. The Land and Water Conservation Fund provided Udall with a new and vitally necessary revenue source to increase the NPS's holdings, especially those with a heavy emphasis on recreational use. During the Great Depression the NPS had identified twelve such potential parks along shorelines. Congress had since established only the Cape Hatteras National Seashore, and the Mellons had paid for it. "All the others

save one—Cape Cod—went into private or commercial development."[17] In the late 1950s the Mellons once again furthered shoreline conservation by underwriting new NPS studies.[18]

Kennedy's personal support for a park in his home state, the backing of Massachusetts's governor, and widespread local enthusiasm
cajoled Congress into approving the Cape Cod National Seashore in
1961. This landmark act provided for tax dollars to purchase private
land for a federal park. Similar authorization for Point Reyes National Seashore in California and Padre Island National Seashore
in Texas occurred in 1962, but Congress then balked at the expense
of any additional land acquisition until the fund solved the money
problem.

Establishment of the Land and Water Conservation Fund had another effect. It increased congressional influence over the national
park system. Heretofore, the NPS had gone to Congress for approval
of free additions. Parks created on federal land only required an
interagency transfer of ownership, and parks resulting from private
or state donations needed similar simple legislative acquiescence.
Congress could afford such generosity. Now new park proposals carried a price tag. Proponents argued that money from the Land and
Water Conservation Fund would cover the costs. Opponents, shorn
of the argument about spending tax dollars for park acquisition,
wrangled interminably about the federal government's right to purchase private land for public parks. Moreover, since Congress held
the power to tap into the Land and Water Conservation Fund, the
cost of each proposed unit became an important element in the
decision-making. Some critics maintained that the existence of the
fund permitted Congress to view national park additions as pork-
barrel projects. In any case the fund provided the wherewithal for
the proliferation of the national park system in the 1960s and 1970s.

By authorizing these additional units, Congress also accentuated
one of the agency's thorniest difficulties—reconciling the NPS's
mission to maintain nature unimpaired and its obligation to provide
for public use. During the Nixon years the unabated demand for
open space convenient to urban populations led to the establishment of the nation's first urban parks, Golden Gate in California
and Gateway East in New York. Congress also restated the purpose
of the NPS in the 1970 General Authorities Act:

> The National Park system, which began with the establishment
> of Yellowstone National Park in 1872, has since grown to in-
> clude superlative natural, historic, and recreational areas in every
> major region of the United States, its territories and island pos-
> sessions; these areas, though distinct in character, are united

through their interrelated purposes and resources into one national park system, as cumulative expressions of a single national heritage; that individually and collectively these areas derive increased national dignity and recognition of their superb environmental quality through their inclusion jointly with each other in one national park system preserved and managed for the benefit and inspiration of all the people of the United States.[19]

Additions to the system received congressional approval at an accelerating rate during the Gerald Ford and Jimmy Carter administrations. However, in 1978 another reorganization removed the NPS's jurisdiction over historic preservation. A new Interior agency, the Heritage Conservation and Recreation Service, combined the functions of the Bureau of Outdoor Recreation for recreation planning and the NPS's role in planning historic preservation. The agency's veterans complained about this change, just as they had at the establishment of the Bureau of Outdoor Recreation—and with the same result. NPS became more exclusively a land management agency, albeit with a greater diversification of properties.

Along with the vast increase in NPS land holdings in the past half century has come a second major development, a steady breakdown in the agency's insulation from politics. More than any other single influence, the politicization of the NPS altered Mather's original concept for the agency: isolation from political influence. His view typified that of most leaders in the early twentieth century. The professional, the expert, he believed, could make impartial and therefore correct decisions if left uncontaminated by the narrowmindedness and corruption of politics. Before the service's establishment, superintendents of individual federal parks in many cases owed their appointments to political connections. Mather worked hard to recruit park superintendents with professional credentials. Similarly, he created a cadre of professional rangers. He succeeded brilliantly in hiring and training park employees whose virtues included cleanliness, courteousness, versatility, and dedication to the NPS's mission. During the agency's early days, such selectivity and indoctrination sufficed. Mather added civil service protection for the rangers, and his successor, Horace Albright, increased the bureau's stature by obtaining the reclassification of the NPS as one of "the largest and most important in the Interior Department."[20] In 1931 he also achieved civil service coverage for park superintendents.[21]

Five of the six succeeding directors of the NPS rose through the ranks, maintaining the professionalism Mather had tried so hard to inculcate. The exception, Newton Drury, came to the NPS from a career in conservation work, which made him equally sensitive to upholding the Mather tradition of nonpolitical appointments. However, secretaries of the interior appoint park service directors, who serve at the secretary's and the president's pleasure. Until the Dwight Eisenhower administration, directors promoted from the ranks had the opportunity to return to their former jobs if dismissed. Interior Secretary Douglas McKay abolished this job security.

The tradition of career appointments for NPS directors ended with the Richard Nixon administration. As part of a general government reorganization, the NPS director and the agency's top management jobs lost their civil service protection. The politicization of the NPS began in earnest. Conrad Wirth described what happened:

> By the last year of Nixon's first term, the National Park Service began to get requests from the White House to give certain people jobs. Many of these applications were returned with the explanation that the individuals were not qualified. Word came back to the National Park Service from the White House to put them on because refusal to do so would interfere with the President's program. About that time, the Director of the National Park Service, a long term career man in his 50's, was asked to resign. Hartzog resigned under protest. In 1973, a White House man with no experience in the parks was appointed Director of the National Park Service. After the new Director took over, it wasn't long before 20 or so additional people were brought into the Service with qualifications unrelated to the positions they filled.[22]

Ronald Walker, Nixon's NPS director, had served previously as a White House advance man. After two years, his lack of qualifications and general ineptitude forced his resignation. With his three successors the NPS returned to the tradition of career appointments, but political pressure forced two of them to resign. Gary Everhardt and William Whalen both lost their posts because of congressional opposition to their policies.

Though the NPS strove to keep its employees immune from political taint, as a government agency it always operated in a political milieu. Dependent on Congress for operating funds and appropriations for acquisitions, it continually wooed influential senators and representatives, especially those who served as chairmen of the interior and parks appropriations committees. Although such relations permeate the federal system, Mather set the pattern of extensive cultivation of these committees to nurture his nascent agency, and his successors followed his path. They carried on the practice, begun in pre-NPS days, of assigning each park superintendent the job of building political fences. This responsibility includes developing good relations with the senators and congressman from the district in which the park is located; these individuals constitute the congressional delegation for matters involving that park.[23]

The increased politicization of the NPS over the past two decades has affected both its leadership and its policies. The NPS adjusted to the advent of new administrations, shifts in secretaries of the interior, and changes in directors. Each new personality influenced the service's philosophy, as did the realignment of the power base caused by the election of different congressmen, senators, and governors in each park locale. The shifting NPS positions make sense only through understanding the national, state, and local politics of each era. The initial establishment of the Indiana Dunes National Lakeshore and its later enlargements provide an illuminating example of how politics influenced the NPS's decision-making.

In 1916, when a Dunes national park proposal first emerged, the combined political influence of Indiana's governor and junior senator and the bistate coalition of conservationists easily outweighed Porter County's opposition. The proponents' political strength made Mather's endorsement of the park politically feasible. Subsequently, since no national political figure backed the project, the NPS could ignore the Dunes for the next forty years.

Following World War II, pent-up demand for housing fostered the development of urban sprawl. Throughout the nation open space began to disappear. In the midst of a booming economy, which brought higher wages, a shorter work week, and more paid vacations, Americans turned to travel to meet outdoor recreation needs. These pressures resulted in mounting use of national park facilities. The NPS, in turn, began surveying for the first time the park land possibilities along the Great Lakes. The study examined "what portions of undeveloped shoreline remained that were worthy of preservation for their scenic, natural or other recreational values."[24] Several of the study's recommendations directly affected the future of the Indiana Dunes. The report proposed that first consideration should go to "the acquisition of potential recreation shoreline near centers of population like . . . Chicago."[25] It warned that "the advent of the St. Lawrence Seaway has increased industrial demands for Great Lake[s'] frontage—especially for new harbor space. Responsible planning groups should carefully evaluate long-range recreation needs and select port sites where a minimum effect on recreation values would occur."[26] In the accompanying detailed description of each shoreline site surveyed, Indiana Dunes received this accolade: "Few other places on the Great Lakes exhibit a greater need for recreation sites than the vast Chicago Metropolitan area. This remaining portion of Lake Michigan shoreline represents a potential major contribution toward the fulfillment of these recreational needs. Its early acquisition for park uses would be in the best interest of public recreation."[27] The report identified a 5,000-acre section between the western boundary of Porter County and the Indiana Dunes State Park with three-and-a-half miles of shoreline as suitable for preservation.[28]

Although the NPS conducted its Great Lakes studies in 1957–58, publication of the findings did not occur until 1960. The report contained a prefatory letter, signed by Interior Secretary Fred Seaton, stating the Eisenhower administration's cautious approach to national park expansion.

> The Department of Interior is supporting the enactment of legislation to permit the designation by the Secretary of Interior of not more than three shore areas as National Recreation Areas. The shorelines of the Great Lakes will be considered along with those of the Pacific, Atlantic, and Gulf coasts in determining which three areas are worthy of preservation by the Federal Government should Congress enact the legislation. Publication of this survey should not be construed as either approval or disapproval of the recommendations contained herein.[29]

Clearly the Eisenhower administration had no intention of promoting a major expansion of national parks. Instead, the NPS continued to make study upon study of potential additions to the system. It took the advent of a president committed to conservation as one of his "New Frontiers," an interior secretary interested in expanding national park land, and a Congress willing to pay for public ownership of private property for the realization of shoreline parks. Preservation of the Indiana Dunes proceeded against this backdrop of policy change.

From 1959 to 1963 the Douglas bills proposed federal purchase of the very land identified as worthy of preservation by the NPS survey. With the strong support of Secretary Udall, the NPS backed enactment of a Dunes park in Congress. However, in spite of the Kennedy administration's enthusiasm, the opposing political influence of Indiana's Democratic leaders, as well as that of Congressman Charles Halleck, blocked congressional authorization.

Midwest's and Bethlehem's ownership and development of that land deprived the NPS of a contiguous 5,000-acre park with three-and-a-half miles of shoreline. The agency grew fainthearted about embracing the post-1963 Douglas bills. The prospect of administering a noncontiguous lakeshore seemed a doubtful proposition to Director Hartzog.[30] He presciently saw the difficult management problems that a small park bisected by a massive industrial complex would possess. In addition, some NPS officials worried about the continuing base of political support for a Dunes lakeshore, which suffered from the adamant opposition of the local congressman and the halfhearted acquiescence of state government. The anti–Dunes lakeshore elements in the agency also revived the old battle cry of national significance for areas controlled by the NPS. They claimed that the proposed park lacked the characteristics of spectacular, pristine scenery that they regarded as the *sine qua non* of their properties. Finally, NPS traditionalists viewed the lakeshore as the latest in a series of new parks that threatened to tilt the agency's orientation toward recreation. In their view the NPS had no business administering park lands with bathing beaches as their chief asset. They compared the hundreds of thousands of pristine acres in the western parks to the miniscule thousands of acres in Indiana Dunes; they considered the Dunes further degraded by heavy human contact; they concluded that such an addition would bring only monumental headaches to the agency.

Dunes supporters within the NPS based their position on Udall's perceptions of the agency's mission. In essence, they subscribed to the totality of arguments that Indiana Dunes proponents had preached for half a century—and they won. At Udall's insistence and with the blessings of President Lyndon Johnson, even the diehards in the NPS officially had to accept the political decision to preserve the Indiana Dunes. The traditionalists' discontent festered, however, and reappeared in the subsequent attempts to enlarge the park.

More than the covert opposition of a faction within the NPS shaped the agency's stance when a campaign to enlarge the lakeshore began in 1971. A new set of political circumstances decided the NPS's position. In the intervening half decade between the lakeshore's authorization and the beginning of the expansion effort, a groundswell of public support for the environmental movement resulted in a Congress more sympathetic to park enlargements. Even the Nixon administration seemed to have caught park fever. Though conservationists had not greeted Nixon's appointment of Alaska businessman, Walter Hickel, as secretary of the interior with much enthusiasm, Hickel surprised them. Under his aegis the NPS moved steadily toward favoring the establishment of urban parks with heavy recreational use. President Nixon enunciated the new approach in his message to Congress on environmental quality.[31] Hickel coined the phrase that symbolized the new policy—"parks to the people"—and pushed for its implementation during the remaining years of his tenure.[32] NPS teams made exhaustive studies of lands near the nation's urban centers that retained relatively natural characteristics and identified twenty-five potential locations for urban national recreation areas. Two such sites, Gateway National Recreation Area near New York City and Golden Gate National Recreation Area near San Francisco, received congressional approval before the Nixon administration pulled back from the urban park concept, ostensibly in the name of budget retrenchment.[33]

Though lakeshore expansion proponents sought to position their proposal under the urban park umbrella, they did not find much favor for their plan with the Nixon administration. Hickel lost his cabinet seat after publicly opposing Nixon's Vietnam war policy. His replacement, Rogers Morton, favored neither urban parks nor the enlargement of the Indiana Dunes. Neither did Porter County's Republican Congressman Earl Landgrebe, who had assumed Halleck's old seat. Not surprisingly, therefore, a NPS study team investigating the first lakeshore enlargement proposal managed to endorse only 1,800 of the proposed 7,024 acres.[34] They rejected the remaining land as either too expensive, too far from the existing park boundaries, or below national park standards. The report suggested that the State of Indiana or Porter County acquire some of the rejected acreage for additions to the Indiana Dunes State Park or for a county park system that did not exist.

Despite the administration's and Morton's unwillingness to enlarge the lakeshore, its existence provided an event for the 1972 Nixon reelection campaign. The NPS found itself arranging a media extravaganza when ceremonies nominally held for the formal establishment of the park became part of the president's political strategy.

JULIE IN DUNELAND

In spite of overcast skies, the beauty of the Dunes touched the assembled dignitaries and audience. Towering oaks in full foliage and early red-tinged sumac framed the backdrop of tall Dunes. Glimpses of the vast expanse of Lake Michigan waters added to the natural ambiance while an offshore breeze cooled the late summer heat. Today, Friday, September 8, 1972, the crowd awaited formal establishment of the Indiana Dunes National Lakeshore.

Few of the gathering observers understood why six years had elapsed between legislative approval of the park and the ceremonies scheduled to begin at 9:30 A.M. The NPS ascribed the interval to regulations requiring substantial land acquisition before a new park could officially join the system. Conservationists suspected political foot-dragging.

Politics certainly permeated the atmosphere. Porter County Republican women greeted each member of the growing assemblage with homemade signs touting the reelection of President Nixon, two months in the future. Many of the arrivals, clutching American flags and campaign balloons, had come to see the president's younger daughter, Julie, who just yesterday had become the program's star speaker. Appropriately, second district Nixon Reelection Committee Chairman William Conover had announced her participation.

Some of those watching and waiting found the locale for the event wryly amusing. Officialdom had chosen the parking lot of the Indiana Dunes State Park for the festivities, ostensibly because of easy access. However, almost everyone present realized that the 2,500 acres of state land, though technically included within the federal park's boundaries, would never come under federal control. The lakeshore's legislation provided for acquisition of the state park land by donation only. Hoosier Republicans, including Governor Edgar Whitcomb in one of his rare forays to northwest Indiana, knew that would never happen.

As 9:30 came and went, Master of Ceremonies and Lakeshore Advisory Commission Chairman Bill Lieber, grandson of Colonel Richard Lieber, founder of the Indiana state park system, decided the program ought to begin, though neither Julie Eisenhower nor Secretary of Interior Morton had arrived. The crowd, now swelled to more than 1,000, had become impatient. Lieber urged the coterie of officials onto the platform, carefully protected by a blue and white canopy against a sun that would rarely appear. The Republican tilt of the speakers' list became more apparent. Governor Whitcomb made a welcoming address that emphasized the compromise between industrial development and conservation that had produced the lakeshore. Congressman Earl Landgrebe postponed his remarks with the assurance that Julie and Morton had begun the trip from Chicago's O'Hare Airport to Indiana.

For a brief interval, the Democrats took over. Lake County Congressman Ray Madden and Fort Wayne Congressman J. Edward Roush joined Illinois Congressman Abner Mikva in praising the lakeshore and paying tribute to Senator Paul Douglas, whose illness kept him in Washington. All three used the occasion to urge expansion of the park and funding for its development. Landgrebe knew his turn to counter their arguments would come later. The absence of Indiana's two Democratic senators caused comment. Only insiders knew they had wanted to participate by telephone from Washington. Ostensibly the length of the program had caused their request to be denied. Dorothy Buell, who had made the trip from California especially for the event, sat on the platform, though she, too, had not been invited to speak.

Now a parade of cars rolled into the parking lot. Everyone's eyes turned to see Secret Service men jump out and move to strategic locations atop the surrounding Dunes. Julie, with Secretary and Mrs. Morton in tow, made her way to the stage.

Slim and girlish, dressed in yellow and orange knit, Julie proceeded to change the atmosphere with a graceful talk that heartened even the most cynical conservationists. Noting she "was proud to be able to represent my father at this historic occasion," Julie paid tribute to "these magnificient dunes" and praised Senator Douglas.[35] Her low-key, positive speech captured both Republicans and Democrats and set the tone for Secretary Morton's principal address.

Before introducing the secretary, Congressman Landgrebe interposed his anti-lakeshore position. He reiterated the complaints of lakeshore opponents—lack of clear boundaries, lack of intensive development of the park, lack of funds to complete land acquisition, loss of tax valuation, and controversy over purchase prices.

Next, Morton, a gray-haired, tall man, strode to the rostrum to read his prepared text, which ignored his fellow Republican's point of view. He began with obligatory praise for Nixon as "the first President to make the environment a national priority."[36] Remembering that Morton had voted against the lakeshore's authorization when he had served as Maryland's first district congressman in 1966, conservationists began to squirm uneasily at this dose of partisan rhetoric. Morton's further remarks calmed their apprehension and even brought delight. He honored Buell, among a long list of those with "tenacity and vision" who had produced "the success of a momentous legislative effort."[37] He particularly singled out Douglas's contribution, declaring "this great Lakeshore will be a lasting tribute to Senator Douglas' efforts."[38] The remainder of Morton's speech sounded like an environmentalist's paean. "Together, we must commit ourselves to our great national goals . . . restoring air and water of our environment and preserving the magnificent achievement of nature, such as the dunes. . . . More than any other generation of Americans, we can shape the quality of life for those who follow us."[39]

Edmund Thornton, chairman of the National Parks Centennial Commission, spoke next, but his talk seemed anticlimactic. He reminded his audience that the Indiana Dunes dedication occurred as the first such event during the one hundredth anniversary year *of the establishment of Yellowstone. However, Thornton's remarks lacked the emotional impact that Morton's talk had engendered. Park proponents wondered if they had heard correctly. Not only had a former congressional opponent praised the lakeshore, but as interior secretary he had promised funds for imaginative development and creative programming.*

Next came an even more incredible occurrence. Instead of rushing away to the next campaign stop, Julie and Morton decided to take a walk along the shoreline with most of the audience, many newspaper reporters, and TV camera crews accompanying them. They appeared in no hurry to leave the Dunes. Instead, they chatted amiably with members of the trailing entourage. Julie reminded her listeners of her Hoosier grandmother, and Morton said, "If we are in error, let's err on the side of conservation." Not even the Secret Service detail hovering around her seemed willing to interfere with what Julie called "this magnificent day." Even the sun cooperated, finally peeking through the clouded sky.

Armed with a Dunes painting and an American flag pin inscribed with the dedication's date, the party prepared to leave. Local, county, and state police announced the departure through their walkie-talkie radios. Secret Service men disappeared from their Dunes vantage points and reappeared ready to climb into waiting cars.

As the caravan of official cars moved out of the parking lot, the audience, too, prepared to leave. All knew that the morning affair had cemented the lakeshore's existence. Even diehard opponents grudgingly admired the pictures of Julie flanked by the cabinet officer strolling along the beach that appeared in Saturday papers from coast to coast.

The glow of the ceremonies soon vanished as the hard realities of Nixon's second term became evident. With the appointment in 1973 by Secretary Morton of Walker as the NPS's first strictly political director, the agency's stand against enlargement of the lakeshore hardened. At the 1974 House hearings the Department of Interior strongly recommended against enactment of the latest version of the lakeshore's expansion.[40]

However, expansion proponents had assembled a formidable coalition of Indiana, Illinois, and national environmental and labor support as well as the backing of the Republican governor of Indiana. Both Indiana's Democratic senators cosponsored the legislation, and the Democratic party controlled both houses of Congress. Responsive to this political alignment, NPS spokesman Richard Curry appeared at a House hearing to voice his agency's willingness to accept 1,152 acres of the proposed 5,300. This position represented a cut of 750 acres from the NPS's 1971 assessment. In answer to sharp questioning by Representative Joseph Skubitz (R., Kans.), Curry could not explain why the agency, which in 1966 had supported an 11,000–acre Dunes park, now would not endorse additions that kept the lakeshore's acreage far short of that figure. Obviously Curry could not articulate the political factors that had influenced the NPS's decision-making process.[41] However, Curry's repeated statement that his agency's position reflected "our thinking for this area" revealed both the administration's political stance toward the Indiana Dunes and the resurrection of the NPS's negative feelings toward the park. In neither the Department of Interior nor the NPS did the Indiana Dunes enjoy the political backing and support that might have produced a more favorable administration position. Curry served as spokesman for the anti-lakeshore political elements existing both in the Republican party and in the NPS. Consistently opposing more than token additions to the park, he repeated the same message at the Senate hearing three months later.[42]

In 1974, following the election of Floyd Fithian as the Democratic congressman representing Porter County, the political chemistry changed once again.

FLOYD FITHIAN

After forty-two years of unremitting defeat, a Democrat finally won Indiana's second congressional district seat. Floyd Fithian bounded into office on the tide of voter reaction to the Watergate scandals. Incumbent Landgrebe unwittingly assisted the Democratic campaign with his mulish support of the disgraced president. Landgrebe's famous utterance, "Don't confuse me with the facts," when questioned about his blind devotion to Nixon, and his offer to "be shot with him if necessary" received nationwide publicity, much to the discomfort of local Republicans.[43]

Fithian's credentials revealed little of the political acumen and skill he used four times to woo and win the predominantly conservative voters of the Dunes district. A transplanted Hoosier, he could not even appeal to Indiana roots, a tactic that Indiana's Democratic senators, Vance Hartke and Birch Bayh, had effectively employed. Born, reared, and educated in Nebraska, Fithian had served in the Navy as a radar specialist during the Korean War. Be-

fore coming to the district he taught high school in his native state. Then, moving up the academic ladder, he won an appointment to teach American history at Purdue University. Though he downplayed his intellectualism in public, preferring to emphasize his part-time farming experience, he could not shed his professorial manner of speaking.

Fithian's political involvement began with volunteer work for Robert Kennedy's successful 1968 presidential primary campaign in Indiana. A product of a staunchly Republican family, Fithian nevertheless found himself drawn to the younger brother of the assassinated president and his vision for America. In 1970 Fithian again volunteered to assist in a Democratic race. This time he served as Tippecanoe County coordinator for Michigan City businessman Phillip Sprague in his ill-fated race against second district Congressman Landgrebe. The campaign taught Fithian a great deal about district voters and made him known to party professionals. By the 1972 election the Republican-dominated legislature had redrawn the boundaries of the second district to eliminate Michigan City. Fithian, nevertheless, urged Sprague to relocate and make a second try against Landgrebe, but Sprague demurred. On the last filing day Fithian decided to take on the challenge himself. The Democrats, unable to conceive of winning the congressional seat, happily accepted him. Landgrebe easily won reelection.

The campaign seasoned Fithian and made him eager to try again in 1974. His sense of history and his opponent's record convinced him that a middle-of-the-road Democrat could triumph—and 61 percent of the voters proved him right.

Fithian came to office with a vast storehouse of knowledge about American political history but no experience as an officeholder. A firm believer in pragmatic politics, he operated on the principle that rational people can resolve any problem. The new congressman subscribed to the conviction that communication between interest groups can produce a solution to any controversy. Before taking office he put this conviction to the test by endeavoring to resolve the district's most heated controversy—expansion of the Indiana Dunes National Lakeshore.

Fithian first held a mammoth public hearing on the issue. He invited all interested parties to present testimony concerning every section of land proposed for addition to the park. Virtually ignoring the NPS, Fithian concentrated on assembling various factions of his constituency for a day-long presentation of their views.

Following the public hearing, Fithian convened a private negotiating session to which he invited representatives of industry, the affected communities, scientists, and the Save the Dunes Council, again omitting the NPS. He attempted to pressure each participant into making concessions in the time-honored fashion of American consensus politics; however, none of the representatives of the key interest groups modified their stands. All had long experience in the Dunes struggle and remained steadfast in their respective positions. Fithian had to take responsibility for deciding among the opposing viewpoints—something he had sought to avoid. Thereupon, the freshman congressman developed a bill, which proposed substantial enlargement of the park but omitted some land that industry sought to keep. Fithian proudly boasted that his legislative proposal, when passed, would end the controversy over the boundaries of the lakeshore. He learned soon enough how unrealistic a goal he had set.

Fithian's 1975 public hearing on Dunes legislation stood in sharp contrast to Mather's 1916 public hearing. Then the director of the NPS came from Washington to hear the views of the park supporters. Mather himself played a large role in orchestrating the hearing, making sure that an impressive roster of nationally known speakers, as well as Illinois and Indiana officials, endorsed the establishment of a Sand Dunes Park. No one uttered a word in opposition. The agency had complete control of the speakers and the field inspection that followed; it prepared the follow-up report endorsing the proposal to Congress.

The 1975 hearing took a very different tack. This time Congress held the reins while the NPS sat on the sidelines. The shift in power between Congress and the NPS during the intervening half century caused the change. Fithian determined the speakers' list and made sure, in a much more democratic fashion, that a spectrum of witnesses testified. Instead of soliciting testimonials from nationally known speakers, he concentrated on getting local evidence in favor of or opposed to park enlargement. He conducted the field investigation and wrote the report of the hearing in the form of proposed legislation. Not only did NPS local management stay completely aloof, but NPS officials in Washington also remained apart. Only when Fithian's bill came to the stage of committee hearings would they present their comments.

Fithian, characteristically, walked a tightrope on the Dunes expansion issue, trying to placate all the interest groups. Though he stated repeatedly that the lakeshore did not represent an issue of particular concern for the vast majority of second district residents, he knew full well that the park and its expansion had paramount importance for those living and doing business in the Dunes. He balanced his support of conservationists' concerns with equal time and attention to industrial interests.

As promised, Fithian sponsored expansion legislation after paring the proposed addition to 4,686 acres. His bill overcame predictable NPS and administration negativism and passed the House in February 1976. Three months later, at the Senate hearing, the last-ditch opposition of the Republicans surfaced. There, Assistant Secretary of the Interior Nathaniel Reed appeared to testify for a 987-acre addition to the park. He further emasculated his proposal by asking for an immediate appropriation for 203 acres and later funding for the remaining 784 acres. Using the cost of the addition as the reason for the administration's opposition, Reed flatly stated that many of the additions "are excessively expensive as well as impossible to manage."[44] The Senate, like the House, ignored the NPS's and administration's judgments and voted to enlarge the lakeshore, though reducing the addition to 3,300 acres.

Throughout the five years of congressional consideration of lakeshore expansion, the NPS steadily decreased the acreage it supported, bowing to mounting pressure from first the Nixon and then the Ford administrations. Land that one year won agency support as desirable in the next year became too costly or more suitable for state acquisition. Lack of support for the park in Republican circles heavily influenced the NPS's decision-making. In response to the agency's vacillation, the Democratic Congress legislated additions to the Indiana Dunes without regard for the NPS's shifting positions. The agency's presentation of its viewpoint amounted almost to an obligatory exercise in rhetoric, politely heard by congressional committees and then ignored. The NPS clearly lost its role as the agent for conservation. Its official pronouncements became far removed from the results that nonpartisan field study teams reported. Instead of basing decisions about additions on their value to the lakeshore's purposes, the agency stand became a vehicle for administration cost-consciousness.

Passage of the first lakeshore expansion bill in 1976 did not end the pressure for additions to the park. In the legislation Congress had included a directive to the NPS, ordering it to make a further study of two sections dropped at the time of final passage. By the time another NPS study team appeared at Indiana Dunes to investigate the value of these parcels to the lakeshore, the political picture had again changed. President Jimmy Carter occupied the White House; Cecil Andrus was secretary of the interior; and the new director of the NPS, William Whalen, had served as superintendent of the Golden Gate National Recreation Area, one of the new urban parks. The study team report recommended one of the areas, the Beverly Shores Island and Strip, for acquisition.[45] Previously labeled as too expensive by successive NPS pronouncements, it now won approval. Political support for the incorporation of this land into the park included both the state's senators, Congressman Fithian, and Indiana's governor, Otis Bowen. The study team rejected the second area, land sandwiched between a utility plant on the west and the lakeshore on the east, as unnecessary in spite of its value as a buffer zone between industrial land and the lakeshore. Again politics, not merit, influenced the NPS's views. Only Indiana's senior senator, Birch Bayh, supported this addition. Indiana's junior senator, Republican Richard Lugar, who had replaced Vance Hartke in the 1976 election, opposed any expansion of the lakeshore that intruded on industrial land. Both Bayh and Fithian, who sponsored the second expansion bill in the House, insisted on Lugar's support. Ultimately neither the Beverly Shores tract nor the buffer zone won congressional approval in the expansion bill of 1980.[46] Ignoring the NPS's views once again, the legislators approved almost 500 other acres for addition to the lakeshore. This second increase in the park's holdings resulted after four years of effort against a backdrop of indifference on the part of the Carter administration. The appearance of Assistant NPS Director Ira Hutchinson instead of NPS Director Whalen to speak for the administration at one set of congressional hearings signaled the executive branch's low priority for the Indiana Dunes.[47]

In addition, the House and Senate dragged their heels on the issue, each body passing a version of an expansion bill in different sessions, thus canceling each other's work. The senatorial sponsor, Bayh, preoccupied with his wife's terminal illness and a bitter reelection campaign (which he ultimately lost), displayed less than his usual interest. The resultant act typified the incremental end product of much of the American legislative process—it incorporated bits and pieces into the lakeshore's domain; it pleased no one, giving expansion proponents far less than they had wanted and disappointing opponents who had hoped to block any additions. The NPS lost the land it considered most necessary for proper management of the lakeshore. A newly aggressive Republican minority in the Senate successfully blocked passage of a larger expansion bill by raising the banner of expense, a prelude to the Ronald Reagan era.

The NPS in its role as the administrative agency most concerned with land preservation played a decisive role in the ultimate land use of the Indiana Dunes. In retrospect, Mather's concept of the agency as a politically shielded bureau restricted to managing transferred public lands or donations seems at best naive and unrealistic and at worst open to charges of elitism and tyranny. Under his charismatic leadership, his vision sufficed for thirteen years. House Speaker Joseph Cannon's dictum "not one penny for scenery" gave way to a slowly developing trend that enlarged the agency's responsibilities and budgets. During the New Deal the NPS added historic preservation and national recreational planning to its mandate, while steadily expanding its land base. After World War II it concentrated on modernizing its properties, with the assent of a Congress now willing to invest more federal dollars in the upkeep of the national park system.

Until the Kennedy-Johnson years the NPS kept a low political profile. Successive directors worked amiably with various administrations, accepting additional jurisdictions as offered, concentrating on the management of its holdings, and practicing fiscal austerity. The agency functioned like a traditional mission-oriented bureaucracy, never questioning publicly the policies and procedures under which it operated.

From 1960 to 1980 the NPS struggled to cope with political change. First, the executive branch directed the agency to increase its holdings substantially by modifying long-held standards for additions to its domain. No longer did the emphasis rest solely on spectacular scenery, nor did the avenues for acquisition remain limited to public land transfers or donations. With the passage of the Land and Water Conservation Fund federal purchase of private land became permissible with the approval of Congress. Though internal resistance to such dramatic shifts in the agency's parameters existed, publicly the NPS acquiesced but remained cool to the new trends.

Frustrated by the agency's unresponsiveness to the growing number of conservation activists, who reflected a rise in American participatory politics, these groups turned to Congress to achieve their goals. The legislative branch became more directly involved in the selection of new parks. Certainly the selection became more responsive to public influence. Advocates of a particular park, through congressional sponsorship for their proposal, could hope for a public hearing in both the House and Senate. Adherents soon learned that introduction of legislation never ensured a hearing. Political pressure had to push the NPS, the Department of the Interior, and the administration to declare their positions publicly at a hearing. However, congressional involvement did mean that NPS had less influence over park enactments than the proponents and opponents of each project. Only the naive assumed that merit alone decided the NPS's position, even in Mather's day. A constellation of forces influenced each decision to enlarge the system. In the past, away from the glare of intense public interest, the agency could weigh each addition's political benefits and liabilities and perhaps reach a balanced conclusion. As Congress took center stage in decision-making, the NPS, in most cases, and certainly in the case of Indiana Dunes, became the public mouthpiece of the administration in power. No matter what the agency had enunciated in the past, it obligingly changed its stance with any shift in Interior Department and/or White House policy. Increasingly in the 1970s Congress paid less attention to the agency's views and more to the pleadings of constituents.

No park service director after Mather possessed his stature or ability to win political support for the agency without suborning its independent decision-making ability. In light of the NPS's politicization during the past two decades, some have suggested its removal from the Department of the Interior. For example, former NPS Director Whalen proposed an independent status akin to the Smithsonian Institution.[48] Though the desirability of this solution remained questionable in terms of accountability, national support for perpetuation of the national park system continued unabated. Americans' delight in the system that expanded following World War II made the NPS more visible and inevitably more controversial. The increase of parks resulted in a more accessible agency and one open to criticism. The NPS itself never resolved internal division over its purpose, its holdings, and the use of its land. Founded in an era when conservation and incrementalism seemed responsible politics, the NPS appeared still rooted in that tradition when the nation moved to an age of environmentalism and public participation.

NOTES

1. William Lienesch, "How Much Will We Pay to Save the Parks?" *National Parks*, Feb. 1981, p. 11.

2. The latter were authorized by various presidents under the authority of the Antiquities Act of 1906.

3. For an extended analysis of the genesis of the NPS units, see Ronald E. Lee, *Family Tree of the National Park System* (Philadelphia: Eastern National Park and Monument Association, 1972).

4. Shankland, *Steve Mather*, p. 232.

5. U.S. *Statutes at Large*, 39 (1915–17), "An Act to Establish a National Park Service and for Other Purposes," Aug. 25, 1916.

6. Lee, *Family Tree*, p. 18.

7. Ibid., p. 21.

8. Additions to the national park system included national memorials such as the Washington Monument and the Statue of Liberty, national military parks such as Gettysburg and Antietam and their adjacent military cemeteries, the National Capitol parks, and the George Washington Memorial Parkway.

9. Wirth, *Parks, Politics and the People*, pp. 176–90.

10. Ibid., p. 198.

11. Ibid.

12. Ibid., pp. 174–76, 282–83.

13. Authors' interview with Stewart Udall, Washington, 1977.

14. Lee, *Family Tree*, p. 63.

15. Ibid., p. 43.

16. U.S. *Statutes at Large*, 78, pt. 2 (Jan. 1964–Oct. 1964), "Land and Water Conservation Provisions," Sept. 3, 1964.

17. Lee, *Family Tree*, p. 58.

18. U.S. Department of the Interior, National Park Service, *Our Vanishing Shoreline* (1955); *A Report on the Seashore Recreation Survey of the Atlantic and Gulf Coasts* (1955); *Pacific Coast Recreation Area Survey* (1959); and *Our Fourth Shore: Great Lakes Shoreline Recreation Area Survey* (1959).

19. U.S. *Statutes at Large*, 84, pt. 1 (Feb. 1970–Nov. 1970), "An Act to Improve the National Park System by the Secretary of the Interior," Aug. 18, 1970.

20. Donald C. Swain, *Wilderness Defender: Horace Albright and Conservation* (Chicago: University of Chicago Press, 1970), p. 191.

21. Ibid., p. 192.

22. Wirth, *Parks, Politics and the People*, p. 365.

23. William Everhart, *The National Park Service* (New York: Praeger, 1972), p. 172.

24. *Our Fourth Shore*, p. 3.

25. Ibid., p. 8.

26. Ibid., p. 9.

27. U.S. Department of the Interior, National Park Service, *Remaining Shoreline Opportunities in Minnesota, Wisconsin, Illinois, Indiana, Ohio, Michigan, Pennsylvania and New York* (Washington, 1959), p. 41.

28. Ibid.

29. *Our Fourth Shore*, p. 1.

30. Authors' interview with George Palmer, associate regional director, NPS northeast region, Valparaiso, 1977.

31. U.S. President, *Public Papers of the President of the United States* (Washington: Office of the Federal Register, National Archives and Records Service, 1968), Richard M. Nixon, 1971, p. 105.

32. News Release, U.S. Department of the Interior, Sept. 14, 1970, Save the Dunes Council Files.

33. For an extended discussion of the urban parks program, see J. William Futrell, "Parks to the People: New Directions for the National Park System," *Emory Law Journal*, 25 (1966), 225–316.

34. U.S. Department of the Interior, National Park Service, *National Park Service Study Team Report on Proposed Expansion of the Indiana Dunes National Lakeshore* (Washington, 1971).

35. "Lake Front Dedication," Valparaiso *Vidette Messenger*, Sept. 9, 1972, p. 1; Bob Jackson, "Morton Asks Everyone to Preserve Heritage," Michigan City *News-Dispatch*, Sept. 9, 1972, p. 1.

36. U.S. Department of the Interior, News Release of "Remarks of the Secretary of the Interior, Honorable Rogers C. B. Morton at Dedication of Indiana Dunes National Lakeshore Near Gary, Indiana," Sept. 8, 1972, p. 1, Save the Dunes Council Files.

37. Ibid.

38. Ibid., p. 2.

39. Ibid., p. 4.

40. U.S. Congress, House Committee on Interior and Insular Affairs, hearings before a subcommittee of the Committee on Interior on HR 357, 93rd Cong., 2nd sess., 1974.

41. Ibid., p. 34.

42. U.S. Congress, Senate Committee on Interior and Insular Affairs, Indiana Dunes National Lakeshore, hearings before a subcommittee of the Interior Committee, Senate, on S.B. 820, 93rd Cong., 2nd sess., 1974, pp. 17–49.

43. U.S. Congress, House, 88th Cong., 2nd sess., Aug. 17, 1964, *Congressional Record*, E 5502.

44. U.S. Congress, Senate Committee on Interior and Insular Affairs, S. 3329 and H.R. 1455, hearings before a subcommittee of the Interior Committee, Senate on S.B. 3329 and H.R. 1455, 89th Cong., 1st sess., 1965, p. 37.

45. U.S. Department of the Interior, National Park Service, *Special Study, Areas, III-A, III-C & II-A*, June 1977, Indiana Dunes National Lakeshore.

46. U.S., *Statutes at Large*, 94, pt. 3 (Dec. 1980), "An Act to Provide for the Establishment of the Indiana Dunes National Lakeshore," Dec. 28, 1980.

47. He testified before the House Subcommittee on Public Lands and National Parks on July 26, 1979. No published report of this hearing exists. See also U.S. Congress, Senate Committee on Energy and Natural Resources, S. 599, hearings, before a subcommittee of the Committee on Energy and Natural Resources, 95th Cong., 1st sess., 1979, Publication 96–73.

48. "Make Park Service Independent Entity, Recommends Past Director," *Conservation Report* (Washington: National Wildlife Federation, June 30, 1982), p. 3.

9 Limited Victory

Clamor for environmental protection reached a crescendo between 1969 and 1973. As public attention turned to domestic affairs, due to the destruction, discord, and disillusionment of the Vietnam War, a series of environmental disasters focused national awareness on the need for new federal controls. New and stringent legislation protecting basic resources resulted from citizens concerned about pollution of the air and water and the contamination of the land.

Professor Wallace Stegner of Stanford University sounded an alarm typical of the period: "Unless, being men and not bacteria, and living not in an agar dish but on a renewable earth, we apply to ourselves and our habitat the intelligence that has engendered both. That means drastically and voluntarily reducing our numbers, decontaminating our earth, and thereafter husbanding, building and nourishing, instead of squandering and poisoning."[1] In addition, the militancy of the antiwar movement carried over into protests against environmental degradation.

The new national consensus fueled an ecological crusade. Heretofore, aesthetic conservationists had concentrated on incremental and isolated attempts to preserve public land holdings for parks, wildlife refuges, and bird sanctuaries. Now they swelled their membership by focusing on larger issues involving the preservation of the land, water, and air from the impacts of a growing chemically dependent society. In addition, a new breed of conservation organization, such as the Wilderness Society and the Friends of the Earth, emerged. Along with such later additions as the National Resources Defense Council, Environmental Action, and the League of Conservation Voters, these more militant associations increased the political visibility and viability of environmentalism.

This broadened coalition of conservationists increasingly criticized the National Park Service (NPS) for a narrow interpretation of its role. Historically, the agency viewed its mandate as primarily that of managing the land under its jurisdiction for maximum public use.

Reluctant Ally

Its other function, that of preserving the natural resources within its borders, received less attention. The NPS neither exhibited much sensitivity about how its actions affected its own holdings nor accepted responsibility for protecting its domain from external threats. Instead, the NPS maintained that its authority stopped at the boundary lines established by Congress for each unit. The agency seemed helpless to prevent deterioration caused by any source outside of its jurisdiction. It relied solely on persuading Congress to enlarge a unit's boundaries. Obviously such expansion could not mitigate external threats to park resources that originated at some distance from NPS land. The agency also lacked both the scientific knowledge and political strength to advocate criteria such as ecosystems or animal habitats as the basis for a park's boundaries and settled for a congressional determination, which generally used arbitrary political subdivision borders.[2] The Indiana Dunes particularly suffered from the NPS's approach to resource protection. Beginning with the establishment of the lakeshore, the NPS and conservation organizations clashed over how to preserve the park's natural qualities from both the agency's decisions and industrial contamination. The NPS's weak stance, along with the broadening environmental perspective of the Save the Dunes Council and its allies, forced these groups to become the lakeshore's advocate in confrontations with the agency and the park's industrial neighbors.

Park proponents used the tools provided by the upsurge of national environmental concern with varying success. The National Environmental Policy Act (NEPA) of 1969 compelled the consideration of environmental values in federal decision-making.[3] The following year the creation of two new agencies, the Council on Environmental Quality (CEQ) and the Environmental Protection Agency (EPA), both independent of existing federal departments, provided the institutional framework for the federal response to environmental problems.[4]

NEPA required all federal agencies, including the NPS, to examine how their actions might affect the quality of the environment.[5] The law did not make rejection of a project mandatory because of adverse environmental effects, but its framers hoped that public scrutiny of the environmental impact statements would generate sufficient public pressure to accomplish that end. "If we only had had NEPA in the 1960s, the Port of Indiana would never have been built," one consultant involved in formulating NEPA claims. He further maintains that the existence of NEPA would have precluded federal funding for the project.[6]

Consolidation of the often diffuse and fragmented federal efforts to control pollution occurred with the formation of the EPA. The new agency's jurisdiction included such key environmental challenges as determination of standards for air and water quality, management of solid wastes, and establishment of standards for use of pesticides and levels of noise to which people could be exposed. For the NPS, EPA's formation offered hope that the nation's park lands might escape further agricultural and industrial contamination and once again enjoy clean skies and pure water.

Establishment of the CEQ meant that for the first time in the nation's history the executive branch of government had an advisory group focusing on the environment and able to offer input into policy formation. The influence of CEQ waxed and waned, depending on the interest of a particular president and the quality of the appointees. The CEQ's activities, largely those of a clearinghouse, had little direct effect on NPS. However, CEQ's annual report most often gave a detailed account of NPS activities and accomplishments and thereby informed a larger constituency.

The expectations initially aroused by these environmental advances soon dissipated. As John Quarles, EPA's first director, relates, "The year 1973 witnessed a dissolution of the national consensus that had supported demands for environmental reform. This was in part the result of the difficulties in carrying out the environmental programs already established and in part the consequence of the energy crisis. The situation was aggravated a year later by the recession. The inertia was also a result of the movement's success in helping to obtain legislation to deal with several of the major environmental problems; that very success created the impression that public pressure was no longer needed." Moreover, the courts held that agencies did not have to pay heed to their NEPA statements and had the prerogative to decide whether or not adverse environmental impacts should prohibit projects.[7] Nevertheless, the genuine accomplishments of EPA in the 1970s did ameliorate many blatant pollution problems and did assist the NPS in difficulties with external threats. At Indiana Dunes conservationists turned again and again to the EPA for help in combatting the impacts of industrial pollution on lakeshore land, and EPA standards and enforcement did improve northwest Indiana's air and Lake Michigan's water. Without legislative authority to concern itself with pollution emanating beyond its own lands, the NPS preferred to rely on the conservationists to battle the despoilers. The Save the Dunes Council and its allied organizations found dealing with both EPA and Indiana on these matters their most difficult problem. (Enforcement of EPA air-quality standards belonged to a state once the federal agency had accepted its plan for remediation.)

The NPS's unwillingness to tackle external environmental threats to its property at Indiana Dunes matched the agency's general and longstanding inability to recognize that some of its own actions resulted in undesirable environmental impacts. At first, NPS did not adequately understand how to manage its land so as to minimize environmental damage. A series of studies in the 1930s resulted in the publications entitled *The Fauna of the National Parks of the United States*. These reports as well as later *Scientific Monographs* contained management recommendations based on the identification of ecological problems.[8] However, it would take thirty more years and the appearance of two reports prepared by blue-ribbon panels, which criticized NPS's ecological vision, to effect change. They spurred Secretary of Interior Stewart Udall into appointing the agency's first chief scientist. The Leopold Committee report in 1963 dealt with protection of wildlife habitats within the agency's holdings.[9] The Robbins Committee report of the same year decried the lack of scientific research by NPS.[10]

Further protection for park land from the effects of NPS's actions occurred in 1964. The Wilderness Act mandated that certain portions of the national park system remain pristine.[11] Passage of this legislation resulted from charges by a growing band of conservationists that the agency had compromised its stewardship by overconstruction. They argued, as did a later report, that "Mission 66, instead of being a far-sighted planning operation to conserve [these] choice areas, seems to have been conceived to allow more complete infiltration and uncritical use."[12]

Wilderness designation for some park lands put the spotlight on the NPS's concern for the ecological safety of all of its holdings. More searching questions arose about the environmental sensitivity of the agency's operation. Conservationists believed all parks, including recreational units, should emphasize an individual's relation to nature and decried a tendency toward grandiosity in park planning. They urged the construction of the fewest possible unobtrusive facilities.

At Indiana Dunes the NPS seemed bent on repeating the mistakes that had brought nationwide criticism of its environmental blindness. Reluctantly, the Save the Dunes Council learned both to contend with the agency's unwillingness to rebuff external threats to the lakeshore's domain and to care for the natural resources of its holdings. Much of the impetus for the council's continued activity and broadened environmental focus stemmed from the leadership of its second president, Sylvia Troy.

SYLVIA TROY

In the mid-1960s Sylvia Troy assumed leadership of the Save the Dunes Council. Like Bess Sheehan and Dorothy Buell, Sylvia exuded fire and determination. Unlike them, she fought not only to save the Indiana Dunes from industrial development but also to protect it from a new and unexpected enemy. Recognition that the NPS would not necessarily guard and secure the lakeshore came slowly indeed. When Troy assimilated that reality, she and the council embarked on a new undertaking.

Self-possession and ability to lead did not always characterize Sylvia Cranberg Troy. As a bashful adolescent in the 1930s, she attended an all-girl public high school in the Bronx, followed by matriculation at all-female Hunter College. Both choices resulted from her extreme shyness. Fortunately, however, Sylvia compensated for her discomfort with people by taking refuge in a love for nature, particularly the water. She credits her mother with having developed and nurtured this lifelong enjoyment. "My mother was very creative about getting the kids away in the summer. We always went to Rockaway Beach along the Atlantic Coast. One year, we lived in a tent for the summer. Other times, we rented a cottage. During the depression, she operated a concession and rented out lockers—one way or another she saw to it that we were out of the city."[13]

Sylvia Troy graduated from Hunter in 1944 with a degree in medical social work. In 1946 she married a young doctor, Jack Troy, and a year after that gave birth to a daughter. The couple spent their first two summers on Fire Island, New York, where Jack worked as the community's only doctor. They adored the beaches, dunes, and ocean and dreamed of settling somewhere scenic, the Pacific northwest perhaps. When a clinic position opened up in Whiting, Indiana, they accepted, considering it a stepping-stone to the ideal location they envisioned. Now, over thirty years later, Jack Troy still works at the northwest Indiana clinic.

In 1948 the Troys moved to Whiting without knowing anything about it. "On the map it looked fabulous. It was close to Chicago's large medical centers and cultural activities and close to the shores of Lake Michigan, which I knew were beautiful from articles I had read in the National Geographic." The map did not prepare them *for Standard Oil's contribution to scenic Lake County, Indiana. They hated Whiting on sight, finding it both horribly ugly and depressingly dirty.*

Indescribable odors from Lever Brothers' Corn Products plant and from Standard Oil and smoke, which produced instant night, assailed their senses and sent them immediately in search of escape. They found respite and refuge in the Indiana Dunes. To some extent, Whiting's people compensated for its dreary physical setting. "At that time, all Standard Oil employees had to live in the city. Over 100 Ph.D.'s lived in that one little town. It was a great people resource. Although we lived on the railroad track because of the [postwar] housing shortage, we had wonderful neighbors and good friends from the clinic." Nevertheless, the Dunes provided Sylvia and Jack with a greatly needed escape. Twice a week the Troys packed up their growing family for excursions to the Indiana Dunes State Park. These outings offered salvation and allowed survival in a place far removed from the fantasy of life in a beautiful place.

A life-threatening miscarriage, the subsequent birth of a second daughter and a son, preoccupation with husband, children, schools, temple, and community kept Sylvia Troy close to home during her first ten years in Whiting. She lived a comfortable middle-class life without resentment and without complaint. Her natural shyness and hesitancy helped her to blend with her peers. She desired neither career nor cause, and she showed no glimmer of talent for her future roles: actress, leader, partisan political tactician.

About 1960 Sylvia went alone to a Save the Dunes Council dinner at Jackson's Restaurant in Miller. She had read about the event in the newspaper, and, although she knew something of the preservation effort as a result of her attempts to buy land in the Dunes, she did not know any of the people nor the specific goals of the organization. "I was immediately impressed with the quality of the people, and I approved of their objectives. They were all nature lovers—non-political, non-activist, not organizers, not joiners, not cause-oriented. They sought out the Dunes because they loved it. They all came from somewhere else and joined together out of that love. As a group they lacked personal animosity and self-serving motivation. They trusted each other and were utterly devoted to Dunes preservation."

A butterfly poised to emerge from its cocoon, Sylvia began her metamorphosis with that meeting. She, who had disliked the League of Women Voters for its failure to take a stand on issues, found both an issue and a stand. She viewed the cause in the most absolute of terms; she divided all Dunes questions into good or bad, black or white, right or wrong. *She deemed it so good and right that she could shed her inhibiting shyness. In a later reflection on her Dunes experience Sylvia concluded, "I think that the Dunes did more for me than I did for it. The Save the Dunes Council experience changed me dramatically. It became a vehicle for my personal growth. I learned a lot about my own capabilities, my own strengths, and my own assertiveness in behalf of a cause."*

As her first Dunes project Sylvia started the Calumet chapter of the Save the Dunes Council. She found it easy to get support. With most of the region already fallen to industry, people in Lake County could easily support preservation of what remained. She recruited about fifteen active members who, between 1960 and 1966, contacted thousands of people. The chapter's activities differed little from those of the chapters in Fort Wayne or Indianapolis: promotion of Dunes preservation through a speakers' bureau, a film about the Dunes, a tape and slide program, two to three meetings a month, year after year all for the goals of money, members, and support. In contrast to the "one-man-band" nature of the outlying chapters, Sylvia's effort flourished, and with success her self-confidence and organizational abilities blossomed as well.

In those early years most of the world viewed the council members as "irresponsible, flighty butterfly chasers." They had no status. Because they operated apart from the mainstream, the establishment, the politicians, and the press found them easy to ignore. Sylvia destroyed this image. With her pretty, animated face and memorable feminine figure, she exorcised the "little old lady in tennis shoes" by representing the council in her highest heels and most stylish outfits. Not easily forgotten, she exuded a charm and self-possession she did not always feel.

The combination of Sylvia's natural administrative abilities and her ever-expanding fervor for saving the Dunes made increased activity and responsibility a foregone conclusion. Tom Dustin recalls, "I've never seen anyone so singleminded in my life—I don't think she thought of a thing except the Dunes, and she would wear you down. There was no way you could avoid being impressed with her arguments, and if she had a weakness, it was that disagreement with her was the equivalent of domestic treason."[14]

Between 1965 and 1968 Sylvia served as Buell's assistant. As Hal Buell's health failed and Dorothy's domestic responsibilities increased, Troy assumed more and more of the work load. Finally, in 1968, a reluctant, rather naive Sylvia Troy took over the helm. Despite her years of experience, she maintained an ingenuous belief in how things ought to work. The Save the Dunes Council as a whole *shared her view, one as yet untempered by the realities of the way administrative agencies of the government function. Moreover, her innocence did not dissipate easily. Even after the lakeshore bill passed in 1966, Sylvia Troy did not grasp political actuality. "We had some visionary notion that once the Park Service was here our services would no longer be needed. We thought of [the NPS] as our saviors—that they would move in and take over and do everything that was needed."*

The idea that NPS would protect its hard-won resource neither from internal encroachments nor from external environmental degradation took time to penetrate the consciousness of the council's leadership. Awareness of this new threat meant a new role for the organization, that of agency oversight. Under Troy's stewardship, the council slowly changed its direction. Not only did it continue to press for legislation to expand the lakeshore, it actively prodded Congress to appropriate funds for land acquisition, operation, and development; it evaluated and criticized park service plans; and it attempted to keep NPS officials on the straight and narrow path of doing the job entrusted to them.

As Dustin aptly observed, "Sylvia quickly learned how to attract some lightning."[15] When, for example, she discovered that NPS officials looked the other way while private industry sand-mined in the lakeshore, she worked herself into the kind of rage that produced instant results. She demanded that the NPS regional director view the damage and then told him, "Look, they're hauling sand out by the truckload—you're entrusted with the park and you have to do something." She recalled, "I made a great big scene, said this has got to stop and it's going to stop and that's it. I just intimidated him."

Troy cultivated a wide assortment of contacts; she possessed an intuitive understanding of "realpolitik," which she employed with increasing skill over the years. "I was more political than Dorothy. I lived in Lake County. I knew a lot of the political people, and I cultivated them. I think politics is all personal. Politicians are very social beings by their nature, and a lot of decisions are made in social situations. I knew Sam Evett, the head of the steel workers union—his daughter babysat for me. I developed and used all the contacts I had."

As she developed her political contacts, she expanded her associations with environmentalists, scientists, unions, and people in the media. In addition, she nurtured an innate theatrical talent, which allowed her to produce tears or a torrent of righteous rage seemingly at will. Unbeknownst to her audience, like any good ac-

tress, she rehearsed. Although the idea of staging a tantrum in a congressional office, for example, filled her with self-deprecating terror, she could, by stewing over an evil at hand, work herself into a state of indignation sufficient to unleash the desired reaction at the desired time. Less talented Save the Duners greatly admired her performances that, as often as not, had a remarkable effect on their recipients.

Troy grew to see clearly that the council's two roles, legislative stimulation and agency oversight, would of necessity have to continue. She recognized the crucial role of politics and the significance of maintaining broad support. Moreover, she believed in making the system work. Looking back, she points to the formation of coalitions as the council's most significant activity. The coming together of the steelworkers, the auto workers, the teachers unions, conservation groups, and others played the critical part in the organization's successes.

While Sheehan could retire when the Indiana Dunes State Park became a reality and Buell could slow down with the authorization of the Indiana Dunes National Lakeshore, Troy had no such visible end product to mark her accomplishment. Instead she bore the knowledge that Dunes preservation had no end that she could anticipate, no milestone except the invisible inevitability of continued effort. After a decade of leadership, Sylvia longed to begin a new phase in her life. She continued the annual pilgrimages to Washington, the ceaseless lobbying and political campaigning for sympathetic candidates in the hope that she could see the expansion legislation through to some final conclusion. Eventually, the unending nature of the endeavor wore her down. The realization that no definitive end would occur finally enabled her to withdraw gratefully and hand the reins to another.

Today Troy views her Dunes experience as significant for her past and formative for her life to come. She takes great pride in what she learned and what she accomplished. She particularly values the Conservation Service Award, the highest citizen honor conferred by the Department of the Interior, which she received in 1979. Now, as she seeks new horizons and conquers new challenges, Troy will not predict where her enthusiasm for new experiences will lead. She plans to go in freedom, participate with self-confidence, and see as much of the world as she can.

The Save the Dunes Council's realization of the NPS's limitations developed slowly and gradually. Far more aware of the natural resources of the lakeshore than agency newcomers, council members hovered protectively over every inch of park land, like an anxious mother attempting to ward off any deleterious influence from her pampered darling. The group's long history of constant association with the terrain made it especially sensitive to any change that might affect the status quo. Unhampered by bureaucratic restraints, members pursued, with dogged concentration, the preservation of the land now part of the park.

While the NPS pushed land acquisition as its first priority, council members, scattered throughout the environs, watched for any hint of incipient threats to the natural qualities of the Dunes. Requests for water discharge permits by Bethlehem, Northern Indiana Public Service Company (NIPSCO), and Midwest caused consternation. The council, failing to get the NPS to take up the cause, sued against their issuance by the EPA. Leaders especially worried about potential pollution of lakeshore beaches and the impact on the lakeshore's wetlands. The courts turned down their challenges. The Save the Dunes Council then realized that the NPS could not and would not battle against the contamination caused by the lakeshore's industrial neighbors and that it would have to undertake that task. Without the political influence of Paul Douglas to sway Lyndon Johnson, the NPS's stance reflected its concern about the political instability of the lakeshore. The local congressman, Earl Landgrebe, did not rank as a park advocate. Indiana's two senators, Birch Bayh and Vance Hartke, did not rate the lakeshore a top priority. In Illinois the picture did not appear any brighter. Paul Douglas's replacement, Charles Percy, though professing the same attachment for the Dunes as his predecessor, had no seniority or influence. No one from the Chicago congressional delegation stepped forward to assume Douglas's mantle. No wonder the NPS busied itself with administrative duties and left controversy to the Save the Dunes Council.

If opposing Bethlehem, Midwest, and NIPSCO on the lakeshore's behalf seemed like a comfortable role to the council, attacking the NPS decidedly did not. However, the agency did not always behave as the group expected. Instead of making decisions on substantive bases, zealously guarding its land and embracing other prized environmental values, the NPS often took positions based on political assessment and bureaucratic considerations. Soon after the lakeshore became a reality, the prospect of NPS's agreement to industrial use in the park shattered any remaining council illusions.

In 1966 the Chicago, South Shore and South Bend Railroad developed plans for a new marshalling yard within the park. Historically the railroad had served primarily as a passenger line. Now its new owners, the Chesapeake and Ohio Railroad, saw a bright future for the company in the freight business. South Shore could haul coal from Chessie mines in southern Indiana and Illinois to Bethlehem's Burns Harbor plant. Congress had exempted the line's right of way, which traverses the park, from federal acquisition. However, the South Shore decided it needed adjacent land upon which to construct a freight yard. The railroad's management saw an opportunity to proceed with the project while the NPS awaited a congressional appropriation with which to begin buying lakeshore land. (Land within the authorized boundaries of a park does not come under federal control until purchase.) However, South Shore officials knew that the NPS could apply for emergency funds to acquire property threatened with development. To forestall such a move, company representatives decided to negotiate with the NPS to gain approval for their plan. After several meetings, including at least one attended by NPS Director George Hartzog, the preservationists discovered the scheme.[16] They reacted predictably and threatened to make public the agency's apparent willingness to negotiate away park land.[17] They vowed to fight the giveaway of any land that the conservationists had fought so hard and so long to include in the lakeshore.

Save the Dunes Council members well understood that the NPS would respond far more quickly to political pressure than to their entreaties. So they turned to friendly Indiana and Illinois congressmen for support. The conservationists accurately saw the South Shore request as precedent-setting: Unless the NPS rejected this industrial use of lakeshore land, other requests for similar boundary adjustments would follow. "This is the method, whittling away, chisel-chisel-chisel, until much of the originally authorized park is gobbled up."[18]

Their House sponsor, Congressman Edward Roush, stated the case. "The time has come to set the record straight. No one is going to be permitted to trespass the boundaries of the Indiana Dunes National Lakeshore. Threats and ultimatums will not deter our position. I strongly urge that this and all future requests for land within the Dunes that are not compatible be flatly refused. The battle for this park was too dearly fought to throw away the sweet fruits of victory."[19]

The Save the Dunes Council also used the same tactics it had employed in its successful legislative campaign. It enlisted friends and members in yet another letter-writing campaign to the NPS, the Department of the Interior, and friendly legislators, protesting the

South Shore plan. It generated friendly press comment.[20] Meanwhile the railroad continued its effort, obtaining the rezoning of the land it wanted for the freight yard from residential to industrial use.

The NPS responded to congressional inquiries with the reassurance that the agency "was doing everything possible to work [out] a desirable solution with the railroad."[21] The conservationists remained uneasy, for they knew the town of Porter's rezoning made the land available for the railroad's development while the NPS's coffers remained empty.

The council proceeded on two fronts. First, it worked hard to ensure that Congress passed a $10 million appropriation for land acquisition. Second, it involved more and more congressmen in questioning the desirability of the freight yard. It knew the railroad had a behind-the-scenes friend in Charles Halleck.

The protesting letters produced a form response from the NPS. In it the agency revealed heretofore undisclosed details of the South Shore proposal. The railroad planned a four-mile-long marshalling yard, with twelve parallel sets of tracks, extending from the eastern boundary of the lakeshore to the Bethlehem plant.[22]

In June 1968 Congress approved half of the requested funds. The future of the freight yard remained unsettled. The conservationists happily settled for half of their funding goal, since with an assured appropriation the NPS could now acquire any industrially threatened land—if the agency had the will to do so. Save the Dunes Council members traveled to Washington. Supported by Indiana's two senators, they reviewed the South Shore's latest freight yard plan with NPS officials and continued to express their dissatisfaction with the proposal. Though the railroad admitted that "the original area where we would like to have placed the marshalling yard probably would have had adverse effects on the Park," it now maintained that the latest site would have no deleterious impact. The conservationists disagreed. The South Shore also offered to "at least partially replace land used for the yard with other acreage, so that the total acreage of the park is not substantially affected."[23] The conservationists refused to budge. They insisted on one of two alternatives: Either the railroad locate the yard entirely outside lakeshore boundaries or it replace lakeshore land with an identical number of equally suitable acres.

The council continued to monitor each round of the continuing negotiations between the NPS and the South Shore. Finally a proposed agreement came before the organization and the Lakeshore Advisory Commission, now headed by the council's former public relations chairman, Tom Dustin, for concurrence. Both groups refused endorsement without two additional stipulations. First, they insisted on the railroad's commitment not to use its right of way or the adjoining utility right of way for any future freight tracks. Second, they stood firm on the requirement for an even land swap.[24]

Negotiations resumed. The conservationists worried that the advent of the Nixon administration might persuade the NPS to concur with the terms of the rejected pact, in which the NPS had agreed to acquire the marshalling yard site and lease it back to the railroad for a nominal sum. The railroad had agreed to give the secretary of the interior the right to approve the design and construction plans for the marshalling yard in order to "protect park qualities to the maximum feasible extent."[25] The conservationists had counted on Secretary of Interior Udall to support their position. They feared Nixon's appointee, Walter Hickel, might "be more sympathetic to the railroad."[26]

The conservationists' anxiety seemed justified by an incident that occurred two months later. The Indiana State Senate passed a resolution memorializing Congress to redraw the lakeshore's boundaries so as to exclude any land "within the economic development area of the public port of the State of Indiana."[27] The Save the Dunes Council interpreted the resolution as part of a growing campaign to deauthorize the marshalling yard site. They also found ominous the reappearance of a former port commission attorney in his new role as railroad lobbyist.

Barely a month later, the conservationists' campaign ended happily. Responding to their urgent pleas, Senator Bayh intervened in the stalled negotiations. With influence derived from his membership on the Senate Transportation Committee, he convinced the railroad to locate its marshalling yard entirely outside the lakeshore's boundaries. The Save the Dunes Council leaders could hardly believe the outcome. President Sylvia Troy wrote to their ailing mentor, Paul Douglas: "We had thought it hopeless. Our only explanation is persistent pressure by a great many people. The moral here, apparently, is never give up."[28] The council publicly thanked Bayh for his pivotal role, but in a report to its membership it took part of the credit, too. "Behind the scenes, Save the Dunes Council was working, talking, buttonholing everybody who had connection with the fracas and some who didn't. For a while all we got was promises—promises that turned out to mean nothing. That's when we turned obstinate. We wouldn't be surprised to learn that they finally gave up just to get rid of us."[29]

Self-congratulations notwithstanding, the council had learned several lessons from the marshalling yard episode. Clearly the NPS needed constant watching. The organization also realized that the agency responded most directly to political pressure. The council's most significant lesson came from the recognition that it knew how to mount that pressure.

In the midst of the freight yard controversy, the NPS unveiled the first of its master plans for the Indiana Dunes National Lakeshore.[30] The agency has an elaborate procedure for preparing long-range development proposals for each of its units. On the basis of the legislative mandate for each park, the NPS prepares a document that describes the physical features, regional setting, and proposed uses. The conceptual plan also includes material on the projected circulation system and cost of development. At Indiana Dunes the agency experienced immediate pressure to make the park available for public enjoyment. Three factors pushed the agency into publishing the initial plan in 1967: the high cost of land, the emphasis on recreational benefits used to convince Congress to approve the lakeshore, and continued local opposition. The agency apparently believed that prompt opening of federal land for public use would stifle critics of the park and engender Indiana political support. A revision of the plan, issued in 1969, proposed a more detailed delineation of specific uses for each section of the park.[31]

Despite the publication of these two plans, from 1966 to 1973 the NPS made little visible progress toward developing visitor facilities at the lakeshore. Conservationists and opponents alike chafed at the inactivity. Both groups' positions stemmed partly from lack of experience with the tangled web of relationships within a bureaucracy, its department, Congress, and the White House. Former EPA Director Quarles explained the reason, "The dynamics of government operations arise from the interplay of politics in setting government policy and the hard realities of running government programs."[32]

Outside observers, friend and foe alike, looked for instant results following authorization of the lakeshore. Instead, the complicated process of starting up a new park made any hope of quick development illusory. The NPS has to decipher the will of Congress in approving a new unit. The intraagency debate over the ambiguities of the law establishing the park ultimately results in a strategy for carrying out the legislation as interpreted. In the case of Indiana Dunes decisions about where to buy land first and what acquisition practices to use formed part of that strategy. Difficult questions of access, security, and facilities for visitors followed. A set of regulations that decides final implementation becomes the end product of agency interpretation of the law. In the case of the Indiana Dunes National

Lakeshore, the NPS did not publish these regulations until 1972.[33] Conservationists, unsophisticated in the ways of the bureaucratic world, played no part in the development of the regulations. They did not understand that the final document represented dozens of preliminary decisions made by unseen and unknown NPS staffers, whose cumulative effect would mold the future of the park.

Fortunately the lakeshore had an advocate in Allen Edmunds, then assistant to the NPS regional director. He spent many days during 1967 and 1968 speaking to local groups, primarily to allay their fears about land acquisition. He also backed the nascent park in intra-agency disputes. The substantial faction within the NPS that did not accept the lakeshore as established by Congress continued to voice concern about the lack of contiguousness, the common boundaries shared with industries, and especially the lack of strong political support in Indiana for the park. They pointed to repeated stories about the continued opposition of the district's congressman emanating from the NPS's legislative liaison with Congress. "Charlie Halleck wants to see the Lakeshore die on the vine," he reported.[34] Lakeshore opponents in the NPS argued that the agency stood to lose support for its total program by bucking the former "Mr. Republican" over the lakeshore. They counseled inactivity. Caught between the push of the conservationists and the pull of congressional, Indiana, and Porter County Republicans, the NPS chose a cautious, vacillating approach to translating legislative intent into an operating park.

Subsequently, early in his term, Interior Secretary Rogers Morton seriously discussed teaming up with Congressman Landgrebe, Halleck's congressional replacement, to support legislation to nullify the lakeshore.[35] With Morton lukewarm to the park, the NPS followed the safe course of going as slowly as possible. These political considerations delayed planning for development. More than six years passed after Congress established the park before the NPS revealed its grand design in 1973.

SWIMMING POOLS IN THE LAKESHORE

For the first and only time the Indiana Dunes National Lakeshore Advisory Commission scheduled its January 19, 1973, quarterly meeting in Indianapolis, 150 miles from the park. The commission's agenda notice for that cold January day listed a presentation on the NPS's plans for development of West Beach. For conservationists, the inclusion of that item meant mandatory attendance.

To reach the state capital involved a four-hour drive on icy roads. However, they decided the issue's importance made the effort worthwhile.

An hour before daybreak, Save the Dunes Council President Sylvia Troy met future Executive Director Charlotte Read and Porter County Chapter Izaak Walton League President Herbert Read to begin the trip. With the meeting set for 10 A.M., they had allowed leeway for delays caused by road conditions as well as for the difference in time zones between northwest Indiana and their destination.

As they headed south along lightly traveled Interstate 65, with only an occasional truck to keep them company on the road, they wondered what the NPS would unveil. Almost seven years had passed since the lakeshore's establishment without any tangible evidence of visitor facilities, and the trio knew that with 50 percent of the lakeshore's land already in NPS hands, the agency felt mounting pressure to provide for visitor use of the acreage.

The three speculated about the heretofore secret development plans. They believed the lakeshore's enabling act had laid down specific guidelines. The law provided:

> *No development or plan for the convenience of visitors shall be undertaken therein which would be incompatible with the preservation of the unique flora and fauna or the physiographic conditions now prevailing or with the preservation of such historic sites and structures such as the Secretary may provide for the public enjoyment and understanding of the unique natural, historic, and scientific features within the lakeshore by establishing such trails, observation points, and exhibits and providing such services as he may deem desirable for such public enjoyment and understanding.*[36]

However, the travelers understood that the NPS's interpretation of the legislative mandate might not jibe with theirs. Up to now, planning had remained closely guarded; the NPS had permitted no public input. Today the first presentation of the plans would occur.

Stopping midway for coffee, Charlotte Read voiced her concern about the influence of the Nixon administration's urban parks orientation on the Indiana Dunes. Troy added another dimension to the conversation. Congress had added the 475-acre West Beach tract to the lakeshore shortly before approving the park. Proponents had argued successfully for this parcel of vacant land with its mile of shoreline to provide space for development of water-related visitor activities. However, she pointed out, the West Beach section contained more than flat, sand-mined land with access to Lake Mich-

igan. Its natural features included Dune ridges, Long Lake, an
interdunal pond, which provided an important habitat for water
fowl, and significant examples of Dunes vegetation. "I hope the Park
Service's plan protects and preserves as well as promotes use," she
commented.

Herb Read echoed her sentiments. He pointed out how little they
all knew about the NPS's planning process. Four years before the
agency had issued a revised master plan for the lakeshore. The
twelve-page document had discussed development of each part of
the lakeshore and had classified West Beach for the most intensive
recreational use. Departing from NPS practice, the agency had hired
outside planning consultants, the Milwaukee firm of Howard,
Needles, Tammen and Bergendoff, to design West Beach facilities.
"We don't know what these guys consider intensive recreational
use," Herb groused. "Or even if they've ever seen the site and know
what's there."

With increasing apprehension, the conservationists drove on to
the State Office Building. There, in Room 602, they found their long
time ally, Tom Dustin, now executive secretary of the Indiana Division of the Izaak Walton League, and Ernie Hernandez, statehouse correspondent for the Gary Post Tribune. The five formed the
entire audience for the commission session.

Commission Chairman William Lieber, grandson of Richard Lieber, called the meeting to order promptly. After hearing routine reports, the commission members and the limited public eagerly
turned to the West Beach item. Robert Steenhagen, northeast manager of the NPS's Denver Service Center (the NPS planning office),
began to talk. With a few cursory remarks about the "tentative"
nature of the plans, Steenhagen turned the podium over to Richard
Sinclair of the consulting firm. Sinclair displayed a series of photographs, architectural drawings, and maps. Then he asked for dim-
ming of the room's lights and drawing of the window curtains in
order that he might show slides illustrating the proposed facilities.

The conservationists listened and watched in horror as he metic-
ulously proceeded to detail the plan. Methodically, Sinclair covered
twenty-six separate and distinct facilities. They ranged from two
Olympic size swimming pools "to provide for bathers when the beach
is too cold to use" to two steel bathhouses for 5,100 users replete
with overhung roofs "to provide shade."[37] Sinclair also described a
three-story parking garage for 2,000 cars, a pavillion, sports fields,
winter coasting slopes, a manmade dune, a bandshell and amphi-
theatre, an ice-skating rink, basketball courts, a viewing terrace
overlooking the swimming pools, a general field game area, a boat-

ing and fishing lagoon, five day-use shelters, storage and maintenance facilities, an administration building, and sixteen residential
units for NPS employees. The proposal called for cutting through
the foredune "to improve access."

Oblivious to the growing outrage of the conservationists and un-
aware of objections forming among commission members, Sinclair
completed his description of the West Beach development. Chairman Lieber turned to his colleagues for their reactions. John Hillenbrand, chairman of the Indiana Natural Resources Commission,
minced no words: "We have the finest beach in the world, with
5,000 feet of beach, so we build swimming pools.... What's the
beach for? Couldn't we spend the money for a broader experience?
You could do something else for the same money." [38] John Schnur-
lein, Porter County's representative, echoed Hillenbrand's opposition to the bathhouse design. Hillenbrand had called the roofline
"compatible to the steel mills rather than to the Dunes." [39] In an
attempt to balance the outpouring of criticism, Lieber praised the
substitution of a parking garage for "acres and acres of parking lots"
and the elimination of earlier suggestions for a monorail in favor of
less conspicuous minibuses to transport visitors around West Beach.
However, Hillenbrand continued to find fault with the scheme. He
questioned locating the bathhouses high on Dunes instead of in
more inconspicuous locations. "You shouldn't see anything," he insisted. "We try to screen steel mills, and then we do something like
this." [40]

With Sinclair's proposals obviously in trouble, Steenhagen assumed the role of the plan's defender. Brushing aside the comments, he asserted that the plans had already received the agency's
approval and went on to announce the timetable for their implementation. After completion of the required environmental impact
statement within forty-five days, he estimated the NPS could open
bids for the first phase of the project by May. Lieber, sensing the
growing antipathy to Steenhagen's indifference to commission
comments, adjourned the meeting.

The conservationists, denied any opportunity to make their opin-
ions heard, jumped up to consider the drawings more carefully. As
they rushed up for a closer inspection of the maps, photographs,
and illustrations, Steenhagen interposed. "None of this material is
available to the press or public." He then barked an order to Sinclair, "Let's wrap it up and get out of here." Within a few minutes,
they and their materials disappeared. "They act like they're handling C.I.A. documents," Charlotte Read quipped, shaking her head.
"No, they act like we're the enemy," Troy remarked.

*Hernandez received the same rebuff when he approached Steen-
hagen for copies of the maps and drawings. Steenhagen bluntly replied, "No." Pressed for an explanation of his refusal, the NPS official
stated, "Because they are the property of the National Park Service."*[41]

*Steenhagen's arrogant behavior made Hernandez even more re-
ceptive to the conservationists' comments. They voiced three objections to the West Beach plans, which became the dominant
themes of the ensuing three-year controversy. First, they protested
the lack of opportunity for public comments; second, they disagreed with the scope of facilities and the intensity of use envisioned; and third, they called for local involvement in the planning
process.*

*After a gloomy lunch during which they vented their frustration
at exclusion from commenting at the meeting and their mounting
anger at the quality of planning exhibited, the conservationists
headed for home. The trip sped by quickly as they planned a coun-
terattack. They knew the time-tested ingredients needed to pressure the bureaucracy by now: fire up the press, interest their allies,
bombard the department with protests, and call in the Congress.
"This is too dangerous to believe," Charlotte Read exclaimed. "We'll
change those plans in spite of Mr. Steenhagen."*[42]

The conservationists turned to their tried and true formula of protest: letters to Interior Secretary Morton and to NPS officials, visits
to the press, and cultivation of allies. As a result of the uproar, by
March 1973 the agency retreated and made the West Beach development plan available for public review. The Lakeshore Advisory
Commission agenda became dominated by the controversy over the
proposal. Further study of the projected use for the beach area made
the critics even more angry. The NPS now faced a barrage of adverse
comments about the degree of development within the small confines of the West Beach unit. In addition, the access route produced
intense opposition from the City of Gary and the Northwestern Indiana Regional Planning Commission.

The Save the Dunes Council and their newly formed coalition
reiterated the need for local input into the planning in order to scale
down development and improve the access. Finally, in December
1973 Richard Curry, special assistant to the Assistant Secretary for
Fish, Wildlife and Parks Nathaniel Reed, "offered a short term, temporary solution for local comment."[43] This latest NPS proposal provided for parking pads with a 600-car capacity instead of 2,000.

The NPS delay in issuing the required environmental impact statement continued the furor. The regional planners, at long last, informed the agency it would have to comply with the procedure of public review.[44] The long-sought public hearing occurred on October 16, 1974. It followed widespread newspaper accounts of the agency's differences with conservationists and the City of Gary over the West Beach design. The hearing provided an opportunity to put these complaints on the record.[45] To soften the impact, Interior Department officials began admitting that the agency had erred in not providing for local consultation.

The NPS made further accommodations at the hearing. A spokesman presented a modified beachhouse design and a first-phase development package. Speakers urged the NPS not to replicate a city park's recreational features but instead to offer a quality natural experience for West Beach visitors.

Two-and-a-half years later, the NPS formally opened West Beach to the public. Its bathhouse design still displeases some. EPA Director Russell Train in 1976 said it "stands up like a sore thumb."[46] However, the thousands who come to swim ignore the building for the beach. The NPS has built little more than its first phase, much to the delight of all who fear further construction. The access road remains a problem.

Because of the difficulties surrounding West Beach, the conservationists successfully pressed Congress to add a planner to the lakeshore staff. The NPS itself became more sensitive to the early involvement of local interests in the planning process. Still, the West Beach experience reinforced the apprehensions of the conservationists. The agency's performance did little to reassure them that the NPS would carefully protect the natural resources of its holdings. The agency's record in dealing with external threats to the lakeshore displeased them even more.

NIPSCO, the region's gas and electricity supplier, caused two of the most serious external threats to the lakeshore's natural resources. In the case of ash pond seepage into Cowles Bog, environmentalists prodded the Department of Interior into negotiating an agreement with the company to stop the damage. In the other, the NPS and the Interior Department, though occasionally willing to speak in opposition, did not join in legal challenges. Instead, with little federal support, environmental, union, and local citizen groups won an eleven-year battle against construction of a nuclear plant on the lakeshore's border.

NIPSCO proved a formidable opponent in both instances. With assets of $1.5 billion and annual operating revenues of $1.2 billion, the company also counted on its more than a century of operations in the state to combat problems caused by the new federal presence. Its longtime president, Dean Mitchell, characterized corporate philosophy and image: "[Northern Indiana Public Service Company] prides itself in being as Hoosier as the Tippecanoe and the Wabash, as James Whitcomb Riley's 'When the Frost Is on the Punkin,' as the covered bridges still sentimentally standing, and as down to earth as Vice President Marshall's 'All the Country needs is a good 5¢ cigar.' Its entire holdings and the largest concentration of its stockholders are in Indiana."[47] The company developed into the public utility monopoly for the thirty northern counties of Indiana through a series of mergers and consolidations. Samuel Insull, the Chicago utilities magnate, played a decisive role in combining the various companies into a single regionwide power producer. By 1926 NIPSCO had established its present dominion over the northern one-third of Indiana.

Three years later, the company acquired 300 acres in the Dunes. A later land swap with the Bethlehem Steel Corporation increased the acreage to 350. Sandwiched between Bethlehem's Burns Harbor Works to the west and southwest, Lake Michigan to the north, the South Shore Railroad right of way to the southeast, and what became the lakeshore to the east, the site at first promised the company enormous benefits. It constructed two coal-fired generating stations producing 523,900 kilowatts, a 345,000-kilowatt substation, and a transmission line corridor as well as support facilities to serve the power needs of its industrial neighbors, Bethlehem and Midwest. Its environmental problems resulted from the juxtaposition of industrial and park lands provided in the compromise establishing the lakeshore. The industrial corridor, which bisected the park, included NIPSCO property abutting the lakeshore's Cowles Bog section.

The two coal-fired generating plants produced (as do all coal-fired generating stations) industrial waste in the form of flyash. NIPSCO dumped this unwanted industrial by-product on its undeveloped property nearest to the lakeshore. The utility used a disposal system that mixed water with the flyash for easier handling. At first the company constructed a dike on its land, behind which it placed the wet flyash. The dike, an earthen wall, had flyash as one of its components. When the flyash-laden water seeped through the dike and threatened to erode the nearby South Shore Railroad embankment, the company scooped out one and then ultimately five ponds behind the dike where it disposed of the flyash. Claiming that ownership of land sanctioned all uses, the utility at first turned deaf ears to fears of environmental damage to adjoining lakeshore land caused by the seepage of ground water from the ash settling basins. In fact, a nosey Save the Dunes Council member had first discovered the waste disposal system and protested to the NPS about the potential damage that the contaminated water could cause to the native vegetation in the adjacent Cowles Bog wetlands. After several years of urging action and getting very little result, the council pursued a new course. It included the NIPSCO dike in the first expansion bill. The company objected vehemently, claiming it needed the land and disputing the polluting effect of ash pond seepage.

The passage of the 1976 lakeshore enlargement bill occurred without the inclusion of the NIPSCO property but with the stipulation that the NPS make a special study of the land in question and report its findings to the Congress. The NPS study did not recommend acquisition of NIPSCO land for the lakeshore. However, continuing controversy over flyash pollution did convince the company of the necessity for accommodation. Illinois Congressman Sidney Yates, chairman of the House Interior Appropriations subcommittee, backed the Save the Dunes Council's plea for protection of the lakeshore from this industrial contaminant; the NPS heeded his power. A 1978 agreement between the Department of Interior and the company provided for discontinuance of wet flyash disposal on the lands bordering the lakeshore and for sealing of the ponds.[48] In 1981 NIPSCO completed reclamation of the last of the ponds. Though gratified with the outcome, Save the Dunes Council members still worry about the long-term effect of flyash-contaminated water on the Cowles Bog ecosystem.

In contrast, neither the NPS, nor the Department of Interior played a significant role in thwarting NIPSCO's plan to build a nuclear plant adjacent to the lakeshore. The episode clearly revealed the political weakness of both in combating the environmental degradation of NPS's holdings. Pitted against another federal agency interested in expanding the use of nuclear energy, as well as Oval Office support of this energy source, neither had the political muscle to obtain a presidential review. Although the lakeshore resulted from President John Kennedy's intervention in the 1960s, a decade later administrations committed to nuclear energy foreclosed such a course. As a result, the NPS stood by helplessly, unable to prevent an industrial development that portended widespread damage to the park's natural resources, while a citizens' coalition took up the challenge. Using skillful legal appeals to delay construction, the coalition waged a mounting campaign to enlist public opinion against the projected Bailly plant.

During the decade from 1971 to 1981 the Bailly fight served as a barometer of the Save the Dunes Council's growing political sophistication and increasing professionalism. Instead of assuming the mantle of public leadership against the utility's plan, the council initially joined with other sympathetic organizations. A Chicago-based public interest law firm, Business and Professional People for the Public Interest, took on the important legal end of the struggle. The Porter County Chapter of the Izaak Walton League accepted the role of chief environmental opponent. Dune Acres residents who lived in the community adjacent to the proposed plant site organized the Concerned Citizens against Bailly. Because of the plant's location, less than six miles from downtown Gary and thirty miles from downtown Chicago, Democratic Gary Mayor Richard Hatcher and William Scott, Republican attorney general of Illinois, joined the opposition, too.

NIPSCO's construction plans for the nuclear generating station required a giant excavation on its land 800 feet west of the lakeshore. Environmentalists feared the hydrological consequences of a hole 32 feet deep, 200 feet wide, and 675 feet long on the neighboring Cowles Bog watershed. They worried as well about the probability of safely evacuating lakeshore visitors in case of a nuclear accident. They also questioned the long-term effects of the reactor's cooling system on Lake Michigan's waters and objected to the unaesthetic effect of the 400-foot cooling tower on the shoreline adjacent to the park.

The NPS, though sensitive to these considerations, first counted noses and found most of Indiana's politicians solidly on the utility's side. NIPSCO's position that nuclear energy represented a new, efficient, and cheap source of power found many adherents in the state government, the construction unions, and the public in northwest Indiana. The company proclaimed that the growing industrialization of Porter County required an increasing energy output. Few questioned the utility's energy demand projection, though the economic downturn in later years proved it false. In a virtual rerun of the clash in values that had preceded the establishment of the lakeshore, private property rights formed the basis of NIPSCO's case and found great acceptance.

The utility first announced its plan to build a nuclear generating station at Bailly in 1967. Preoccupied with nurturing the establishment of the newly authorized lakeshore, neither the Save the Dunes Council nor the NPS paid serious attention to the announcement. At that time atomic power for electric power generation seemed the safe, cheap method that both the government and the utility industry heralded. None of the subsequent safety and environmental thoughts had surfaced.

In August 1970 NIPSCO applied to the Atomic Energy Commission (AEC) for a construction permit, set the plant's cost at $185 million, and scheduled completion for 1979. Faced with the imminent reality of the plant's operation next door to the park, both the NPS and the environmentalists voiced apprehensions. At first both the agency and the Department of Interior joined the anti-Bailly campaign. Nathaniel Reed gave strong testimony against Bailly at hearings AEC conducted on the construction permit application.[49] Though he joined a long parade of witnesses in enunciating all the environmental concerns during the thirteen months of the hearing, neither Reed nor other opponents prevailed. On May 3, 1974, the AEC gave NIPSCO permission to start construction, and the utility soon began excavation. For the next two-and-a-half years Bailly opponents battled in court to set aside that ruling. Initially, an appellate court enjoined construction and ordered the excavation filled, but on November 8, 1976, the U.S. Supreme Court sustained the original decision.

As soon as the AEC granted NIPSCO its construction license, the NPS and the Interior Department assumed a position of official silence and passive bystander. Both refused to participate in the subsequent legal challenges. In spite of claims by environmentalists that the water level in the Cowles Bog wetlands began to recede as NIPSCO proceeded with construction, the NPS refused to reconsider its position. Alarmed, frustrated, and bitter, the anti-Bailly forces implored the agency to take action. In response the lakeshore acquired a scientist to oversee the problem. Dissatisfied, the environmentalists turned to Yates, the lakeshore's most powerful political supporter. He inserted a requirement in the NPS's 1977 appropriation for a study of the hydrological consequences of the plant's construction on the lakeshore's water system. To comply with this mandate, the NPS added a science staff to the lakeshore's management team. Though the environmentalists found the park's chief scientist hostile to their concerns about the nuclear plant's impact on the water quality and quantity at Cowles Bog, they welcomed the addition of water- and air-quality experts at Indiana Dunes. They hoped these scientists would provide solid evidence to prove their case.

Meanwhile, NIPSCO ran into trouble in constructing the foundation for its nuclear reactor. The company originally planned to use bedrock pilings. In 1977 the company asked permission to adopt a shorter piling system. This change offered a new opportunity for the opponents to request public hearings on questions of construction safety. Concurrently, new allies joined the original coalition of Bailly opponents. The United Steel Workers, who had supported the lakeshore since its inception, expressed concern for the safety of its members. Its Bethlehem local raised questions about how any evacuation plan could protect the lives of employees working 630 feet away from the nuclear plant in case of a meltdown. Heretofore, NIPSCO had always received complete support on Bailly from its prime industrial customers, Bethlehem and Midwest. Now the Bethlehem local broke ranks with its employer.

Moreover, a new group, the Bailly Alliance, composed of local residents, union activists, and environmentalists, took over leadership of the anti-Bailly movement. A local version of the nationwide antinuclear protest, the Alliance adopted the militant tactics of marching, leafleting, and confrontation to press their case.[50]

Along with mounting public opposition to the Bailly nuclear plant and to nuclear power throughout the country, NIPSCO also had problems with the Nuclear Regulatory Commission (NRC) a newly established agency which took over the licensing function that the AEC had handled. The NRC questioned the short piling system that the company proposed and delayed approval while costs for the nuclear facility escalated. As the years dragged on, with opponents continually resorting to the courts to challenge NRC decisions, the company postponed its completion date for the Bailly plant time and time again. By March 1980 NIPSCO reported the expenditure of $184,200,000, and the plant was still a hole in the ground. With interest rates soaring, the utility faced a further round of regulatory and legal challenges to an extension of its construction permit. The company estimated in 1981 that the plant would cost $1.1 billion and could not go into operation until 1987. Burdened with almost a 1,000 percent cost increase, unabated local opposition fueled by the Three Mile Island incident, and the probability of nine more years of delay, NIPSCO in October 1981 announced the end of its effort to build a nuclear facility at the Bailly site. In May 1982 the NRC terminated the construction permit.

Park proponents admit the company's decision stemmed mainly from cost considerations. Though enormously pleased at the outcome, they continue to state their concern over the long-term effects on the Cowles Bog wetland produced by the utility's activities.

Balancing requirements for public use against protection of natural resources remains a continuing dilemma for the NPS. Within the complex system of federal decision-making, the agency responds to political influences rather than substantive considerations. While NPS's charter calls for preservation of its holdings, translation of that concept into effective management policies presents difficulties. In a dynamic society the inevitability of change precludes the absolute maintenance of the status quo.

Yet as the Indiana Dunes experience demonstrates, NPS has done little to prepare for possible change. Its organizational structure, formed in Stephen Mather's day, has not adapted to modern requirements. Security and visitor interpretation still receive primary emphasis. Neither scientific study nor resource protection has the attention or funding they deserve. In the best of times the agency has allocated only 2 percent of its budget and 150 out of its 9,000 employees to resource protection.[51] Nor has the NPS developed effective strategies to deal with external threats to its resources. A 1982 House bill proposed several promising techniques: interagency assessment of impacts caused by federal projects affecting park lands, priority attention by the EPA to threats to park lands, and technical assistance by the NPS to neighboring communities in order to mitigate development threats on park boundaries.[52]

The agency continues to operate in a reactive mode, responding to threats to its natural resources only in crisis. The protective isolation of the system's crown jewels, its great western parks, has vanished, and perhaps the pressures of development that crowd Yellowstone, Yosemite, and the Grand Tetons will jolt the NPS into protective activity. The record at Indiana Dunes should provide ample evidence that every park needs basic scientific studies of its natural resources. Without them evaluation of development proposals lacks an authoritative data base.

Every park also needs a constituency of concerned citizens who will fight to protect its integrity. Only a determined and politically sophisticated group of park advocates can exert the countervailing force that the national park system requires to escape becoming an endangered species.

NOTES

1. "Conservation Equals Survival," *American Heritage*, Dec. 1969, p. 14.
2. For an extended discussion of the legal ramifications of external threats, see Joseph Sax, "Helpless Giants: The National Parks and the Regulation of Private Lands," *Michigan Law Review*, 75 (Dec. 1976), 239–74.
3. U.S. *Statutes at Large*, 83 (Jan. 1969–Jan. 1970), "National Environmental Policy Act of 1969," Jan. 1, 1970.
4. Ibid., 84, pt. 1 (Feb. 1970–Dec. 1970), "An Act to Amend the Federal Water Pollution Control Act," Apr. 3, 1970.

5. U.S. Council on Environmental Quality, *Environmental Quality*, first annual report (Washington, 1970), pp. 21–22.

6. Authors' interview with Lynton Caldwell, Beverly Shores, 1980.

7. John Quarles, *Cleaning Up America: An Insider's View of the Environmental Protection Agency* (Boston: Houghton Mifflin, 1976), pp. 213–14.

8. U.S. Congress, House Committee on Interior and Insular Affairs, Robert M. Linn, Chief Scientist (Retired), National Park Service, *Statement*, before a subcommittee of the House Committee on Interior and Insular Affairs, H.B. 5552, 97th Cong., 2nd sess., Feb. 5, 1982.

9. U.S. Department of the Interior, Advisory Board on Wildlife Management, *Wildlife Management in the National Parks* (Washington, 1963).

10. U.S. National Academy of Science, National Research Council Advisory Committee to the National Park Service, *Report* (Washington, 1963).

11. U.S. *Statutes at Large*, 78 (Jan. 1964–Sept. 1964), "An Act to Authorize the Exchange of Public Domain Lands . . . ," Aug. 31, 1964.

12. F. Fraser Darling and Noel D. Eichhorn, *Man and Nature in the National Parks*, 2d ed. (Washington: The Conservation Foundation, 1969), p. 77.

13. Authors' interview with Sylvia Troy, Beverly Shores, 1981. All of the Troy quotations in this section are from this interview.

14. Dustin interview.

15. Ibid.

16. J. Jenson, NPS deputy associate director, to Edward Osann, Jr., Nov. 22, 1967, Save the Dunes Council Files.

17. Sylvia Troy to Allen Edmunds, Nov. 27, 1967, Save the Dunes Council Files.

18. *Newsletter*, Save the Dunes Council, Oct. 1967, p. 1, Save the Dunes Council Files.

19. Edward Roush to Stewart Udall, Jan. 18, 1968, Save the Dunes Council Files.

20. See, for example, "Of Men and Dunes," New York *Times*, May 16, 1968, p. 14E.

21. Enclosure in letter of Congressman Donald Rumsfeld to Mrs. Mildred L. Batchelder, Jan. 30, 1968, Save the Dunes Council Files.

22. U.S. Department of the Interior, National Park Service, Indiana Dunes National Lakeshore, *Statement* (Chesterton, Ind.: Indiana Dunes National Lakeshore, Feb. 6, 1968), Save the Dunes Council Files.

23. James B. McCahay, president of the South Shore Railroad, to Mrs. James Hect, secretary of the Illinois Audubon Society, July 8, 1969, Save the Dunes Council Files.

24. Sylvia Troy to Paul Douglas, Nov. 29, 1968, Save the Dunes Council Files.

25. Tom Dustin to Otis Bowen, Speaker of the Indiana House of Representatives, Mar. 9, 1968, Save the Dunes Council Files.

26. News Release, Save the Dunes Council, "South Shore Railroad Waiting for Hickel on Marshalling Yards," Jan. 14, 1969, Save the Dunes Council Files.

27. Indiana Senate, Resolution 63, Mar. 8, 1969.

28. Troy to Douglas, Apr. 10, 1969, Save the Dunes Council Files.

29. *Newsletter*, Save the Dunes Council, May 1969, Save the Dunes Council Files.

30. U.S. Department of the Interior, National Park Service, *A Master Plan for Indiana Dunes National Lakeshore* (Chesterton, Ind., 1967).

31. U.S. Department of the Interior, National Park Service, *Master Plan: Indiana Dunes National Lakeshore* (Chesterton, Ind., 1969).

32. Quarles, *Cleaning Up America*, p. 93.

33. *Federal Register, Sept. 20, 1972,* Vol. 37/183 (Washington, 1972), p. 19389.

34. Palmer interview.

35. Authors' interview with Charlotte Read, Beverly Shores, 1976.

36. U.S. *Statutes at Large,* 80, pt. 1 (Jan. 1966–Nov. 1966), "An Act to Provide for the Establishment of the Indiana Dunes National Lakeshore," Nov. 5, 1966.

37. Howard, Needles, Tammen and Bergendoff, architects' plans, "West Beach Comprehensive Design Plan, Indiana Dunes National Lakeshore," 1972, Indiana Dunes National Lakeshore Administrative Headquarters, Porter, Ind.

38. Ernie Hernandez, "Dunes Lakeshore Plan Hit," Gary *Post Tribune,* Jan. 20, 1973, p. A–2.

39. Ibid., p. A–1.

40. Ibid.

41. Ernie Hernandez, "Park Service Secrecy Hit," ibid., Jan. 21, 1973, p. B–10.

42. Charlotte Read interview.

43. Nathaniel Reed to Tom Dustin, Mar. 8, 1974, Save the Dunes Council Files.

44. Statement of the Northwestern Indiana Regional Planning Commission to Indiana Dunes National Lakeshore Advisory Commission, Aug. 21, 1974, Save the Dunes Council Files.

45. *Transcript of the Public Hearing on Indiana Dunes National Lakeshore, West Beach Development Plan and Environmental Impact Statement* (Highland: Northwestern Indiana Regional Planning Commission, 1974).

46. Dave Hawk, "EPA Director Raps Dunes Bathhouse," Gary *Post Tribune,* Jan. 24, 1976, p. 1.

47. Dean E. Mitchell, "Northern Indiana Public Service Company Serving Today—Building for the Future in the Workshop of America," an address given before the Newcomen Society in North America, Chicago, May 21, 1960.

48. U.S. Congress, Senate Committee on Interior and Insular Affairs, *S. 260,* before a subcommittee of the Committee on Interior and Insular Affairs, Senate on S. 260, 95th Cong., 2nd Sess., 1970, p. 19.

49. U.S. Atomic Energy Commission, Hearing in the Matter of the Northern Indiana Public Service Company, Bailly Generating Station, Nuclear Unit 1, Docket 50–367, Valparaiso, Sept. 20, 1973, pp. 9ff.

50. Dave Hawk, "Dunes Form Stage for Nuclear Debate," Gary *Post Tribune*, July 13, 1980, p. 1.

51. Linn statement before House Committee.

52. U.S. Congress, House Committee on Interior and Insular Affairs, *H.B. 5552*, before a subcommittee of the House Committee on Interior and Insular Affairs on H.B. 5552, 97th Cong., 2nd sess., 1982.

CHAPTER 10 Reflections

Before the conflict over the Dunes erupted, the politics of plenty dominated land use decision-making in the United States. Economic development of abundant lands signified great progress to private and public sectors of the society alike. Both culture and law fully supported a value that lacked foresight and recklessly disregarded environmental consequences. An unending supply of open land presented developers with immediate and prospective benefits; such riches supplied ample justification for ignoring future noneconomic costs.

The Dunes controversy took place during a period of national transition from land plenty to land scarcity. It resulted from a fierce competition between industrial developers and conservationists for use of property once considered worthless. The conflict unleashed political forces and conflicting values always present in the formation and resolution of such struggles. As undeveloped open lands continue to decrease, similar battles will erupt with increasing fire and frequency. Competing demands for their use will strain existing decision-making processes and tax public officials to discover better means of resolving the inevitable discord. Leadership, or lack of it, will prove critical for the future.[1]

Prior to the 1960s prodevelopment forces easily succeeded in getting their interests on the nation's political agenda. They established and maintained a vast network of private power geared to assuring the legislative, administrative, and judicial advancement of those interests.[2] They met little resistance from the public and even less from the political power structure because their interests corresponded with the dominant values of American society.

Then, during the "environmental decade" of the 1970s, environmentalists came to believe that at last new values had superceded the old. Progress no longer meant profligate growth and expansion, but the ability to control and manage dwindling resources. Giddy with new-found national recognition and support, the environmentalists flooded the political agenda with their concerns, positing the emergence of a shift in national values and a change in the nation's priorities; public opinion studies supported their view. The 1980 election of Ronald Reagan and his appointment of James Watt as secretary of the interior left environmentalists reeling. The philosophy and actions of the new administration demonstrated quite clearly that the politics of the country had returned to business as usual.

The struggle over the Indiana Dunes illustrates crucial national concerns. As a case history, it examines the broader issues of land use policy and its relation to national park development, the interaction between political and economic processes and land use decisions, and the inadequacy of solutions arrived at by current methods. It raises important and continuing national issues. As a prototype of struggles between private and public use of our national heritage, the Dunes case merits serious study.

Beyond these considerations, the Dunes controversy initiated changes in the nature of the conflict between development and conservation that extended to the national scene. It elaborated and elevated the role of citizen input and paved the way for environmentalists to play a major part in policy formulation. Moreover, the Dunes case presented many firsts.

In 1916, for the first time in history, Stephen Mather proposed government funding for a national park—Sand Dunes National Park—as a new concept for park acquisition. It took forty-six years for Congress to accept that radical suggestion. The Dunes became the first national park that Congress established in the wake of extended nationwide conflict and public controversy and the first realized through the efforts of a citizen group. During the course of the conflict preservationists successfully challenged the cost-benefit calculations of the Army Engineers. In addition, the conflict produced the pioneering Save the Dunes Council, the first citizens' organization of its kind and a model for many environmentally oriented citizens' groups that followed. Probably most important, the battle in the Dunes provided direct impetus to the shaping of America's first national environmental protection legislation, the National Environmental Policy Act, in 1969. For the first time, Indiana Democrats and Republicans united behind a single goal in an unprecedented fashion. Finally, a powerful congressman (Charles Halleck) accepted humiliating defeat on a public works project in his own district.

Ultimately the Dunes case serves to illuminate two major processes: the nature of decision-making and the transition in values. The resulting insights comprise its most important contribution. The Dunes conflict makes a particularly good vehicle for the study of broad policy problems and perplexing value questions. Through

looking at the how, the why, and the who of the Dunes controversy—its politics, its values, and its people—we may perhaps learn
more about similar situations far from Lake Michigan's shore.

Decision-making for the Dunes occurred in two stages: a nonfed-
eral one between 1916 and 1958 and a federal one between 1958 and
the present. Before 1958 no federal agency participated directly in
producing land use decisions or policies for the Dunes. This period
divides into three phases in terms of the decisions that took place:
first, the federal government failed to make a decision; second, the
decisions reverted to Indiana; and third, conflict directed the outcome.

During the first phase Stephen Mather, the first director of the
National Park Service (NPS), together with a coterie of scientific,
cultural, and political elites from Illinois and Indiana, attempted to
obtain federal purchase of twenty-five miles of duneland in three
Indiana counties for a national park. Participants in the 1916 effort
consisted of well-organized but politically unrealistic preservation
proponents whose success lay only in the eloquent articulation of
their goal. An unorganized but vocal group, exclusively from Porter
County, Indiana, opposed a national park. Their spokesman, A. J.
Bowser, defined in general terms the reasons for Porter County's antipark position. Conflict during this phase remained submerged. While
the propreservation faction formed a bistate constituency and achieved
a bipartisan coalition of conservation organizations and civic and
philanthropic leaders, the prodevelopment people represented the
interests of a narrower constituency, a small but noisy group of Republican businessmen from Porter County. They did not attempt to
acquire a national political sponsor for their position; they had no
positive proposal to put forward. The conservationists had both an
easier and a harder time in dealing with more than one political
jurisdiction. On the one hand, they could enlarge their coalition and
garner broad support; on the other, they required greater coordination and resources to achieve their goal. They had to cover many
bases; the opposition needed only one. In this phase no decision
resulted. Governmental inaction did not stem from conflict between opposing land use proposals but from the combination of an
unfavorable national political climate and a lack of support within
Congress for a park.

During the second phase, beginning in 1919, the preservation effort shifted to a smaller arena, the state of Indiana. Proponents no
longer needed to attract supporters outside the state. This narrower
"scope of conflict" simplified the prospects for a decision. Further
simplification resulted because the state park proposal involved only

two political jurisdictions, Porter County and the state. Moreover, since the new proposal trimmed lake frontage demands to nine miles, proponents and opponents had less land to dispute. Opposition to a park remained the same, Porter County businessmen, led by former state Senator Bowser; as in the first phase, they had no positive proposal of their own for Dunes land use. They merely sought to reduce proposed park acreage in order to reserve as much land as possible for hypothetical future development.

Except for Richard Lieber's attempts to get out-of-state funds, the entire Indiana Dunes State Park effort developed and concluded within the arena of state politics. Proponents and opponents marshalled support within Indiana and lobbied legislators who submitted the issue to the customary political process. Although each side would have liked more land, each accepted both the process and the result.

The third phase, 1927–58, unfolded as a period of conflict consolidation, economically motivated and politically fostered. Encouraged by the completion of Burns Ditch and Midwest Steel's land purchase, the prodevelopment forces coalesced behind the proposal to build a public harbor in Porter County. Supported by a coalition of businessmen and chambers of commerce identical to themselves in outlook and values, these forces held to a single goal. They courted a congressman and elected a state senator from their own ranks. They initiated a series of moves on the state level to acquire bipartisan support and provide state mechanisms to achieve their goal. The creation of the Indiana Board of Public Harbors and Terminals as well as the passage of various appropriation bills by the legislature erased hurdles in a step-by-step fashion, thus reducing the number and magnitude of the decisions remaining for federal discretion. Private interests often merged with public positions, making it difficult to determine who controlled the decision-making process. For example, John Van Ness participated in the port issue as a member of the Valparaiso Chamber of Commerce, as a state senator, and as an employee of Midwest Steel. Furthermore, the nucleus of young men who began the port effort in the 1930s constituted a stable and unchanging group. With few exceptions, these same individuals saw their dream reach fruition in the 1960s. Between 1929 and 1949 port promoters had no opposition. During those years they failed to achieve their goal because of the Great Depression and World War II and an unfavorable political climate on the federal level. Democratic control of Congress, the presidency, and, consequently, the Army Engineers prevented Porter County spokesman Charles A. Halleck from obtaining favorable decisions on the federal level.

Unlike port proponents, preservationists had no goals that called for immediate government decisions during the third phase. Leaders decried industrial expansion and promoted saving the Dunes in the most general and nonspecific terms. Instead of attempting to influence government action, preservationists addressed the necessity of establishing the legitimacy of the Dunes' national, scientific, and recreational value. Because they had little significant local support, they widened their constituency by becoming a national organization. They solicited memberships outside Indiana and rejoiced at coverage in such national publications as *National Geographic* and *Life*. The Save the Dunes Council concentrated on making sure the Dunes satisfied the NPS's criterion of "national significance" for admission to the national park system. Prior to 1958 the council did nothing to effect policy decisions in any political jurisdiction. Instead, it pursued a strictly educational and promotional program, which acquired a national constituency. The council established itself as the authoritative and legitimate voice of the Dunes cause and developed expertise and prestige that it maximized in later years.

After 1958 the Dunes conflict reached the national political arena. Paul Douglas's attempts to gain national park status together with Halleck's continued efforts to obtain federal port funds removed the issue forever from state and county jurisdiction. The usual congressional-administrative decision-making process did not resolve the controversy. Instead, the conflict, which should not have interested many outside the extended local area, reached the desk of the president whose special counsel orchestrated a compromise. Why didn't the normal decision-making apparatus suffice in the case of the Dunes? How did the dispute get to the highest possible level for mediation?

R. H. Platt in *The Open Space Decision Process* describes the Dunes conflict as a "nested set of conflicting interests between peer units of land use management: private; local; county; and state."[3] He notes that "conflicts between peer units of land use management are resolved at the next higher level of authority . . . [therefore] we find the federal government playing a critical albeit ambivalent role in the final stages of the Dunes conflict."[4] Platt details the series of decision-making standoffs that occurred in the Dunes case, and his analysis bears attention. What transpired at the county and state levels suffices to explain the barriers to enough of a consensus for the decision-making procedure to go forward as though no opposition existed.

In the 1960s Porter County still compared poorly with both Lake and LaPorte counties in relative economic status.[5] Porter County leaders maintained total commitment to economic development and saw construction of the port as an absolute means of catching up. Beyond its aspirations for development, Porter County had reasons to reject the idea of a national park. The county eschewed lakefront usage, which might produce further nontaxable recreation facilities. Moreover, Porter County residents shrank from the thought of becoming an enlarged weekend and vacation haven for the urban industrial, ethnic, and minority populations of the surrounding counties. Since the state park had never stimulated any taxable tourist facilities to offset property tax losses, Porter County probably would have opposed a national park even if no industrial development materialized. Conversely, Lake and LaPorte counties welcomed the prospect of a national park in the county next door. Their populations could thus enjoy close-to-home recreation without having to pay. Lake and LaPorte county leaders supported the park for yet another reason. They viewed the industrialization of Porter County as undesirable competition in good economic times and an intolerable threat in bad. They also feared loss of skilled workers to more modern plants. Easier and more politically acceptable than opposing the harbor project outright, Lake and LaPorte counties took the high road and supported preservation.

The genuine conflict of interest between the three Dunes counties prevented consensus on either proposal. Because of the weakness of county government in Indiana, municipal leaders and state and federal representatives expressed the counties' positions. Porter County, particularly, diligently courted these representatives. First District Congressman Ray Madden, however, succumbed to pressure from Sylvia Troy and others who spoke for a wider constituency. He recognized that the park served his county's interest far more than did a port in Porter County.

The conflict took a different form on the state level. Although Indiana produced solid bipartisan support for a port and could justifiably demand that decision-making protect its interests, Illinois had a different interest to preserve. "It stood to gain a major nearby recreation facility at no tax loss to itself if the National Park were enacted. Concomitantly, Illinois' economic position . . . would be threatened if new competition were to arise in Porter County, Indiana."[6]

Given the nature of federalism, Illinois could not interfere directly in the affairs of another state, but it could speak to issues of national concern. Through Douglas and, to a lesser degree, public officials in Chicago and private organizations and individuals, Illinois pressed its claim at the federal level. The Prairie State needed to establish and maintain the legitimacy of the Dunes conflict as a national is-

sue. In this way Illinois overcame Indiana's charges of outside interference by one state in the affairs of another.

When the Dunes conflict reached the federal arena, changes occurred that had implications for decision-making. First, the process
became more complicated. Rather than following a single, legislative path toward resolution, the conflict simultaneously followed
the administrative procedures of two agencies of the executive
branch—the Army Corps of Engineers and the National Park Service (NPS). Each side in the dispute tailored its campaign to the
policies and behavior of those agencies. The port promoters hoped
to benefit from the particular interaction that had developed between the Corps of Engineers and the Congress.

> Over the years, a symbiotic relationship evolved; the Corps sought
> and received congressional support in its struggle with other
> federal agencies for a large share of the public works budget. In
> turn, congressmen seeking public works projects for their dis-
> tricts needed and received sympathetic consideration from the
> Corps. The more powerful and prestigious the congressman, es-
> pecially those on the House Public Works and Appropriations
> Committees, the greater the sympathy received.[7]

Port backers expected that Halleck's well-established position of
power and prestige would prove more than adequate to take advantage of this situation. Park promoters tried to shape their demands
to shifting NPS policies. Proposals for preservation took the form of
national monument, national park, scientific landmark, national
lakeshore, urban park, or recreation area, according to which NPS
designation applied at any given time. Administrative manipulations took place concurrently with the legislative process.

Beyond increased complexity, everything took longer. In the broader
arena more delays occurred and more decision points developed, allowing both proponents and opponents many entrances into the
decision-making system. Each side now had a range of places from
which to intervene in the proceedings or win interim decisions.
Furthermore, because success in the federal arena required greater
lobbying pressure on decision-makers, advocates needed larger, better-
organized, better-staffed, and better-financed support groups.

Port proponents tended to lose ground as the arena widened. They
could reach their goals most easily by narrowing, not expanding, the
number of decisions, by having decisions made quickly, by reducing
the number of agencies and legislators involved, by restricting litigation to local and state courts, and by courting the already favorable
local and state communications media. Preservationistis, on the other
hand, had everything to gain by widening the arena and slowing the

process. They, therefore, encouraged such activities as multiple studies by the NPS and studies of alternative sites by the Army Engineers. They undertook a wide array of litigation, attempting to gain federal jurisdiction, and they worked assiduously at attracting the attention of the national media. In addition, they tried to block decisions favorable to the opposition. Their successful challenge to the Army Engineers cost-benefit calculations produced lengthy delays. Moreover, this confrontation marked the first instance of effective citizen challenge to the Corps' economic and engineering criteria.[8]

Transfer to the national stage and subjection to the decision-making apparatus of two agencies in the executive branch as well as Congress still did not resolve the Dunes conflict. The port proposal followed its course through the machinery of the House Committee on Public Works while the park proposal pursued its path through the Senate Interior Committee as though no conflict existed between the two plans. Each committee held hearings and reached an interim decision incompatible with that reached by the other. "The benefits of each proposal to the national welfare were extolled and each committee reported out its measure favorably."[9] A new standoff occurred between two peer units, forcing the conflict up one more level for resolution. It took a year of behind-the-scenes work on the part of Special Counsel to the President Lee White and representatives from both factions and the Bureau of the Budget to reach a compromise. Strong but equal pressure from each side forced an administrative rather than a legislative decision. Its framers attempted to satisfy all parties with a solution that, in the short run, accommodated everyone. Concurrently, the decision resolved the many political difficulties faced by the decision-makers. One could justifiably argue, however, that over the long run the Kennedy compromise began and ended as a prodevelopment decision. As political scientist David A. Caputo observed: "Anyone with any sense would have recognized that dunes could not coexist with surrounding industry."[10]

The Kennedy administration emerged as the chief beneficiary of the compromise. It successfully minimized political losses and eliminated future pressure by sending further Dunes decisions back to lower jurisdictions. By the time the long-range implications of the compromise became clear, that administration had gone, no longer accountable for the results.

Although the Kennedy compromise proclaimed both sides "winner," it eventually stimulated new definitions of the term. Since that Dunes decision, environmentalists have applied new criteria to the determination of winners and losers in other land preservation conflicts. They no longer accept mere physical division of disputed territory as a winning solution, even though politicians may employ the same compromise strategies.

In terms of the use of the Dunes land, proindustry forces emerged the clear victors. Port proponents acquired the sites they wanted for the purpose they proclaimed. Though they might have wished to save the rest of the land for future industrial and commercial development, they gave up not an inch of the contested land until the 1976 expansion legislation penalized both Bethlehem and Midwest. Park supporters won a park that in no way compared to what they wanted in the first place. Nevertheless, Douglas hailed the park as a great victory for conservationists and for the nation. In what ways could Douglas view such obvious defeat as victory? How, if at all, did port proponents lose? What factors besides land usage merit attention?

Considering the inequality of the contending forces, any park at all in the Dunes stands out as a remarkable achievement. During the struggle, the Save the Dunes Council had available none of the legislative and judicial safeguards that might have evened up the sides. Lynton K. Caldwell, an authority on environmental affairs, contends that the requirement for environmental impact statements could have prevented Dunes industrialization had it then existed. "If there had been NEPA, five or six years earlier, we could have saved the Dunes. If there had been NEPA, the Corps would have had to assess the impact of industrial development on the entire lake shore. . . . NEPA could have been a delaying preventative technique forcing federal agencies to look at a whole range of alternatives."[11]

Furthermore, the strategy of invoking injunctions for environmental conflicts had not yet gained acceptance. Because of the paucity of federal environmental law, environmentalists seeking judicial solutions could not reach federal courts; state and lower courts seldom rendered judgments consonant with preservation. At best court procedures bought time, delaying decisions until the emergence of a more favorable climate.

Finally, the national environmental consciousness, which was ignited at the end of the 1960s, came too late to influence the outcome of the Dunes struggle. The Save the Dunes Council did not benefit from mass public support or national environmental coalitions. Moreover, even during federal involvement, the goals and values espoused by the port proponents still mirrored those of the American public as a whole.

Park proponents did garner sufficient political strength to cause the standoffs that produced the compromise, a victory that should not be underestimated. The Save the Dunes Council's fortuitous and largely serendipitous recruitment of Douglas constituted the heart of its success. His political skill did not help as much as his complete accord with their goal. He demonstrated astonishing willingness to allow the Dunes conflict to assume a high priority in his activities. The Save the Dunes Council never needed to keep its political sponsor on the track, usually one of the primary activities of lobbying groups.

The development of strength, longevity, and political sophistication constitutes another victory for park proponents. Through and with Douglas, the council became an effective political instrument, perceived by its industrial opposition as bigger, stronger, richer, and more formidable than the members ever imagined themselves. This group pioneered in using the courts and in challenging the Army Engineers. The council took on Halleck and embarrassed him in his own district. It inspired other citizens' groups to try to beat the odds. These efforts provided a model for the institutionalization of citizen environmental efforts. What members learned by hit or miss, by trial and error, they passed on to similar groups who now employ those hard-learned strategies and tactics as a matter of course.

Park proponents could claim a third victory in having contributed to a major shift in public values. The popularity of the idea of preserving the Indiana Dunes probably shocked port proponents more than any other aspect of the conflict. At its beginning these men expressed and reflected the nation's dominant values; they emerged from the conflict scorned by a larger public and castigated by the national media for their formerly acceptable views.

While prodevelopment forces survived the conflict with lands intact, they lost in a few significant ways. First, they acquired a new and permanent watch dog. No longer could they operate without public scrutiny and possible public censure. Second, they never again enjoyed a position of progressive leadership. As these boosters of industry surfaced from the struggle, the nation had already begun to redefine progress. The same ideas that once brought national approbation now brought national disdain. Industrial leaders faced a period of declining tolerance for their values; in disbelief, they found themselves regarded as "bad guys" punished by ever-increasing regulatory restrictions.

The Kennedy compromise that produced a port and a national park also had a number of unintended consequences. It resulted in an inherently unstable area characterized by incompatible land uses. The incompatibilities ran from the visual—a sand dune and a steel mill do not look right side by side—through the ecological—industrial deterioration of plant and animal habitats, air and water pollution, accelerated beach erosion, and drainage altered by massive land fills. These injuries to the fragile Dunes environment have had consequences beyond the immediately affected sites.

Because the compromise satisfied no one, the land remained subject to constant pressure for new decisions, both from within and without. Since 1966, for example, the Save the Dunes Council has persuaded congressmen to introduce park expansion legislation many times. Two of the bills have resulted in additions. Although the council has generally applauded the broad goal of increasing park acreage, specific parcels have not always pleased individual members. Dissent among some property owners has produced concerted pressure on legislators to include or exclude particular sites. Industry has put much effort and money into keeping bordering lands out of expansion plans. Such lobbying has occasionally resulted in bizarre decisions, which have caused inequities to property owners and produced hostility toward the capriciousness of government. Intended as fair or as compromise positions, these decisions have often created more problems than they have solved.

The preservationists themselves have exerted opposing pressures for land uses within the park. One element among them decries "development," defined as NPS construction of structures and recreational facilities. They eschew dune buggies and other off-road vehicles, hang gliders, motorcycles, motor boats, paved roads, and unlimited visitation. This faction believes in and lobbies for land use restricted to scientific study and preservation. The recreationists, on the other hand, envision a wide range of facilities available to the broad constituency in whose name Congress authorized the park in the first place.

Simultaneously, strong pressure for change has continued on the part of the proindustry faction. Since 1966 antipark forces have attempted to reduce the size of the lakeshore, tamper with its boundaries, or deauthorize it altogether. Whether these attempts have originated with the local congressman as they did with Earl Landgrebe in 1973 or with the secretary of the interior as with James Watt in 1981, they have had the support of industry as well as some vocal and well-organized local property owners.

Such pressures for change have destabilized the Dunes region. NPS has had difficulties in formulating a comprehensive management plan responsive to incompatible interests. Local park officials feel continually bombarded with ideas, plans, and objections from an alert and disagreeing public. They cannot count on constancy in funding because the lakeshore remains an appropriations football. The park superintendent spends a disproportionate amount of time lobbying for basic necessities in order to operate the park. In addition, the park's urban characteristics and compact, noncontiguous nature present management problems never before encountered by the NPS. Because no precedents exist, local park management must broker solutions to these headaches on a case by case basis.

The pressure has also taken its toll on local communities. All have had to deal with impact due to increased numbers of park visitors as well as the presence of an additional layer of bureaucracy. Hard hit Beverly Shores, which had two-thirds of its land included in the lakeshore in 1966, suffers a declining tax base as well as greater visitor impact. Moreover, its small permanent population remains deeply and bitterly divided over the park's existence.

The region's instability has had significant political fallout as well. Pressure for Dunes action continues to appear on agendas of legislators from Indiana and Illinois far beyond its relative importance. Try as they may, affected congressmen and senators cannot seem to put an end to the din. For example, in 1981 Congressman Sidney Yates earmarked funds in the 1982 budget for the lakeshore—a far from routine procedure. The Dunes has probably seen more final bills than most disputed areas.

Industry's problems add to the pressures for change. Although its supporters do not easily admit it, the Port of Indiana has not produced the economic panacea so glowingly predicted twenty years ago. Bethlehem's Burns Harbor plant, the most modern in the nation, cannot compete with Japanese steel, which ironically constitutes the chief cargo unloaded at the Burns Waterway Port. Moreover, the Indiana Port Commission has, at least once, taken Bethlehem to court to settle a dispute over dockage fees. Midwest Steel has shelved its plans to build an integrated plant in the foreseeable future; few satellite industries have located in the Dunes industrial corridor. The Port of Indiana, like the other Great Lakes ports, suffers from the shortcomings of the St. Lawrence Seaway and joins with them in grumbling about the government's failure to utilize Great Lakes port facilities.[12] Despite the disappointments, however, Porter County has thrived. Between 1970 and 1980 its population rose from 87,114 to an estimate of more than 118,000. It grew over 3 percent a year—three times the national average over the past twenty years—and its per capita income ranked fifth in the nation. Yet, because 62 percent of the population hold manufacturing jobs, prosperity becomes tenuous in times of recession.[13]

Halleck's claims that a park would turn Porter County Democratic have probably proved most accurate of the many rhetorical claims. The increase in and makeup of Porter County's population finally produced a Democratic congressman in 1976, 1978, and 1980.[14] Floyd Fithian's 1980 victory, won in the face of Ronald Reagan's capture of the government, represented his last in the district, as once again the Republican legislature changed the boundaries of the second district. This time lawmakers put northern Porter County together with its neighboring Democratic lakefront counties and attached the Republican southern section to solidly Republican companions.

The decision of the Kennedy administration proclaimed both port and park. Though it succeeded politically, it failed to address long-range consequences or the broader questions raised by the controversy. An understanding of the nature of the decision-making process holds the key to why the Dunes decision could not produce a better, more workable result.

The process has a dynamic nature: groups and individuals representing a wide spectrum of interests continually press legislators for action; Congress articulates broad policy, and administrative agencies interpret it more narrowly; their decisions produce consequences, both intended and unintended, which result in pressure for new policies and new decisions. Final solutions, enduring dispositions do not exist; change emerges as the only constant.[15] Unfortunately, some decisions produce final, irretrievable consequences; the heart of the Dunes, once lost, disappeared forever.

Moreover, many factors intrinsic to the system contribute to unsatisfactory decisions. Incrementalism and fragmentation, for example, help to perpetuate the status quo and generate resistance to creative change. Walter A. Rosenbaum notes that "incrementalism favors the making of new policy on the basis of past experience, careful and prolonged consultation among all the major parties affected by decisions, bargaining and compromise among interested parties, and modest policy change rather than comprehensive or radical alterations in policy."[16] He goes on to say that it favors delay and virtually assures that no problems, save those of war or national emergency, get solved. The practice of incrementalism precludes long-range comprehensive planning that might have resolved the Dunes conflict more rationally. However, it does provide a measure of political safety for officials. It perpetuates conservatism by supporting dominant values and the existing political system. While no one would wish policies so static that they could not respond to changing political, economic, and social conditions, the nation nonetheless needs decisions and policies stable enough to resist the inevitable onslaught of every pressure for change.

Fragmentation—diffusion of power among many participants both in and out of government—helps to create incrementalism. It affects policy-making in ways that inhibit sound decision-making. Moreover, it gives a tactical advantage to the opponents of a major policy change. They can often defeat innovative proposals by withholding support in one strategic place. Proponents, on the other hand, must satisfy a coalition of interests throughout the government. They have to work harder, spend more, and invest more inventiveness in their efforts.

Even Douglas fell prey to the seductiveness of incrementalism and fragmentation. He often consoled the Save the Dunes Council by saying, "Don't worry if we don't get as much as we want now. It's always easier to add more later."[17] While he directed the council masterfully in the arts of legislative strategy, he did not fully apprise the members of the necessity for monitoring the policy-implementation aspects of the decision. Rosenbaum aptly generalizes the problem the council faced, noting that "both friends and foes of public policy must fight a two-front war if they are to be effective. Those favoring a public policy must take care that not only is it made in Congress but also faithfully executed administratively." He then formulates the lesson the council learned on its own through bitter experience. "Vigilance over administration is the price of victory in the policy process . . . successful interests in the struggle are those that create stable access and influence within the administrative branch."[18] This the council accomplished by relinquishing its ad hoc status and by establishing its legitimacy as *the* informed spokesman for Dunes preservation.

While some observers attributed the quality of the Dunes compromise to those factors intrinsic to the decision-making process, others blamed the system's deficiencies. Lynton Caldwell views the Dunes case not as an example of how America's political process works but as a demonstration of its failure. "[It was] a classic case of a failure of institutions in civic responsibility—a lack of foresight on the part of so many who could not see the enormous asset Indiana had in the Dunes. The institutional structure was against it. The nature of civic responsibility was against it because the responsibility that was exercised by politicians was not to future generations, nor to a broader point of view, nor to the American people. It was a civic tragedy that had a not wholly tragic ending."[19]

According to Caldwell and others, the nature of the decision-making process supplies only a partial answer as to why policymakers reached a less than satisfactory compromise over the Dunes. For the crux of the answer, they look to values. They inquire into questions such as: What constitutes the nature of civic responsibility? What relationship exists between values and public policy? Who defines and speaks for the public interest? What change must occur in order to produce workable environmental policy?

Harold and Margaret Sprout in *The Context of Environmental Politics* delineate the scope of such value questions. They note that those attempting to institute environmental programs must first deal with ethical questions: Who ought to set standards for the public's air, water, land, and noise? Who determines how society will pay for environmental benefits? Whose priorities shall take precedence? They conclude that only the federal government has the obligation of putting the common good above private interests, regardless of how well or badly it may fulfill this responsibility.[20]

Many environmental writers and thinkers of the 1970s believed that as the only entity with sufficient power and access to required expertise the federal government must originate and disseminate the information that can affect environmental values. However, they often differed about how to accomplish that end. According to the Sprouts, elected officials must take responsibility for determining the public interest by actively seeking assistance from many sources, including the media, the business community, and intellectuals.[21]

Caldwell believes that existing political remedies will not produce public policy based on environmental values. "The solution to the major problems of man-environment relationships is neither in exhortation nor regulation but rather in the redesigning of social institutions and the reordering of political and economic priorities. . . . Solutions are 'radical' in the exact meaning of this word, their tendency being to alter values, to redefine the responsibilities of government and to reinterpret the practical meaning of many so-called human rights." He posits a federally funded environmental science institute as one means of achieving informed, mature, rational decisions. He contends that the cost-benefit approach to policy-making, while an essential element in rational planning, in itself contains value judgments.[22] The definition of costs and benefits must expand to include long-range consequences and effects.[23]

Rosenbaum contends that land use remains the only major environmental concern as yet untouched by the federal government. Conflicts arising from competition for open space require federal attention for adequate resolution. He suggests a greater degree of centralized planning and authority as a means of setting policy for these and other environmental issues. Such centralization, however, would first require some changes in the way the government sets policy. As first steps in that process he recommends new priorities: greater attention to long-range environmental consequences, less on short-range economic gains, recognition that growth does not equal progress, and less concern with the politics of compromise.[24]

In the 1970s these writers and others of equal reputation believed that the heady events of the decade indicated that a shift in national values had occurred. Moreover, their writings implied that these new values could serve as the starting point for a radical revision of the decision-making process, which included "major changes in government, politics, and lifestyle."[25] Even before the policies of Watt made a mockery of the optimistic predictions of the 1970s, some writers had already disagreed with such inclusive statements. According to Michael Kraft, the core American values remained unchallenged. The nation still adhered to belief in private property, self-interest, limited government, material abundance, and the necessity for economic growth. Kraft concluded that environmental problems continue to elicit incremental decision-making in the halls of Capitol Hill.

> The dominant political response to the ecological crisis has been characterized by marginal and superficial attention to, understanding of, and concern for ecological problems; a weak and uncertain commitment to new environmental priorities both on the part of the American public and on the part of political leaders; timidity and moderation at best in public policy developments adversely affecting the basic economic system and the values of our central (though possibly outmoded) political philosophies; the frequent use by politicians of rhetorical and symbolic gestures as a substitute for material, real accomplishments; dedication to palliative measures and technological fixes aimed at relieving highly visible symptons rather than treating underlying social and economic causes of environmental problems; and, of course, devotion in the customary fashion to incrementalism—that is, to "muddling through," to business as usual, to satisfying behavior as a way of life, to preoccupation primarily with short-range goals that are immediately "feasible" or "realistic," to dealing with problems in a piecemeal and fragmented rather than [a] comprehensive and coordinated manner.[26]

Other writers denied that expanded roles for the federal government could guarantee the protection of the environment. Joseph Sax in *Defending the Environment* asserted that the promises of politicians would no longer suffice. Citizens could determine the fate of

their own environment by taking decisions out of the hands of bu-
reaucrats. He contended that citizens did not need a "bureaucratic
middleman" to protect their interest in environmental quality.[27] Sax
viewed the struggle to achieve policy decisions that reflected concern for the environment as a protracted war. In this long battle citizens proceeded on a case by case basis to resolve environmental
conflicts in the courts. Each decision strengthened the next case;
each victory added to the perceived power of the litigant. Recently
Sax has included negotiation as an ingredient in resolving environmental conflict. He talks of possible compromise only when environmentalists achieve a position of power equivalent to that of their
adversaries.[28]

    While the theoreticians argue about such intangibles as public in-
terest and values, practicing politicians concern themselves only with
the political agenda as brought to their attention by the ongoing
dynamics of the political process. To them, the success of an issue
depends entirely on the ability of its proponents to organize and present their case effectively. The better-organized proponents develop
more clout and have a greater chance of seeing their cause enacted
into policy. When equally strong and well-organized groups contend
for the same objective, policymakers attempt to accommodate both
interests equally. They assume that each side serves the public interest and that the underlying values of each have equal validity.
Although groups attract a constituency by articulating the merits of
an issue and its underlying values, politics alone determines the
outcome. In this scenario politicians do not make decisions according to some preexisting set of values of their own nor do they attempt to define the public interest. Instead, they reflect the interests
and values of individuals and groups who gain greatest access to
them.[29]

    As the Dunes case illustrates, the political system does not need
radical restructuring for change to occur. Nevertheless, some alterations must take place. To influence change, environmentalists must
find effective ways of keeping their values before the public and on
the political agenda. Groups wishing to affect governmental policy
on national park land or other environmental matters must work to
make decision-makers responsive to their concerns. It is hoped that
they can preserve policies formed under favorable political conditions from annihilation when the inevitable political swings occur.
They can use the courts and enlist the media. The Save the Dunes
Council pioneered these techniques and tactics, providing an enduring model for a new generation of militant environmentalists.

    In their attempt to persuade the decision-makers during the 1950s and 1960s port advocates and park supporters both claimed that their proposals served the public interest. The rhetoric of each position rested on ideas and assumptions about what constituted such interest and what kinds of policies would best enhance the public good. The positions rested on two vastly different systems of values about what constitutes proper land use. Port proponents expressed the majority view, one long-held, long-accepted, and long-established in the nation's political agenda. Their equation of growth and development with progress had such wide popular acceptance and had such institutionalized links to the political system that even the language of decision-making, as exemplified by the term "costs and benefits," sometimes biased the decisions. All too often, "decision-making rules have been 'loaded' in the sense that they have favored some policy outcomes over others."[30] Knowing that the value underlying their quest—economic concerns—held high priority on the political agenda gave the port proponents an added advantage.

Park proponents, on the other hand, claimed that preservation of the Dunes better served the elusive entity called public interest. Their primary task lay in making the new value of preservation a viable part of the political agenda. Certainly conservation values had had high priority during the administrations of Theodore and Franklin Roosevelt, John Kennedy, and Lyndon Johnson. When other political climates take hold, however, as with the administrations of Warren Harding, Richard Nixon, and Ronald Reagan, such values lose their influence with politicians.

If the values espoused by Stephen Mather, Henry Cowles, Bess Sheehan, Reuben Strong, Dorothy Buell, and the thousands who supported Dunes preservation deserve a place in the formation of relevant land use policy, and if the values of conservationists, preservationists, environmentalists, and ecologists *ought* to continue to influence the formation of quality-of-life policies, their advocates must make these values a permanent part of the nation's political agenda. Groups wishing to achieve this end must take advantage of the lessons it took the Save the Dunes Council thirty years to learn.

The Dunes case amply demonstrates that environmental problems depend on political solutions and that advocates must possess a thorough understanding of the political process. Groups must find a political sponsor. The more power he or she has—which translates into ability to manipulate the system—the more likely that satisfactory results will follow. If a group cannot discover such a sponsor, they must educate one; few groups find a Paul Douglas. They must lobby in the best sense, that of providing legislators and administrators with accurate data and perspective about their cause. They should place the most knowledgeable person they can afford as close to the decision-makers as they can. Credibility and legitimacy constitute the lifeblood of a citizens' movement. When decision-makers recognize a group as *the* spokesman and authority for its cause, they will consult it at each step, assuring its members of continuing input into the process.

Despite some obvious advantages in attaining tax-exempt status, citizens' groups should carefully consider the potentially greater advantages of direct participation in politics as a means of furthering their cause. Nor should they cease activity after the conclusion of positive legislation. The make-or-break substance of policy resides in implementation and interpretation as performed by administrative agencies. To insure the inclusion of their expertise in administrative implementation, citizens' groups must establish and maintain a working relationship with relevant agencies. Mindful of the fine line between cooperation and cooptation, groups must continually refine the functions of oversight, community liaison, and constructive critic. In fact, they must recognize that in the "environment business" the task never ends. While they may begin as ad hoc organizations favoring a particular solution to a narrow or strictly local problem, they must realize that solutions invariably lead to new problems requiring other solutions and new goals to pursue. Moreover, policies based on values not broadly held tend to erode more easily, thus requiring continued vigilance on the part of supporters. Those groups that have disbanded upon achieving their goal have often regretted that decision.

Tom Dustin contends that groups such as the Save the Dunes Council have changed over the years. Whereas they once operated with a kind of charismatic bloom—naive, idealistic, and emotional—they have since become technicians. They now know how to gain access to the press and other media. They have learned how to organize and to establish their credibility; they have learned to "locate the power outlets and the switches. They have institutionalized their techniques and gained technical competence; they have become paper shufflers, and they have lost the spirit to win against insuperable odds. Conservationists are never better than when faced with virulent opposition. Somehow, they need powerful, high profile enemies."[31]

The arduousness of protecting quality-of-life values lies in their elusiveness. They do not fit neatly into existing political jurisdictions; they remain intangible and difficult to grasp. Moreover, because people do not easily accept the notion of paying heavy costs now to reap unknown benefits in the future, reversion to traditional values occurs rapidly in times of uncertainty. The citizens' effort to protect the environment, therefore, must seek the widest possible constituency, form the broadest possible coalitions and alliances, even with competing interests where necessary, make optimum use of the media and the courts, and not be afraid to imitate Sylvia Troy and "threaten public officials with everything in sight" in the service of keeping such questions permanently on the political agenda.[32] Finally, all such groups must recognize the necessity for and legitimacy of compromise. Not compromise dictated from above, as occurred with the Dunes, but compromise among equals, arrived at on the basis of rational, comprehensive consideration of long-range consequences. For the foreseeable future, unfortunately, neither the mechanisms nor the necessary good will for such an accomplishment seems possible. In the final analysis the job of disseminating and protecting, of defining and defending the environment falls to those citizens who will, as in the Dunes, devote their talents, energies, and lifetimes to the cause.

NOTES

1. Walter A. Rosenbaum, *The Politics of Environmental Concern* (New York: Praeger Publishers, 1977), pp. 35, 36.

2. Grant McConnell, *Private Power and American Democracy* (New York: Alfred A. Knopf and Random House, 1966), chs. 5 and 8.

3. Platt, *Open Space Decision Process*, p. 169.

4. Ibid., p. 143.

5. Ibid., p. 162.

6. Ibid., p. 168.

7. Daniel A. Mazanian and Jeanne Nienaber, *Can Organizations Change? Environmental Protection, Citizen Participation and the Corps of Engineers* (Washington: The Brookings Institution, 1979), p. 12.

8. Ibid., p. 19. Although Mazanian and Nienaber pick the Sangamon River conflict of 1967 as the first case of citizen challenge to the Corps' figures, they missed the mark by five years. The Save the Dunes Council had initiated such tactics in 1962. Not surprisingly, Paul Douglas had a hand in the Sangamon River dispute as well.

9. Platt, *Open Space Decision Process*, p. 170.

10. Authors' interview with David A. Caputo, West Lafayette, Ind., 1980.

11. Caldwell interview.

12. James O'Shea, "At 20th Birthday Seaway Falls Far Short of Promises," *Chicago Tribune*, July 8, 1979; Richard O. Bacon, "Port Indiana's Brightest Jewel," *Gary Post Tribune*, July 8, 1979.

13. 1970 and 1980 Bureau of Census figures quoted in *Michigan City News Dispatch*, Porter County Section, Dec. 16, 1980.

14. Halleck interview.

15. *The Politics of Policy Making in America*, ed. David A. Caputo (San Francisco: W.H. Freeman and Co., 1977), pp. 1–6.

16. Rosenbaum, *Environmental Concern*, pp. 95–96, 100.

17. Troy interview.

18. Rosenbaum, *Environmental Concern*, p. 103.

19. Caldwell interview.

20. Harold and Margaret Sprout, *The Context of Environmental Politics* (Lexington: University Press of Kentucky, 1978), pp. 32, 33.

21. Ibid., p. 179.

22. Lynton K. Caldwell, "The Public Administration of Environmental Policy," in *Environmental Politics*, ed. Stewart S. Nagel (New York: Praeger Publishers, 1974), p. 286.

23. Nancy J. Doemel, *The Garrison Division Unit: Science, Technology, Politics and Values* (Bloomington: Indiana University, Advanced Studies in Science, Technology and Public Policy, n.d.), pp. 195–205.

24. Rosenbaum, *Environmental Concern*, pp. 112, 194.

25. Ibid., p. 112.

26. Michael E. Kraft, "Ecological Politics and American Government, a Review Essay," in *Environmental Politics*, ed. Nagel, p. 145.

27. Joseph Sax, *Defending the Environment* (New York: Alfred A. Knopf, 1972), flyleaf.

28. Authors' interview with Joseph Sax, Beverly Shores, 1981.

29. Authors' interview with Warren Stickle, legislative assistant to Floyd Fithian, Beverly Shores, 1981.

30. Rosenbaum, *Environmental Concern*, p. 23.

31. Dustin interview.

32. Troy interview.

Epilogue

Serious destabilizing pressures face the Indiana Dunes in the 1980s. Its two major land uses—the park and the steel mills—reel under attack from national and international forces undreamed of thirty years ago by advocates of either economic growth or preservation.

The nation's sharp economic downturn, combined with high interest rates, the failure to modernize plants and equipment, competition from foreign imports, high labor costs, and a marked shift to the use of plastics and aluminum, proved disastrous to the steel industry in general. By 1982 that industry, once the mighty harbinger of America's progress and productivity, limped along at below 50 percent capacity.[1] At its lowest level of operation since the late 1930s, the industry had "more than 75 million tons of capacity [lying] idle, another six million for sale and some of the remaining plants sputtering along at as low as 35 percent of capacity."[2] Moreover, steel companies laid off 30 percent of their 400,000 steelworkers, and management looked to the unions for wage and benefit concessions. Seven out of ten steel companies, including Bethlehem, Inland, and National, operated at a loss; the other three, including U.S. Steel, merely broke even.[3] Steel economists saw little reason to predict recovery; indeed, they gloomily predicted bankruptcies, the loss of an additional 8 to 17 percent capacity, and the permanent disappearance of 50,000 more jobs. Big steel itself looked to the federal government for a long-term remedy. In doing so, the industry, "long a symbol of emerging industrial capitalism," followed a seventy-year tradition of not-always-willing interaction with Washington.[4] While some managers saw penalties for subsidized foreign steel as the solution, others belatedly recognized the necessity for change in the entire structure of the industry. Still others sought company diversification to protect the stockholders from catastrophic losses. While these capitalists adhered to Ronald Reagan's rhetoric, few shared his optimism that free enterprise would restore America's once booming economy.

Such disastrous times have not left the Dunes steel mills unaffected. At the behest of U.S. Steel, Bethlehem Steel, and Midwest Steel, northwest Indiana's congressional delegation vigorously supported legislation to "stretch out" compliance with federal air pollution requirements. In return, the steel industry promised capital investments in technological advancements to improve its competitiveness; but such investments materialized slowly, given the economic climate. For instance, the once expanding midwestern market, which drew the steel industry to the Dunes, contracted sharply, as orders for tin plate from car and farm equipment manufacturers dwindled. Massive worker layoffs and shortened work weeks occurred at all Dunes's steel plants. U.S. Steel's Gary Works experienced a major decline in employment, in spite of corporate reorganization that placed the South Works under Gary's control. The high fixed costs of the Indiana operations forced U.S. Steel to virtually shut down the South Works in order to channel all possible orders to Indiana. Similarly, Midwest Steel reported 20 percent of its work force on layoff and a depressed order box.

At the same time 1,000 Bethlehem employees were out of work and thousands more worked less than forty hours a week. Burns Harbor managers suffered suspensions of bonuses together with 10 to 15 percent salary rollbacks. Moreover, the company delayed the addition of its much heralded second continuous caster.[5] General Manager C. Richard Hough admitted that "the past twelve months have been perhaps the most difficult period that any of us have faced since we began building the Burns Harbor plant."[6] In 1983, after the signing of an industry-wide union contract that cut pay and benefits in order to provide financial relief for the distressed steel producers, Bethlehem announced a move that strained labor relations at Burns Harbor. It shut down the 110-tin shear operation and shifted the work back to its mill in Sparrow Point, Maryland. The local union vowed to sue the company for breach of contract.

As a result of General Motors' new steel purchase system, which went into effect in June 1982, both the Gary and Burns Harbor works faced further decline. General Motors, the steel industry's largest customer, announced a reallocation of suppliers, with Inland gaining a larger share and Bethlehem and U.S. Steel smaller portions. Since both Bethlehem's and U.S. Steel's northwest Indiana plants produce large quantities of steel for cars, the impact of the decline in orders has significantly affected their Dunes operations.[7]

The economic woes of the steel plants offered cold comfort to Dunes preservationists. Their project, the Indiana Dunes National Lakeshore, faced equally calamitous times. Born in a period when preservation values prevailed, the lakeshore survived as the pendulum swung toward the development ethic of the 1980s. An examination of the legislative and administrative pressures on the park provides in microcosm a picture of present-day conditions in all units of the system. The initiatives of the Ronald Reagan administration, however, have roots in values that predated the Republican return to power. Always present and often pervasive, the prerogatives of private property influenced each stage of the public policy affecting the Dunes land use controversy.

When Stephen Mather first proposed the Sand Dunes National Park, he only considered acquisition of undeveloped land from willing sellers. Similarly, Indiana purchased acreage for the Indiana Dunes State Park from such landowners. The Prairie Club, which leased part of that land, had to demonstrate its allegiance to conservation by acquiescing to the arrangement. In Paul Douglas's first bills for a national park in the Dunes, he, too, avoided all but undeveloped land. When both Bethlehem and Midwest Steel refused to accept the role of willing sellers, Douglas had to revise the park's boundaries, including other undeveloped industrial property as well as undeveloped and developed residential holdings of both willing and unwilling sellers. As a result, the enabling legislation gave the National Park Service power to condemn all commercial properties and unimproved residential land.[8] For built-up residential property, the addition of two sweeteners muted most opposition. Attractive sales terms made most homeowners willing to sell, while exemption from condemnation (perpetual continuation of private property rights) established inholdings and quieted the remaining opposition.[9]

The 1976 lakeshore expansion act contained significantly different terms. It not only deleted noncondemnation rights for residential property owners living in the added sections but also removed such protection for residential owners within the original boundaries.[10] This change infuriated a small group within the lakeshore, who had never sold their holdings to the National Park Service and who had expected to enjoy noncondemnation rights in perpetuity. They charged that Congress had broken agreements made in 1966 and subjected them to its capricious whims. Their anger fueled an already existing mistrust of government and reinforced their dislike of the National Park Service, the federal agency with most influence over their lives. The change in homeowners' terms, moreover, also adversely affected other residential property owners who previously had supported lakeshore expansion.

The opposition of homeowners existed prior to the establishment of the park. Ad hoc groups, such as the Indiana Conservation and

Wildlife Protective Association, espoused the same values that Bethlehem and Midwest held: the right of landowners to use their holdings as they wished.[11] Many of these homeowners convinced Indiana
politicians of the righteousness of their cause and argued that inclusion in the park would result in decreased property values. They also
feared loss of privacy through the increased number of visitors. Consequently, congressional sponsors eliminated some neighborhoods
from the enabling legislation. Other homeowners included within
the park negotiated for noncondemnation certificates. The lakeshore's authorizing act required the secretary of the interior to approve local zoning ordinances before the National Park Service could
issue such certificates. By the time of the passage of the 1976 expansion bill the National Park Service had issued only one, which the
agency later voided.

Subsequent expansion bills proposed inclusion of parts of such
residential communities as Beverly Shores and Dune Acres. Opponents in these towns banded together with angry property owners
to form a new, antipark organization, Home Owners Against Park
Expansion (HOPE). Though the group succeeded in obtaining the
deletion of Beverly Shores from the lakeshore expansion act of 1976,
it could not prevent a congressionally mandated special park service
study of the proposal. Learning from the successes of the Save the
Dunes Council, HOPE affiliated with the National Inholders Association. It thereby gained access to senators and representatives
sympathetic to residential property owners affected by National Park
Service policy changes. Heretofore, lakeshore opponents had successfully pressured the Indiana delegation to plead their case; now
denied such representation because expansion legislation bore the
cosponsorship of both the state's senators and the second district
congressman, they found champions in other states. Moreover,
HOPE's association with a nationwide property rights movement
provided them with other benefits, including an experienced Washington lobbyist, access to the national media, and a means of generating support throughout the country for their cause. Like the Save
the Dunes Council, through its affiliation with national environmental organizations, HOPE's association allowed it to enjoy these
support techniques.[12] The final version of the 1980 expansion legislation excluded most residential property—an outcome directly at-
tributable to HOPE's effectiveness.[13] Though the National Park
Service, the Department of the Interior, the Jimmy Carter administration, the Save the Dunes Council, the Beverly Shores Town Board,
and the bill's sponsors all supported inclusion of part of Beverly Shores,

HOPE's political mentors blocked passage until Congress deleted the 700 acres.

Passage of the truncated expansion bill in December 1980 fore-shadowed lakeshore conditions during the Reagan administration. Proponents found little cause for comfort in James Watt's appoint-ment as secretary of the interior; their anxiety increased with his choice of Charles Cushman as a member of the National Park Ser-vice Advisory Board and of Ric Davidge as assistant to the assistant secretary of the interior for fish, wildlife and parks.[14] Both men had previously served as National Inholder Association lobbyists and had visited lakeshore communities on behalf of HOPE.

The apprehension of organizations like Save the Dunes Council turned to panic when news of a Department of Interior "hit list," targeting the Indiana Dunes National Lakeshore, reached them. An undated memorandum issued by G. Ray Arnett, then acting-assistant secretary of interior for Fish, Wildlife and Parks, to National Park Service Director Russell Dickinson directed the agency to review its files. Arnett asked for testimony and documents raising objections to the creation and expansion of the lakeshore and four other parks. The National Parks and Conservation Association, which released the document to the press, charged it proved "the Reagan Adminis-tration plans to target important units of the National Park system for de-authorization."[15] In response to this ominous threat to the continued existence of the lakeshore, the Save the Dunes Council mustered the full strength of a coalition assembled for over three decades. Resolutions and letters of support for the park flowed into congressional offices and editorials appeared in the bistate press.[16] Even the Valparaiso *Vidette Messenger*, a foe of the lakeshore in an-other era, spoke for its continuance. "It is difficult to imagine in these times, when the cost of travel rules out visits to the great na-tional parks in the west for many, that serious consideration would be given to dropping a park as unique as the Dunes National Lake-shore from the National Park system."[17] The Save the Dunes Coun-cil also joined with other propark groups affected by the Interior move to form the National Park Action Project. This new coalition worked to develop nationwide support for the beleaguered national park system.

In addition, the council called upon Indiana's senior senator, Re-publican Richard Lugar, to intervene with Watt on behalf of the park. In a meeting with the secretary, Lugar succeeded in obtaining a writ-ten disavowal of any Interior plans to eliminate the lakeshore.[18] Clearly, the abortive inquiry had aimed at finding grounds for a legislative attack on the park. In the face of adverse political reaction and without either a congressional mentor or evidence from the investigation, Watt disavowed the gambit. Some viewed the memo as a trial balloon that, for the Indiana Dunes, quickly burst. However, propark adherents looked upon the document as the first indication of a concerted campaign by the Watt forces. They believed the memo notified the National Park Service of the official disfavor of certain parks, including Indiana Dunes.

Watt continued his frontal attack on the lakeshore by trimming land acquisition funds appropriated in the 1981 budget and proposing no lakeshore appropriation for this purpose in both the 1982 and 1983 budgets. In 1982 the lakeshore escaped the effects of Watt's plan because of the strategic position of Chicago Congressman Sidney Yates, chairman of the House Interior Appropriation Committee. Through his considerable influence, the lakeshore received $2.3 million to purchase land. Yet the park never realized the entire amount. The Department of Interior ordered half of the appropriation held in reserve for payment of unsettled condemnation cases. In addition, in order to purchase any individual piece of property, Indiana Dunes like all other park units had to obtain approval from Davidge's office in Washington. At the end of 1982 land acquisition had effectively halted.

Unable to achieve his purposes through congressional action, Watt used administrative pressure to constrain the lakeshore. First, he ordered his department's inspector general to investigate the land acquisition practices of the National Park Service at the Indiana Dunes. He based his directive on "information indicating possible collusion by landowners and National Park Service personnel."[19] After sealing the lakeshore's land acquisition files and conducting the inquiry, the inspector general in a report on Indiana Dunes concluded lamely that "any analysis of the decisions made at that time [several years ago] concerning park boundaries or cost estimates would not be meaningful at this time."[20] In 1982 at the request of HOPE's ally, the Indiana Dunes Conservancy Federation, Watt again ordered the inspector general to investigate the lakeshore, this time on charges of inflating visitor figures.[21] No report on the subject has yet appeared. The results will have great significance because the size of visitation at the lakeshore will play a role in future expansion efforts.

Lakeshore adherents point to these investigations as evidence of harassment of the park by an unfriendly administration. To further support their case, they cite the abrupt termination of *Singing Sands*. The lakeshore had issued this interpretative newspaper to inform the public about park activities. Using a 1972 regulation that "requires Office of Management and Budget approval before a federal agency may produce a publication which has 10% or more of its copies intended . . . for distribution to the public," a May 1982 directive ordered copies removed from the park's visitor centers, in spite of the fact that the paper had appeared six times a year since 1978.[22] In addition, park supporters list the appointment of a HOPE leader to the Lakeshore Advisory Commission as another example of the secretary's antipark bias.

Watt's redirection of the National Park Service affected decision-making at the Indiana Dunes. His new park "protection" policy, which limited land acquisition to willing sellers, severely constrained the lakeshore's ability to purchase property. For residential owners, it meant a de facto return to the 1966 homeowner provisions. Moreover, Watt's prohibition against land acquisition from unwilling sellers also applied to nonresidential holdings. Commercial and industrial property within the lakeshore boundaries also remained untouchable by the park. Watt not only established the new policy for future land purchases but also retroactively applied the new standard. In response the Save the Dunes Council has gone to court to force the Department to continue previously filed condemnation proceedings. With a secretary who has publicly enunciated his advocacy of a systemwide moratorium on land purchases by the National Park Service, the prospects for the lakeshore's acquiring further property from unwilling sellers seem dim.

Watt's emphasis on development of existing park land also influenced National Park Service decisions about Indiana Dunes land acquisition in 1982. Local management concentrated on buying property earmarked for construction projects. HOPE's connections with the Department prevented acquisition of homes even from willing sellers. Purchase of land for resource protection received very low priority. Moreover, the lakeshore's prodevelopment thrust not only reflected departmental policy but also coincided with the interests of the congressman then representing the lakeshore district, Adam Benjamin. He supported construction of three marinas along the shoreline.

Like other units of the national park system, the lakeshore also had its personnel reduced. The 1982 federal budget provided for additional employees at Indiana Dunes, but an employment ceiling imposed throughout the National Park Service prevented the use of this appropriation. This meant fewer interpretative, security, and maintenance staff.

In April 1982 Secretary Watt visited Michigan City to speak at a community forum. Members of the Save the Dunes Council met with him to express their concerns about the lakeshore. At the session Watt suggested that the group undertake air-quality monitoring within the lakeshore to answer their fears about the effects of industrial pollution of the park. He advised the council to provide additional interpretative services for the public if they had doubts about the wisdom of his cut in park employment. He also reiterated his opposition to expansion of the lakeshore and stood firm on his position against further funding for land acquistions.

Moreover, Watt's actions during his first two years as secretary of the interior have created a serious morale problem at Indiana Dunes. Lakeshore employees worry about lack of funds, decreased advancement opportunities, and job security in a department whose chief seems most interested in finding ways to dismantle or radically change the mission of the National Park Service.

The present shaky status of both the steel industry and the lakeshore contributes to continuing discord in the Indiana Dunes. Past compromises, which permitted both land uses to coexist, however uneasily, have not produced permanent decisions. With the long-term future of the steel industry in question and the continued existence of the park under attack, inevitable doubts about the adequacy of public policy for the Dunes persist.

As always, the problems besetting public preservation of the Dunes reflect larger national issues. Today, as in the past, the Dunes park serves as a bellweather, accurately indicating the vitality, stability, and future direction of the national park system and of the environmental movement in American society.

NOTES

1. Robert M. Bleiberg, "Steel's Succor Play," *Barron's*, June 21, 1982, p. 11.

2. Lydia Chavez, "The Year the Bottom Fell Out for Steel," New York *Times*, June 20, 1982, sec. 3, p. 1.

3. Ibid.

4. Bleiberg, "Steel's Succor Play," p. 11.

5. "Westchester C. of C. Honors Wycoff and Bachuchins," Chesterton *Tribune*, June 24, 1982, p. 4.

6. "Government Ruling May Aid Bethlehem," Michigan City *News Dispatch*, June 26, 1982, p. 28.

7. "GM Picks 9 Steel Suppliers for '83 Models; New Plan Realigns Business to Each Firm," *Wall Street Journal*, June 24, 1982, p. 8.

8. U.S. *Statutes at Large*, 80, pt. 1 (Jan. 1966–Nov. 1966), "An Act to Provide for the Establishment of the Indiana Dunes National Lakeshore," Nov. 5, 1966.

9. Ibid.

10. U.S. *Statutes at Large*, 90, pt. 1 (Jan. 1976–Dec. 1976), "An Act to Amend the Act Establishing the Indiana Dunes National Lakeshore to Provide for the Expansion of the Lakeshore, and Other Purposes," Oct. 18, 1976.

11. Authors' interview with Betty Prang, a leader of opposition to lakeshore expansion, Chesterton, Ind., 1977.

12. U.S. Department of the Interior, National Park Service, *Special Study, Areas III–A, III–C & II–A*, June 1977, Indiana Dunes National Lakeshore.

13. U.S. *Statutes at Large*, 94, pt. 3 (Dec. 1980), "An Act to Provide for the Establishment of the Indiana Dunes National Lakeshore," Dec. 28, 1980.

14. Robert Cahn, "Quelling the Storm: What It Will Take," *Christian Science Monitor*, June 18, 1982, p. 14.

15. "Two Area National Parks Periled in U.S. Order," Chicago *Sun-Times*, Apr. 29, 1981, p. 11.

16. See, for example, "Fox Guarding the Hens," Hammond *Times*, Apr. 26, 1981, and "Don't Trifle with Dunes," Chicago *Sun-Times*, May 5, 1981, p. 43.

17. "Park Phase Out," Valparaiso *Vidette Messenger*, May 4, 1981, p. 4.

18. David S. Robinson, "Dunes Not On U.S. Parks 'Hit List,' Lugar Reports," Chicago *Sun-Times*, May 8, 1981, p. 41; Jeanne Wright, "Feds Will Keep Control of Lakeshore, Lugar Assured," Valparaiso *Vidette Messenger*, May 7, 1981, p. 1.

19. Phillip Shabecoff, "Interior Chief Orders Inquiry on Federal Park Land Deals," New York *Times*, May 23, 1981, p. 8.

20. U.S. Department of the Interior, Office of Inspector General, *Special Review of Land Acquisition Policies and Practices in the National Park Service, Part 1—Cost Estimates* (Washington, 1981), p. 5.

21. Indiana Dunes National Lakeshore, minutes of meetings of Indiana Dunes National Lakeshore Advisory Commission, meeting of May 18, 1982, pp. 8–9, typescript, Indiana Dunes National Lakeshore Administrative Headquarters, Porter, Ind.

22. "Singing Sands Newsletter Banned," *Exchange* (Washington: National Parks Action Project, National Parks and Conservation Association, June 7, 1982), p. 2. See also J. R. Whitehouse, superintendent of the Indiana Dunes National Lakeshore, to *Singing Sands'* mailing list, K3819 (INDU), June 9, 1982, Indiana Dunes National Lakeshore Administrative Headquarters.

Bibliographical Essay

Uncovering the history of Indiana's shoreline between 1816 and 1982 presented a seven-year research challenge. As Dunes residents since 1969, we came to the scene after the authorization of the lakeshore. Living in Beverly Shores, we quickly became aware of the passions aroused by the park's establishment, which had not quieted at our arrival and which have continued, often at fever pitch, ever since. Our participation in efforts to expand the lakeshore in the 1970s stimulated our quest to understand what happened during the past 150 years to the forty-five-mile coast at the southern tip of Lake Michigan. Our search for an answer to the central question of this book led us to interview forty-eight of the major actors in the struggle and to investigate both primary and secondary sources exhaustively.

Readers interested in more detailed information about the growth of the American conservation movement should consult:

Paul Buck, "The Evolution of the National Park System of the United States" (M.A. thesis, Ohio State University, 1921), reprinted by the National Park Service in 1946

Allen F. Davis, *Spearheads for Reform: The Social Settlements and the Progressive Movement* (New York: Oxford University Press, 1962)

Samuel P. Hayes, *Conservation and the Gospel of Efficiency: The Progressive Conservation Movement, 1890–1920* (Cambridge, Mass.: Harvard University Press, 1959)

Samuel P. Hayes, *The Response to Industrialism* (Chicago: University of Chicago Press, 1957)

Hans Huth, *Nature and the Americans: Three Centuries of Changing Attitudes* (Berkeley: University of California Press, 1957)

John Ise, *Our National Park Policy: A Critical History* (Baltimore: Johns Hopkins University Press, 1961)

Henry Jarrett, ed., *Perspectives on Conservation* (Baltimore: Johns Hopkins University Press, 1961)

Roderick Nash, *Wilderness and the American Mind*, rev. ed. (New
    Haven: Yale University Press, 1973)
Norman I. Wengert, *National Resources and the Political Struggle*
    (Garden City, N.Y.: Doubleday, 1955)
Robert Wiebe, *The Search for Order* (New York: Hill and Wang, 1966).

For the period before 1952 we examined the files of the National
Park Service in the National Archives, Washington. Unfortunately
the National Park Service records (including Stephen Mather's papers relating to the period of the Sand Dunes National Park) were
moved to Chicago during World War II for safekeeping and have disappeared. We pieced together Mather's relationship to the Dunes from
the records of the Prairie Club and traced his connections to Jens
Jensen, Henry Cowles, and Richard Lieber. The following books and
article have information about Mather, but they mention the Dunes
only in passing:

Robert Shankland, *Steve Mather of the National Parks* (New York:
    Alfred Knopf, 1954)
Donald C. Swain, "The Passage of the National Park Service Act of
    1916," *Wisconsin Magazine of History*, 50 (Autumn 1966), 1–17
Donald C. Swain, *Wilderness Defender: Horace Albright and Con-
    servation* (Chicago: University of Chicago Press, 1970)
Stewart L. Udall, *The Quiet Crisis* (New York: Holt, Rinehart, and
    Winston, 1963).

The Prairie Club made available all of its papers for which we owe
the club a great debt. Similarly, the Chicago Academy of Sciences
allowed us to examine the files of the Conservation Council housed
in its rafters. We also reviewed the collection of National Dunes
Preservation Association materials at the Gary Public Library. The
Morton Arboretum in Lisle, Illinois, serves as the repository for
memorabilia relating to Jens Jensen. The Henry Regenstein Library
at the University of Chicago houses papers relating to Henry Chandler Cowles. The Indiana State Library maintains a Dunes Park collection.
    Jensen awaits a definitive biography. Malcolm Collier has pub-
lished two well-researched articles about him: "Jens Jensen and Co-
lumbus Park," *Chicago History*, 4 (Winter 1975–76), 225–34, and
"Jens Jensen and the Mid-West Prairie," *Morton Arboretum Quarterly*, 13 (Winter 1977), 49–55. She kindly talked with us about her
investigations. Other works about Jensen include: Leonard K. Eaton,
The Life and Work of Jens Jensen (Chicago: University of Chicago
Press, 1964) and Martha Fulkerson and Ada Carson, *The Story of the*

Clearing (Chicago: Coach House Press, 1972). Jensen wrote one book, *Siftings* (Chicago: Seymour, 1935).

Cowles, too, awaits a biographer. Dr. Paul Voth, his colleague in the botany department at the University of Chicago, gave us valuable insights and considerable assistance in gathering reprints of Cowles's writings and biographical materials. Dr. Jerry Olson, a later student in the department and a disciple of Cowles, shared his historical perspective of Cowles's influence. Other accounts of Cowles include W. S. Cooper, "Henry Chandler Cowles," *Ecology*, 16 (July 1935), 281–88; George D. Fuller, "Henry Chandler Cowles," *Transactions of the Illinois Academy of Science*, 33 (1940), 17–18; and May Theilgaard Watts, *Reading the Landscape* (New York: Macmillan, 1957), 127–43. Accounts of Cowles's scientific contributions appear in Donald Worster, *Nature's Economy: The Roots of Ecology* (San Francisco: Sierra Club Books, 1977), and E. Lucy Braun, "The Development of Association and Climax Concepts," in *Fifty Years of Botany*, ed. William Steene (New York: McGraw Hill, 1958), pp. 329–39.

No full-length biography of Thomas Taggart exists. We gleaned data about him from the following sources:

Jonathan Birge, "Past Imperfect," paper presented to the Indianapolis Literary Club, December 3, 1969, typescript on deposit at the Indiana State Library, Indianapolis

Richard Haupt, "History of the French Lick Springs Hotel" (M.A. thesis, Indiana University, 1953)

History of French Lick Springs, undated pamphlet published by the Sheraton Corporation of America

Men of Indiana in Nineteen Hundred and One (Indianapolis: Nenesch Publishing Co., 1901)

Charles Roll, *Indiana: One Hundred and Fifty Years of American Development* (New York: Lewis Publishing Co., 1931)

Alva C. Saterlee, "T.T., the Master Mind That Wrought Brilliant and Bewildering Achievements in Political Legerdemain," undated typescript at the Indiana State Library, Indianapolis

Who's Who and What's What in Indiana Politics (Indianapolis: J. E. Perry, 1944).

For the period 1952 to the present, the files of the Save the Dunes Council, Beverly Shores, Indiana, contain voluminous information, including the papers of Dorothy Buell and Sylvia Troy. Readers can find some of Congressman Ray Madden's papers in the Indiana University–Northwest archives. The Lilly Library at Indiana University houses Congressman Charles Halleck's papers as well as those r

Senator Birch Bayh. Senator Paul Douglas donated his records to the Chicago Historical Society. The John Crerar Library at the Illinois Institute of Technology possesses a large collection of materials about the steel industry. Two concise accounts of the Dunes political struggle have appeared in larger works: Thomas Dustin, "The Battle of the Indiana Dunes," in *Citizens Make a Difference* (Washington: Citizens Advisory Committee on Environmental Quality, 1973), and James J. Kyle, "Indiana Dunes National Lakeshore: The Battle for the Dunes," in *Congress and the Environment*, ed. Richard A. Cooley and Geoffrey Wandesforde-Smith (Seattle: University of Washington Press, 1970).

John F. Lambert, Jr., has made a thorough analysis of Watt's land protection plan and its implications for the Dunes in "Private Landholdings in the National Parks: Examples from Yosemite National Park and Indiana Dunes National Lakeshore," *Harvard Environmental Law Review*, 6 (1982), 35–60.

For a current and more complete assessment of the problems of resource protection in the national parks, see Eugenia Horstman Connally, ed., *National Parks in Crisis* (Washington: National Parks and Conservation Association, 1982).

Two recently published books contribute to the growing Dunes literature. J. Ronald Engel has written a study of the struggle for community in the Indiana Dunes, *Sacred Sands* (Middletown, Conn.: Wesleyan University Press, 1983), and Indiana Dunes National Lakeshore Chief Interpretive Ranger Larry Waldron has published a guide to the park, *The Indiana Dunes* (New York: Eastern Acorn Press, 1983).

Finally, we have compiled a selected bibliography of Dunes references, including scientific materials. See Norma Schaeffer and Kay Franklin, *The Indiana Dunes: A Selected Bibliography* (Hammond: The Regional Studies Institute of Purdue University Calumet, 1980).

Index

Note on the Authors

KAY FRANKLIN and NORMA SCHAEFFER are freelance writers living in the Indiana Dunes. Mrs. Franklin has a master's degree from the University of Chicago. Mrs. Schaeffer has a bachelor's degree from Queens College and co-authored *Doing the Dunes*, a guidebook to northwest Indiana. Both have worked actively for Dunes preservation. Together and separately, they have published numerous articles in regional and national magazines, primarily on Dunes topics. They are the co-authors of *The Indiana Dunes: A Selected Bibliography* (1980).